Acclaim for the international bestseller,

THE RAPE OF NANKING

"A powerful new work of history and moral inquiry. Chang takes great care to establish an accurate accounting of the dimensions of the violence." —*Chicago Tribune*

"Meticulously researched . . . A gripping account that holds the reader's attention from beginning to end." —Nien Cheng, author of *Life and Death in Shanghai*

"Iris Chang's research on the Nanking holocaust yields a new and expanded telling of this World War II atrocity and reflects thorough research. The book is excellent; its story deserves to be heard." —Beatrice S. Bartlett, professor of history, Yale University

"Heartbreaking . . . An utterly compelling book. The descriptions of the atrocities raise fundamental questions not only about imperial Japanese militarism but the psychology of the torturers, rapists, and murderers." —Frederic Wakeman, director of the Institute of East Asian Studies, University of California, Berkeley

"Something beautiful, an act of justice, is occurring in America today concerning something ugly that happened long ago. . . . Because of Chang's book, the second rape of Nanking is ending." —George F. Will, syndicated columnist

"In her important new book . . . Iris Chang, whose own grandparents were survivors, recounts the grisly massacre with understandable outrage." —Orville Schell, *The New York Times Book Review*

"Anyone interested in the relation between war, self-righteousness, and the human spirit will find *The Rape of Nanking* of fundamental importance. It is scholarly, an exciting investigation, and a work of passion. In places it is almost unbearable to read, but it should be read—only if the past is understood can the future be navigated." —Ross Terrill, author of *Mao, China in Our Time,* and *Madame Mao*

THE RAPE OF NANKING

THE
RAPE
OF
NANKING

THE FORGOTTEN HOLOCAUST OF WORLD WAR II

IRIS CHANG

BASIC BOOKS
A Member of the Perseus Books Group
New York

First published in 1997 in the United States by Basic Books,
A Member of the Perseus Books Group
First published in 1998 as a paperback by Penguin Books
This edition published in 2011 by Basic Books

Books published by Basic Books are available at special discounts for bulk purchases in the United States by corporations, institutions, and other organizations.
For more information, please contact the Special Markets Department at the
Perseus Books Group, 2300 Chestnut Street, Suite 200, Philadelphia, PA 19103, or
call (800) 810-4145, ext. 5000, or e-mail special.markets@perseusbooks.com.

Library of Congress Cataloging-in-Publicat ion Data
Chang, Iris.
   The rape of Nanking : the forgotten holocaust of World War II / Iris Chang.
     p. cm.
   Includes index.
   ISBN 0-465-06835-9
   1. Nanking Massacre, Nan-ching shih, China, 1937. 2. Nan-ching shih (China)—
History. I. Title.

DS796.N2C44 1997
951.04'2—DC21 97-24137

ISBN 978-0-465-06836-4 (2011 paperback)
ISBN 978-0-465-02825-2 (e-book)

10 9 8 7 6 5 4 3

To the hundreds of thousands of victims
in the Rape of Nanking

CONTENTS

Foreword by William C. Kirby   xi

Introduction   3

PART I

1 The Path to Nanking   19

2 Six Weeks of Terror   35

3 The Fall of Nanking   61

4 Six Weeks of Horror   81

5 The Nanking Safety Zone   105

PART II

6 What the World Knew   143

7 The Occupation of Nanking   159

8 Judgment Day   169

9 The Fate of the Survivors   181

PART III

10 The Forgotten Holocaust:
A Second Rape   199

Epilogue	215
Epilogue for the 2011 Edition	227
Acknowledgments	243
Notes	247
Index	301

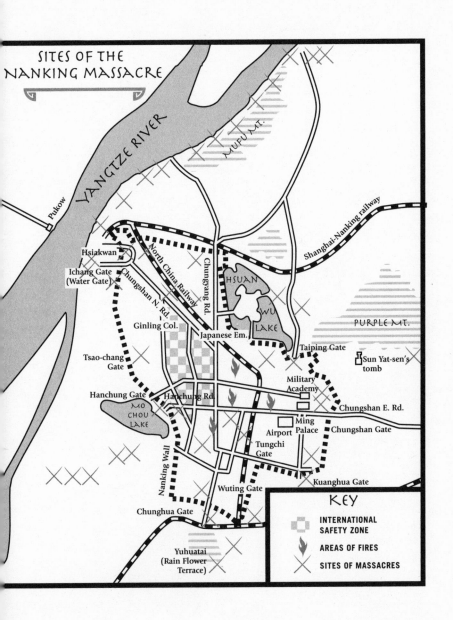

SITES OF THE
NANKING MASSACRE

YANGTZE RIVER

MUFU MT.

Pukow

Shanghai-Nanking railway

Hsiakwan

Ichang Gate
(Water Gate)

Chungshan N. Rd.

North China railway

Chungyang Rd.

HSUAN
WU
LAKE

PURPLE MT.

Ginling Col.

Japanese Em.

Taiping Gate

Sun Yat-sen's
tomb

Tsao-chang
Gate

Military
Academy

Chungshan E. Rd.

Hanchung Gate

Hanchung Rd.

MO
CHOU
LAKE

Airport

Ming
Palace

Chungshan Gate

Tungchi
Gate

Kuanghua Gate

Nanking Wall

Wuting Gate

Chunghua Gate

Yuhuatai
(Rain Flower
Terrace)

KEY

INTERNATIONAL
SAFETY ZONE

AREAS OF FIRES

SITES OF MASSACRES

FOREWORD

O N DECEMBER 13, 1937, Nanking, the
capital city of Nationalist China, fell
to the Japanese. For Japan, this was to
have been the decisive turning point in the
war, the triumphant culmination of a half-year
struggle against Chiang Kai-shek's armies in
the Yangtze Valley. For Chinese forces, whose
heroic defense of Shanghai had finally failed,
and whose best troops had suffered crippling
casualties, the fall of Nanking was a bitter,
perhaps fatal defeat.

We may now think of Nanking as a turning point of a different sort. What happened
within the walls of that old city stiffened
Chinese determination to recover it and to
expel the invader. The Chinese government
retreated, regrouped, and ultimately out-
lasted Japan in a war that ended only in
1945. In those eight years Japan would occupy Nanking and set up a government of
Chinese collaborators; but it would never
rule with confidence or legitimacy, and it

could never force China's surrender. To the larger world, the "rape" of Nanking—as it was immediately called—turned public opinion against Japan in a way that little else could have.

That is still the case in China, where several generations have now been taught of Japan's crimes and of its failure, to this day, to atone for them. Sixty years later, the ghosts of Nanking still haunt Chinese-Japanese relations.

Well they might. The Japanese sack of China's capital was a horrific event. The mass execution of soldiers and the slaughtering and raping of tens of thousands of civilians took place in contravention of all rules of warfare. What is still stunning is that it was *public* rampage, evidently designed to terrorize. It was carried out in full view of international observers and largely irrespective of their efforts to stop it. And it was not a temporary lapse of military discipline, for it lasted seven *weeks*. This is the terrible story that Iris Chang tells so powerfully in this first, full study in English of Nanking's tragedy.

We may never know precisely what motivated Japanese commanders and troops to such bestial behavior. But Ms. Chang shows more clearly than any previous account just what they did. In doing so she employs a wide range of source materials, including the unimpeachable testimony of third-party observers: the foreign missionaries and businessmen who stayed in the defenseless city as the Japanese entered it. One such source that Ms. Chang has uncovered is the diary—really a small archive—of John Rabe, the German businessman and National Socialist who led an international effort to shelter Nanking's population. Through Rabe's eyes we see the dread and courage of Nanjing's inhabitants as they confront, defenseless, the Japanese onslaught. Through Ms. Chang's account we appreciate the bravery of Rabe and others who tried to make a difference as the city was being burned and its inhabitants assaulted; as hospitals were closed and morgues filled; and as chaos reigned around them. We read, too, of those Japanese who understood what was happening, and felt shame.

The Rape of Nanking has largely been forgotten in the West, hence the importance of this book. In calling it a "forgotten

Holocaust," Ms. Chang draws connections between the slaughter in Europe and in Asia of millions of innocents during World War II. To be sure, Japan and Nazi Germany would only later become allies, and not very good allies at that. But the events at Nanking—to which Hitler surely took no exception—would later make them moral co-conspirators, as violent aggressors, perpetrators of what would ultimately be called "crimes against humanity." W. H. Auden, who visited the China war, made the connection earlier than most:[1]

> *And maps can really point to places*
> *Where life is evil now:*
> *Nanking; Dachau.*

> —WILLIAM C. KIRBY,
> Professor of Modern Chinese
> History and Chairman of the
> Department of History,
> Harvard University

---

[1] From W. H. Auden, *Collected Shorter Poems, 1930–1944* (London: Faber and Faber, 1950), "In Time of War," XVI, pp. 279–80.

THE RAPE OF NANKING

INTRODUCTION

THE CHRONICLE of humankind's cruelty to fellow humans is a long and sorry tale. But if it is true that even in such horror tales there are degrees of ruthlessness, then few atrocities in world history compare in intensity and scale to the Rape of Nanking during World War II.

Americans think of World War II as beginning on December 7, 1941, when Japanese carrier-based airplanes attacked Pearl Harbor. Europeans date it from September 1, 1939, and the blitzkrieg assault on Poland by Hitler's Luftwaffe and Panzer divisions. Africans see an even earlier beginning, the invasion of Ethiopia by Mussolini in 1935. Yet Asians must trace the war's beginnings all the way back to Japan's first steps toward the military domination of East Asia—the occupation of Manchuria in 1931.

Just as Hitler's Germany would do half a decade later, Japan used a highly developed military machine and a master-race mentality to set about establishing its right to rule its neighbors. Manchuria fell quickly to the Japanese, who established their government of Manchukuo, ostensibly under their puppet, the deposed emperor of China, but in fact run by the Japanese military. Four years later, in 1935, parts of Chahar and Hopeh were occupied; in 1937 Peking, Tientsin, Shanghai, and finally Nanking fell. The decade of the thirties was a hard one for China; indeed, the last Japanese would not be routed from Chinese soil until the end of World War II in 1945.

No doubt, those fourteen years of domination by the Japanese military were marked by countless incidents of almost indescribable ruthlessness. We will never know everything that happened in the many cities and small villages that found themselves prostrate beneath the boot of this conquering force. Ironically, we do know the story of Nanking because some foreigners witnessed the horror and sent word to the outside world at the time, and some Chinese survived as eyewitnesses. If one event can be held up as an example of the unmitigated evil lying just below the surface of unbridled military adventurism, that moment is the Rape of Nanking. This book is its story.

The broad details of the Rape are, except among the Japanese, not in dispute. In November 1937, after their successful invasion of Shanghai, the Japanese launched a massive attack on the newly established capital of the Republic of China. When the city fell on December 13, 1937, Japanese soldiers began an orgy of cruelty seldom if ever matched in world history. Tens of thousands of young men were rounded up and herded to the outer areas of the city, where they were mowed down by machine guns, used for bayonet practice, or soaked with gasoline and burned alive. For months the streets of the city were heaped with corpses and reeked with the stench of rotting human flesh. Years later experts at the International Military Tribunal of the Far East (IMTFE) estimated that more than 260,000 noncombatants died at the hands of Japanese soldiers at Nanking in late 1937 and early 1938, though some experts have placed the figure at well over 350,000.

This book provides only the barest summary of the cruel

and barbaric acts committed by the Japanese in the city, for its aim is not to establish a quantitative record to qualify the event as one of the great evil deeds of history, but to understand the event so that lessons can be learned and warnings sounded. Differences in degree, however, often reflect differences in kind, and so a few statistics must be used to give the reader an idea of the scale of the massacre that took place in 1937 in a city named Nanking.

One historian has estimated that if the dead from Nanking were to link hands, they would stretch from Nanking to the city of Hangchow, spanning a distance of some two hundred miles. Their blood would weigh twelve hundred tons, and their bodies would fill twenty-five hundred railroad cars. Stacked on top of each other, these bodies would reach the height of a seventy-four-story building.

Using numbers killed alone, the Rape of Nanking surpasses much of the worst barbarism of the ages. The Japanese outdid the Romans at Carthage (only 150,000 died in that slaughter), the Christian armies during the Spanish Inquisition, and even some of the monstrosities of Timur Lenk, who killed 100,000 prisoners at Delhi in 1398 and built two towers of skulls in Syria in 1400 and 1401.

It is certainly true that in the twentieth century, when the tools of mass murder were fully refined, Hitler killed about 6 million Jews, and Stalin more than 40 million Russians, but these deaths were brought about over some few years. In the Rape of Nanking the killing was concentrated within a few weeks.

Indeed, even by the standards of history's most destructive war, the Rape of Nanking represents one of the worst instances of mass extermination. To imagine its comparative size, we must brace ourselves for a few more statistics. The death toll of Nanking—one Chinese city alone—exceeds the number of civilian casualties of some European countries for the entire war. (Great Britain lost a total of 61,000 civilians, France lost 108,000, Belgium 101,000, and the Netherlands 242,000.) Air bombing is considered by those who reflect on these things one of the most awesome instruments of mass destruction. Yet even the worst air attacks of the war did not exceed the ravages of Nanking. It is likely that more people died in Nanking than in the British raids on Dresden and the fire storm that followed. (The figure 225,000 was accepted internationally at the time, but more objective accounts now place the number of Dresden casualties at 60,000 dead and at least 30,000 injured.) Indeed, whether we use the most conservative number— 260,000—or the highest—350,000—it is shocking to contemplate that the deaths at Nanking far exceeded the deaths from the American raids on Tokyo (an estimated 80,000–120,000 deaths) and even the combined death toll of the two atomic blasts at Hiroshima and Nagasaki by the end of 1945 (estimated at 140,000 and 70,000, respectively).

The Rape of Nanking should be remembered not only for the number of people slaughtered but for the cruel manner in which many met their deaths. Chinese men were used for bayonet practice and in decapitation contests. An estimated 20,000–80,000 Chinese women were raped. Many soldiers went beyond rape to disembowel women, slice off their breasts, nail them alive to walls. Fathers were forced to rape their daughters, and sons their mothers, as other family members watched. Not only did live burials, castration, the carving of organs, and the roasting of people become routine, but more diabolical tortures were practiced, such as hanging people by their tongues on iron hooks or burying people to their waists and watching them get torn apart by German shepherds. So sickening was the spectacle that even the Nazis in the city were horrified, one proclaiming the massacre to be the work of "bestial machinery."

Yet the Rape of Nanking remains an obscure incident. Unlike the atomic explosions in Japan or the Jewish holocaust in Europe, the horrors of the massacre at Nanking remain virtually unknown to people outside Asia. The massacre remains neglected in most of the historical literature published in the United States. A thorough examination of secondary-school history textbooks in the United States revealed that only a few even mention the Rape of Nanking. And almost none of the comprehensive, or "definitive," histories of World War II read by the American public discusses the Nanking massacre in great detail. For instance, no photograph of the event, not even one word, appears in *The American Heritage Picture History of World War II* (1966), which for many years was the best-selling single-volume pictorial history of the war ever published. Nor can a word of the massacre be found in Winston Churchill's famous *Memoirs of the Second World War* (1959) (1,065 pages) or in Henri Michel's classic *Second World War* (1975) (947 pages). The Rape of Nanking is mentioned only twice in Gerhard Weinberg's massive *A World at Arms* (1994) (1,178 pages). Only in Robert Leckie's *Delivered from Evil: The Saga of World War II* (1987) (998 pages) did I find a single paragraph about the massacre: "Nothing the Nazis under Hitler would do to disgrace their own victories could rival the atrocities of Japanese soldiers under Gen. Iwane Matsui."

I first learned about the Rape of Nanking when I was a little girl. The stories came from my parents, who had survived years of war and revolution before finding a serene home as professors in a midwestern American college town. They had grown up in China in the midst of World War II and after the war fled with their families, first to Taiwan and finally to the United States to study at Harvard and pursue academic careers in science. For three decades they lived peacefully in the academic community of Champaign-Urbana, Illinois, conducting research in physics and microbiology.

But they never forgot the horrors of the Sino-Japanese War, nor did they want me to forget. They particularly did not want

Throughout the book I use either pinyin or Wade-Giles for Chinese names, depending on the preference of the individual (as specified by business cards or correspondence) or the popularity of one name's transliteration over the other (for instance, "Chiang Kai-shek" instead of "Jiang Jieshi"). For Chinese and Japanese names of people, I use the traditional system of listing the surname before the given name. For cities and landmarks, I typically (but not always) use the form of romanization most commonly employed by Westerners during the era of the narrative, such as "Nanking" instead of the present-day name "Nanjing."

me to forget the Rape of Nanking. Neither of my parents witnessed it, but as young children they had heard the stories, and these were passed down to me. The Japanese, I learned, sliced babies not just in half but in thirds and fourths, they said; the Yangtze River ran red with blood for days. Their voices quivering with outrage, my parents characterized the Great Nanking Massacre, or *Nanjing Datusha*, as the single most diabolical incident committed by the Japanese in a war that killed more than 10 million Chinese people.

Throughout my childhood *Nanjing Datusha* remained buried in the back of my mind as a metaphor for unspeakable evil. But the event lacked human details and human dimensions. It was also difficult to find the line between myth and history. While still in grade school I searched the local public libraries to see what I could learn about the massacre, but nothing turned up. That struck me as odd. If the Rape of Nanking was truly so gory, one of the worst episodes of human barbarism in world history, as my parents insisted, then why hadn't someone written a book about it? It did not occur to me, as a child, to pursue my research using the mammoth University of Illinois library system, and my curiosity about the matter soon slipped away.

Almost two decades elapsed before the Rape of Nanking intruded upon my life again. By this time I was married and living a quiet life as a professional author in Santa Barbara, California, when I heard from a filmmaker friend that a couple of producers on the East Coast had recently completed a documentary on the Rape of Nanking but faced trouble getting funds to distribute the film properly.

His story rekindled my interest. Soon I was on the phone talking to not just one but two producers of documentaries on the subject. The first was Shao Tzuping, a Chinese-American activist who had worked for the United Nations in New York, served as a past president of the Alliance in Memory of Victims of the Nanjing Massacre, and helped produce the videotape *Magee's Testament*. Another was Nancy Tong, an independent filmmaker who had produced and codirected with Christine Choy the documentary *In the Name of the Emperor*. Shao Tzuping and Nancy

Tong helped plug me into a network of activists, many of them first-generation Chinese Americans and Chinese Canadians who, like me, felt the need to bear witness to the event, to document and publicize it, and even to seek restitution for the atrocities of Nanking before all the surviving victims passed away. Others wanted to pass their wartime memories down to their children and grandchildren, fearful that their assimilation into North American culture might cause them to forget this important part of their historical heritage.

What strengthened much of this newly emerging activism was the Tiananmen Square massacre of 1989, which prodded Chinese communities all over the world to form networks to protest the actions of the People's Republic of China. The pro-democracy movement left behind vast, intricate webs of Internet relationships; out of this network a grassroots movement emerged to promote the truth about Nanking. In urban centers with high concentrations of Chinese—such as the San Francisco Bay Area, New York City, Los Angeles, Toronto, and Vancouver—Chinese activists organized conferences and educational campaigns to disseminate information about Japanese crimes during World War II. They exhibited films, videos, and photographs of the Nanking massacre in museums and schools, posted facts and photographs on the Internet, and even placed full-page advertisements on the subject in newspapers like the *New York Times*. Some of the activist groups were so technologically sophisticated that they could at the push of a button send messages to more than a quarter-million readers worldwide.

That the Nanking massacre of my childhood memories was not merely folk myth but accurate oral history hit me in December 1994, when I attended a conference sponsored by the Global Alliance for Preserving the History of World War II in Asia, which commemorated the victims of the Nanking atrocities. The conference was held in Cupertino, California, a San Jose suburb in the heart of Silicon Valley. In the conference hall the organizers had prepared poster-sized photographs of the Rape of Nanking—some of the most gruesome photographs I had ever seen in my life. Though I had heard so much about the Nanking massacre as a child, nothing prepared me for these pictures—stark black-and-white images of decapitated heads, bellies ripped open, and nude women forced by their rapists into various pornographic poses, their faces contorted into unforgettable expressions of agony and shame.

In a single blinding moment I recognized the fragility of not just life but the human experience itself. We all learn about death while young. We know that any one of us could be struck by the proverbial truck or bus and be deprived of life in an instant. And unless we have certain religious beliefs, we see such a death as a senseless and unfair deprivation of life. But we also know of the respect for life and the dying process that most humans share. If you are struck by a bus, someone may steal your purse or wallet while you lie injured, but many more will come to your aid, trying to save your precious life. One person will call 911, and another will race down the street to alert a police officer on his or her beat. Someone else will take off his coat, fold it, and place it under your head, so that if these are indeed your last moments of life you will die in the small but real comfort of knowing that someone cared about you. The pictures up on that wall in Cupertino illustrated that not just one person but hundreds of thousands could have their lives extinguished, die at the whim of others, and the next day their deaths would be meaningless. But even more telling was that those who had brought about these deaths (the most terror-filled, even if inevitable, tragedy of the human experience) could also degrade the victims and force them to expire in maximum pain and humiliation. I was suddenly in a panic that this terrifying disrespect for death and dying, this reversion in human social evolution, would be reduced to a footnote of history, treated like a harmless glitch in a computer program that might or might not again cause a problem, unless someone forced the world to remember it.

During the conference I learned that two novels about the Nanking massacre were already in the works (*Tree of Heaven* and *Tent of Orange Mist*, both published in 1995), as well as a pictorial book about the massacre (*The Rape of Nanking: An Undeniable History in Photographs*, published in 1996). But at the time no one had yet written a full-length, narrative nonfic-tion book on the Rape of Nanking in English. Delving deeper into the history of the massacre, I learned that the raw source material for such a book had always existed and was available in the United States. American missionaries, journalists, and military officers had all recorded for posterity in diaries, films, and photographs their own views of the event. Why had no other American author or scholar exploited this rich lode of primary source material to write a nonfiction book or even a dissertation exclusively devoted to the massacre?

I soon had at least part of an answer to the strange riddle of why the massacre had remained relatively untreated in world history. The Rape of Nanking did not penetrate the world con-sciousness in the same manner as the Holocaust or Hiroshima because the victims themselves had remained silent.

But every answer suggests a new question, and I now won-dered why the victims of this crime had not screamed out for justice. Or if they had indeed cried out, why had their anguish not been recognized? It soon became clear to me that the cus-todian of the curtain of silence was politics. The People's Re-public of China, the Republic of China, and even the United States had all contributed to the historical neglect of this event for reasons deeply rooted in the cold war. After the 1949 Com-munist revolution in China, neither the People's Republic of China nor the Republic of China demanded wartime repara-tions from Japan (as Israel had from Germany) because the two governments were competing for Japanese trade and polit-ical recognition. And even the United States, faced with the threat of communism in the Soviet Union and mainland China, sought to ensure the friendship and loyalty of its for-mer enemy, Japan. In this manner, cold war tensions permitted Japan to escape much of the intense critical examination that its wartime ally was forced to undergo.

Moreover, an atmosphere of intimidation in Japan stifled open and scholarly discussion of the Rape of Nanking, further suppressing knowledge of the event. In Japan, to express one's true opinions about the Sino-Japanese War could be—and continues to be—career-threatening, and even life-threatening. (In 1990 a gunman shot Motoshima Hitoshi, mayor of Nagasaki, in the chest for saying that Emperor Hirohito bore some responsibility for World War II.) This pervasive sense of danger has discouraged many serious scholars from visiting Japanese archives to conduct their research on the subject; indeed, I was told in Nanking that the People's Republic of China rarely permits its scholars to journey to Japan for fear of jeopardizing their physical safety. Under such circumstances, gaining access to Japanese archival source materials about the Rape of Nanking has been exceedingly difficult for people outside the island nation. In addition, most Japanese veterans who participated in the Rape of Nanking are for the most part unwilling to give interviews about their experiences, although in recent years a few have braved ostracism and even death threats to go public with their stories.

What baffled and saddened me during the writing of this book was the persistent Japanese refusal to come to terms with its own past. It is not just that Japan has doled out less than 1 percent of the amount that Germany has paid in war reparations to its victims. It is not just that, unlike most Nazis, who, if not incarcerated for their crimes were at least forced from public life, many Japanese war criminals continued to occupy powerful positions in industry and government after the war. And it is not just the fact that while Germans have made repeated apologies to their Holocaust victims, the Japanese have enshrined their war criminals in Tokyo—an act that one American wartime victim of the Japanese has labeled politically equivalent to "erecting a cathedral for Hitler in the middle of Berlin."

Strongly motivating me throughout this long and difficult labor was the stubborn refusal of many prominent Japanese politicians, academics, and industrial leaders to admit, despite overwhelming evidence, that the Nanking massacre had even happened. In contrast to Germany, where it is illegal for teachers to delete the Holocaust from their history curricula, the Japanese have for decades systematically purged references to the Nanking massacre from their textbooks. They have removed photographs of the Nanking massacre from museums, tampered with original source material, and excised from popular culture any mention of the massacre. Even respected history professors in Japan have joined right-wing forces to do what they perceive to be their national duty: discredit reports of a Nanking massacre. In the documentary *In the Name of the Emperor*, one Japanese historian dismisses the entire Rape of Nanking with these words: "Even if twenty or thirty people had been killed, it would have been a great shock to Japan. Until that time, the Japanese troops had been exemplary." It is this deliberate attempt by certain Japanese to distort history that most strongly confirmed in me the need for this book.

As powerful as this one factor has been, however, the book is also a response to something quite different. In recent years sincere attempts to have Japan face up to the consequences of its actions have been labeled "Japan bashing." It is important to establish that I will not be arguing that Japan was the sole imperialist force in the world, or even in Asia, during the first third of this century. China itself tried to extend its influence over its neighbors and even entered into an agreement with Japan to delineate areas of influence on the Korean peninsula, much as the European powers divided up the commercial rights to China in the last century.

Even more important, it does a disservice not only to the men, women, and children whose lives were taken at Nanking but to the Japanese people as well to say that any criticism of Japanese behavior at a certain time and place is criticism of the Japanese as people. This book is not intended as a commentary on the Japanese character or on the genetic makeup of a people who would commit such acts. It is about the power of cultural forces either to make devils of us all, to strip away that thin veneer of social restraint that makes humans humane, or to reinforce it. Germany is today a better place because Jews have not allowed that country to forget what it did during World War II. The American South is a better place for its acknowledgment of the evil of slavery and the one hundred years of Jim Crowism that followed emancipation. Japanese culture will not move forward until it too admits not only to the world but to itself how improper were its actions during World War II. Indeed, I was surprised and pleased by the number of overseas Japanese who attend conferences on the Rape of Nanking. As one suggested, "We want to know as much as you do."

This book describes two related but discrete atrocities. One is the Rape of Nanking itself, the story of how the Japanese wiped out hundreds of thousands of innocent civilians in its enemy's capital.

Another is the cover-up, the story of how the Japanese, emboldened by the silence of the Chinese and Americans, tried to erase the entire massacre from public consciousness, thereby depriving its victims of their proper place in history.

The structure of the first part of my book—the history of the massacre—is largely influenced by *Rashomon*, a famous movie based on a short story (*"Yabunonaka,"* or "In the Grove") by the Japanese novelist Akutagawa Ryunosuke about a rape-and-murder case in tenth-century Kyoto. On the surface, the story appears simple: a bandit waylays a traveling samurai and his wife; the wife is raped and the samurai is found dead. But the story grows more complex when it is told from the perspective of each of the characters. The bandit, the wife, the dead samurai, and an eyewitness of the crime provide different versions of what happened. It is for the reader to pull all the recollections together, to credit or discredit parts or all of each account, and through this process to create out of subjective and often self-serving perceptions a more objective picture of what might have occurred. This story should be included in the curriculum of any course treating criminal justice. Its point goes to the heart of history.

The Rape of Nanking is told from three different perspectives. The first is the Japanese perspective. It is the story of a planned invasion—what the Japanese military was told to do, how to do it, and why. The second perspective is that of the Chinese, the victims; this is the story of the fate of a city when the government is no longer capable of protecting its citizens against outside invaders. This section includes individual stories from the Chinese themselves, stories of defeat, despair, betrayal, and survival. The third is the American and European perspective. These outsiders were, for one moment at least in Chinese history, heroes. The handful of Westerners on the scene risked their lives to help Chinese civilians during the massacre and to warn the rest of the world about the atrocities being carried out before their very eyes. It is only in the next part of the book, treating the postwar period, that we deal with the convenient indifference of Americans and Europeans to what their own nationals on the scene told them.

The last part of my book examines the forces that conspired to keep the Rape of Nanking out of public consciousness for more than half a century. I also treat the recent efforts to ensure that this distortion of history does not go unchallenged.

Any attempt to set the record straight must shed light on how the Japanese, as a people, manage, nurture, and sustain their collective amnesia—even denial—when confronted with the record of their behavior through this period. Their response has been more than a matter of leaving blank spaces in the history books where the record would have been too painful. The ugliest aspects of Japanese military behavior during the Sino-Japanese War have indeed been left out of the education of Japanese schoolchildren. But they have also camouflaged the nation's role in initiating the war within the carefully cultivated myth that the Japanese were the victims, not the instigators, of World War II. The horror visited on the Japanese people during the atomic bombings of Hiroshima and Nagasaki helped this myth replace history.

When it comes to expressing remorse for its own wartime actions before the bar of world opinion, Japan remains to this day a renegade nation. Even in the period directly after the war, and despite the war crimes trials that found a few of its leaders guilty, the Japanese managed to avoid the moral judgment of the civilized world that the Germans were made to accept for their actions in this nightmare time. In continuing to avoid judgment, the Japanese have become the ringleaders of another criminal act. As the Nobel laureate Elie Wiesel warned years ago, to forget a holocaust is to kill twice.

My greatest hope is that this book will inspire other authors and historians to investigate the stories of the Nanking survivors before the last of the voices from the past, dwindling in number every year, are extinguished forever. Possibly even more important, I hope it will stir the conscience of Japan to accept responsibility for this incident.

This book was written with George Santayana's immortal warning in mind: *Those who cannot remember the past are condemned to repeat it.*

PART 1

1

THE PATH TO NANKING

I N TRYING to understand the actions of the Japanese, the questions that call out loudest for answers are the most obvious ones. What broke down on the scene to allow the behavior of Japanese soldiers to escape so totally the restraints that govern most human conduct? Why did the Japanese officers permit and even encourage such a breakdown? What was the complicity of the Japanese government? At the very least, what was its reaction to the reports it was getting through its own channels and to what it was hearing from foreign sources on the scene?

To answer these questions we must begin with a little history.

The twentieth-century Japanese identity was forged in a thousand-year-old system in which social hierarchy was established and sustained through martial competition. For as far back as anyone could remember, the islands' powerful feudal lords employed private armies to wage incessant battle with each other; by the medieval times these armies had evolved into the distinctively Japanese samurai warrior class, whose code of conduct was called *bushido* (the "Way of the Warrior"). To die in the service of one's lord was the greatest honor a samurai warrior could achieve in his lifetime.

Such codes of honor were certainly not invented by Japanese culture. The Roman poet Horace first defined the debt owed by the young men of each generation to their rulers— *Dulce et decorum est pro patria mori*. But the samurai philosophy went a giant step beyond defining military service as fitting and proper. So harsh was its code that its most notable characteristic was the moral imperative that adherents commit suicide if ever they failed to meet honorably the obligations of military service—often with the highly ceremonial and extremely painful ritual of hara-kiri, in which the warrior met death by unflinchingly disemboweling himself in front of witnesses.

By the twelfth century the head of the reigning (and thereby most powerful) family, now called the Shogun, offered the emperor, who was worshiped as the direct descendant of the Sun Goddess, military protection of his samurai in exchange for divine sanction of the entire ruling class. A deal was struck. In time the code of the samurai, initially followed by only a small percentage of the population, penetrated deep into the Japanese culture and became the model of honorable behavior among all young men.

Time did not erode the strength of the *bushido* ethic, which first emerged in the eighteenth century and was practiced to extremes in the modern age. During World War II the infamous kamikaze suicide missions, in which Japanese pilots ceremoniously trained to fly their planes directly into American ships, dramatically impressed upon the West how ready the young men of Japan were to sacrifice their lives for the emperor. But it was more than a small elite group that held to the view of death over surrender. It is striking to note that while the Allied forces surrendered at the rate of 1 prisoner for every 3 dead, the Japanese surrendered at the rate of only 1 per 120 dead.

Another force that gave Japan its peculiar character was its isolation, both physical and self-imposed. By the late fifteenth and early sixteenth centuries Japan was ruled by the Tokugawa clan, who sealed off the island nation from foreign influence. This seclusion, intended to provide security from the wider world, instead insulated Japanese society from the new technology of the industrial revolution taking place in Europe and left it less secure. For 250 years Japanese military technology failed to advance beyond the bow, sword, and musket.

By the nineteenth century events beyond Japan's control would knock the country out of its cocoon, leaving it in a state of insecurity and xenophobic desperation. In 1852, U.S. President Millard Fillmore, frustrated by Japan's refusal to open its ports to commerce and taking the "white man's burden" attitude toward other societies commonly espoused at the time to rationalize European expansionism, decided to end Japan's isolation by dispatching Commander Matthew Perry to the island. Perry studied Japanese history carefully and decided to shock the Japanese into submission with a massive display of American military force. In July 1853, he sent a flotilla of ships belching black smoke into Tokyo Bay—giving the people of Japan their first glimpse of steam power. Surrounding himself with some sixty to seventy aggressive-looking men armed with swords and pistols, Perry strode through the capital of the Shogun and demanded meetings with the highest-ranking officials in Japan.

To say that the Japanese were stunned by Perry's arrival would be a gross understatement. "A parallel situation," the historian Samuel Eliot Morison wrote of the incident, "would be an announcement by astronauts that weird-looking aircraft from outer space were on their way to earth." The terrified Tokugawa aristocracy prepared for battle, hid their valuables, and held panicked meetings among themselves. But in the end, they had no choice but to acknowledge the superiority of American military technology and to accept the mission. With this single visit, Perry not only forced the Tokugawa to sign treaties with the United States but broke down the doors of Japanese trade for other countries, such as Britain, Russia, Germany, and France.

The humiliation of this proud people left a residue of fierce resentment. Secretly some members of the Japanese power elite advocated immediate war with the Western powers, but others counseled prudence, arguing that war would weaken only Japan, not the foreigners. Those taking the latter position urged that the leadership placate the intruders, learn from them, and quietly plan their retaliation:

> As we are not the equals of foreigners in the mechanical arts, let us have intercourse with foreign countries, learn their drill and tactics, and when we have made the [Japanese] nations as united as one family, we shall be able to go abroad and give lands in foreign countries to those who have distinguished themselves in battle; the soldiers will vie with one another in displaying their intrepidity, and it will not be too late then to declare war.

Although that view did not prevail, the words would prove prophetic, for they described not only the strategy the Japanese would follow but the long-term horizons of those who think of life in terms of the state and not of individuals.

With no clear course open to them, the Tokugawa decided to watch and wait—a decision that signed the death warrant of their reign. The Shogun's policy of appeasement, so different from what it required of its loyal adherents, disgusted many and supplied ammunition for its hawkish opponents, who saw the prudent response of the Shogun as nothing more than kowtowing servility before foreign barbarians. Convinced that the Shogun had lost his mandate to rule, rebel clans forged alliances to overthrow the regime and restore the emperor to power.

In 1868 the rebels achieved victory in the name of the Meiji emperor and ignited a revolution to transform a patchwork of warring fiefdoms into a modern, powerful Japan. They elevated the sun cult of Shinto to a state religion and used the emperor as a national symbol to sweep away tribalism and unite the islands. Determined to achieve eventual victory over the West, the new imperial government adopted the samurai ethic of *bushido* as the moral code for all citizens. The foreign threat acted as a further catharsis for the islands. In an era later known as the Meiji Restoration, Japan resounded with nationalistic slogans, such as "Revere the Emperor! Expel the barbarians!" and "Rich country, strong army!"

With astonishing rapidity, the Japanese hurled themselves into the modern age—scientifically, economically, and militarily. The government sent the best students abroad to study science and technology at Western universities, seized control of its own industry to create factories for military production, and replaced the locally controlled feudal armies with a national conscript army. It also meticulously analyzed the defense cultures of the United States and Europe, favoring above all the German military system. But the knowledge of Western technology and defense strategies brought back by its foreign-educated students shattered the country's old confidence in Japanese military superiority, leaving it deeply uneasy about the inevitability of victory in its future showdown with the West.

By the late nineteenth century Japan was ready to flex its muscles, testing its new strength on Asian neighbors. In 1876 the Meiji government dispatched to Korea a naval force of two gunboats and three transports and forced the Korean government to sign a treaty of commerce—a move hauntingly reminiscent of what Perry had forced on Japan.

Then it clashed with China over Korea. An 1885 treaty had established Korea as a coprotectorate of both China and Japan, but hostilities broke out within a decade when the Chinese tried to quell a Korean rebellion backed by Japanese ultranationalists. In September 1894, only six weeks after war was declared, the Japanese not only captured Pyongyang but crushed the Chinese northern fleet at sea. The Qing government was forced to sign the humiliating Treaty of Shimonoseki, under which the Chinese were made to pay the Japanese 200 million taels in war indemnities and to cede to Japan Taiwan, the Pescadores, the Liaodong region of Manchuria, and four more treaty ports. This was later called the first Sino-Japanese war.

For Japan the triumph would have been complete had it not been later marred by the intrusion of Western powers. After the war the Japanese won the greatest prize of the war—the Liaodong Peninsula—but were forced to surrender the last by the tripartite intervention of Russia, France, and Germany. This further illustration of the power of faraway European governments to dictate Japanese conduct only stiffened Japan's resolve to gain military supremacy over its Western tormentors. By 1904 the nation had doubled the size of its army and gained self-sufficiency in the production of armaments.

That strategy soon paid off. Japan was able to boast of defeating not only China in battle but Russia as well. In the Russo-Japanese War of 1905, the Japanese recapture of Port Arthur in the Liaodong Peninsula and naval victory at Tsushima gained half of the Sakhalin Islands and commercial supremacy in Manchuria. This was heady stuff for a proud country that had been chafing for fifty years under the humiliation dealt it by the Western nations. Giddy with triumph, a Japanese professor summed up the sentiments of his country when he declared that Japan was "destined to expand and govern other nations."

Largely because of these successes, the early part of the twentieth century was a euphoric time for Japan. Modernization had earned for the country not only military prestige but unprecedented economic prosperity. The First World War created a huge demand for Japanese steel and iron production as well as for Japanese textiles and foreign trade. Stock prices skyrocketed, and moguls sprang up from obscurity, dazzling the country with their extravagance. Even Japanese women—traditionally cloistered away in this male-dominated society—were seen gambling away fortunes at casinos and racetracks.

Perhaps if the prosperity had lasted, a solid middle class might have emerged in Japan to provide the people with the strength to check imperial military influence. But it did not. Instead, Japan would soon be faced with the single most disastrous economic crisis in its modern history—a crisis that would wipe out its previous gains, push it to the brink of starvation, and propel it down the path of war.

The 1920s drew down the curtain on Japan's golden era of prosperity. When the end of World War I halted the previously insatiable demand for military products, Japanese munitions factories were shut down and thousands of laborers were thrown out of work. The 1929 stock market crash in the United States, and the depression that followed it, also reduced American purchases of luxuries, crippling the Japanese silk export trade.

As important, many international businessmen and consumers went out of their way to shun Japanese products in the postwar decade, even though Japan had been on the Allied side in the First World War. Although both the European nations and the Japanese expanded their overseas empires with the spoils of the First World War, Japanese expansion was not looked on in the same way. Repulsed by aggressive Japanese actions toward China through the first decades of the new century, and even more so by Japan's attempts at Western-style colonialism in the former German colonies it now controlled as a consequence of the war settlements, Western financiers began to invest more heavily in the Chinese. In turn, China, enraged by the Versailles decision to grant Japan the German rights and concessions in the Shantung Peninsula, organized widespread boycotts of Japanese goods. These developments hurt the Japanese economy still further and gave rise to the popular belief that Japan had once again become the victim of an international conspiracy.

The downturn in the economy devastated the average Japanese community. Businesses shut down, and unemployment soared. Destitute farmers and fishermen sold their daughters into prostitution. Soaring inflation, labor strikes, and a tremendous earthquake in September 1923 only exacerbated the dismal conditions.

An increasingly popular argument during the depression was that Japan needed to conquer new territory to ward off mass starvation. The population had swollen from some 30 million at the time of the Meiji Restoration to almost 65 million in 1930, making it increasingly difficult for Japan to feed its people. With great effort, Japanese farmers had pushed up the yield per acre until it would increase no more, and by the 1920s agricultural production had leveled off. The continually expanding population forced Japan to rely heavily on imported foodstuffs every year, and between the 1910s and the end of the 1920s rice imports tripled. They had once been paid for by Japan's textile exports, but the latter were now subject to reduced foreign demand, intense competition, and often discriminatory tariffs.

By the 1920s young radicals in the Japanese army were arguing that military expansion was crucial to the country's survival. In his book *Addresses to Young Men*, Lieutenant Colonel Hashimoto Kingoro wrote:

> There are only three ways left to Japan to escape from the pressures of surplus population . . . emigration, advance into world markets, and expansion of territory. The first door, emigration, has been barred to us by the anti-Japanese immigration policies of other countries. The second door . . . is being pushed shut by tariff barriers and the abrogation of commercial treaties. What should Japan do when two of the three doors have been closed against her?

Other Japanese writers pointed to the spacious territories of other countries, complaining about the injustice of it all, especially since these other countries were not making the most of their land by achieving the high per-acre yields that Japanese farmers had obtained. They looked enviously upon not only China's vast land resources but those of Western countries. Why, the military propagandist Araki Sadao asked, should Japan remain content with 142,270 square miles, much of it barren, to feed 60 million mouths, while countries like Australia and Canada had more than 3 million square miles to feed 6.5 million people each? These discrepancies were unfair. To the ultranationalists, the United States enjoyed some of the greatest advantages of all: Araki Sadao pointed out that the

United States possessed not only 3 million square miles of home territory but 700,000 square miles of colonies.

If expansion westward to the Pacific Ocean was the manifest destiny of the nineteenth-century United States, then China was twentieth-century Japan's manifest destiny. It was almost inevitable that this homogenous people of high personal esteem would see the socially fragmented and loosely governed expanse of China as having been put there for their use and exploitation. Nor were Japan's covetous intentions limited only to Asia. In 1925, just a short three years after Japan entered into a capital ship limitation treaty with the United States, Great Britain, France, and Italy that afforded it a distinctive role as the world's third largest naval power, Okawa Shumei, a national activist, wrote a book that insisted not only on Japan's destiny to "free" Asia but also on the inevitability of world war between Japan and the United States. In the concluding chapter of his book, he was more prophetic than he realized when he predicted a divine—almost apocalyptic—struggle between the two powers: *Before a new world appears, there must be a deadly fight between the powers of the West and the East. This theory is realized in the American challenge to Japan. The strongest country in Asia is Japan and the strongest country that represents Europe is America. . . . These two countries are destined to fight. Only God knows when it will be.*

By the 1930s the Japanese government found itself mired in intrigue as those who favored using Japan's newly acquired technological skills to build a better society competed for influence with those who wanted to use the nation's military superiority over its neighbors to embark on a program of foreign conquest. Expansionist ideologies gained fervent support from right-wing ultranationalists, who called for a military dictatorship that would limit personal wealth, nationalize property, and dominate Asia. These ideas fueled the ambitions of junior military officers, whose rural backgrounds and youth made them naturally distrustful of Tokyo politicians as well as impatient for immediate access to power. Though the officers feuded among themselves, they shared a similar mission: to overhaul society and eliminate all bureaucratic, economic, and political obstacles to what they believed to be Japan's divine mission to avenge itself against the Europeans and dominate Asia.

Step by step, the interventionists forced a series of compromises from the moderate elements in government. But disappointed by the pace of change, they began to conspire among themselves to topple the government. In 1931 a coup was planned but abandoned. In 1932 a group of naval officers launched a terrorist attack in Tokyo that killed Prime Minister Inukai Tsuyoshi but failed to secure martial law.

On February 26, 1936, a clique of young officers launched a bold coup d'état that took the lives of several statesmen. Though the coup paralyzed downtown Tokyo for more than three days, it ultimately failed and the ringleaders were jailed or executed. Power shifted from the extremists to a more cautious faction within the government, though it is important to point out that even this faction shared many of the young officers' fanatical views when it came to Japan's right to a dominant role in Asia.

It soon became apparent to some Japanese ultranationalists that if they wanted to control China they would have to move fast. For there were signs that China, forced to submit to Japanese demands in 1895, was trying to strengthen itself as a nation—signs that gave the Japanese expansionists a sense of urgency in their mission.

China had indeed used the past two decades to transform itself from a disintegrating empire into a struggling national republic. In 1911 rebel armies defeated the Qing imperial forces and ended more than two centuries of Manchu rule. During the 1920s the Nationalists under Chiang Kai-shek successfully fought the warlords of northern China to unify the country. They also announced as a goal the elimination of unfair treaty agreements foisted upon the Qing dynasty by foreign powers. As Chiang's movement gained momentum, it threatened Japanese interests in Manchuria and Mongolia. Something had to be done, and quickly, before China grew too powerful to be conquered.

With the approval of the Japanese government, the military began to intervene more aggressively in Chinese affairs. In 1928 they engineered the assassination of Chang Tsolin, the warlord ruler of Manchuria, when he failed to give them his full cooperation. The murder only served to infuriate the Chinese people, who organized more boycotts against Japanese goods.

By the 1930s Japan had launched an undeclared war with China. On September 18, 1931, the Japanese army blew up the tracks of a Japanese-owned railway in southern Manchuria, hoping to incite an incident. When the blasts failed to derail an express train, the Japanese killed the Chinese guards instead and fabricated a story for the world press about Chinese saboteurs. This incident gave the Japanese an excuse to seize Manchuria, which was renamed Manchukuo and where the Japanese installed Pu Yi, the last emperor of China and heir of the Manchu dynasty, as puppet ruler. The seizure of Manchuria, however, generated anti-Japanese sentiment in China, which was whipped up by Nationalist activists. Feelings ran high on both sides and erupted in bloodshed in 1932 when a Shanghai mob attacked five Japanese Buddhist priests, leaving one of them dead. Japan immediately retaliated by bombing the city, killing tens of thousands of civilians. When the slaughter at Shanghai aroused worldwide criticism, Japan responded by isolating itself from the international community and withdrawing, in 1933, from the League of Nations.

To prepare for the inevitable war with China, Japan had spent decades training its men for combat. The molding of young men to serve in the Japanese military began early in life, and in the 1930s the martial influence seeped into every aspect of Japanese boyhood. Toy shops became virtual shrines to war, selling arsenals of toy soldiers, tanks, helmets, uniforms, rifles, antiaircraft guns, bugles, and howitzers. Memoirs from that time describe preadolescent boys waging mock battles in the streets, using bamboo poles as imaginary rifles. Some even tied logs of wood on their backs and fantasized about dying as "human bomb" heroes in suicide missions.

Japanese schools operated like miniature military units. Indeed, some of the teachers were military officers, who lectured students on their duty to help Japan fulfill its divine destiny of conquering Asia and being able to stand up to the world's nations as a people second to none. They taught young boys how to handle wooden models of guns, and older boys how to handle real ones. Textbooks became vehicles for military propaganda; one geography book even used the shape of Japan as justification for expansion: "We appear to be standing in the vanguard of Asia, advancing bravely into the Pacific. At the same time we appear ready to defend the Asian continent from outside attack." Teachers also instilled in boys hatred and contempt for the Chinese people, preparing them psychologically for a future invasion of the Chinese mainland. One historian tells the story of a squeamish Japanese schoolboy in the 1930s who burst into tears when told to dissect a frog. His teacher slammed his knuckles against the boy's head and yelled, "Why are you crying about one lousy frog? When you grow up you'll have to kill one hundred, two hundred chinks!"

(And yet with all this psychological programming the story is much more complicated. "There was a deep ambivalence in Japanese society about China," Oxford historian Rana Mitter observes. "It was not all racist contempt, as it was for the Koreans: on the one hand, they recognized China as a source of culture that they had drawn on heavily; on the other, they were exasperated by the mess that China was in by the early twentieth century. Ishiwara Kanji, architect of the Manchurian Incident of 1931, was a big fan of the 1911 Revolution. Many Chinese, including Sun Yatsen and Yuan Shikai, drew on Japanese help and training in the years before and after the 1911 Revolution. The Japanese also sponsored Boxer Indemnity Scholarships and Dojinkai hospitals for the Chinese, and scholars like Tokio Hashimoto genuinely appreciated Chinese culture. Japan's Foreign Office and army experts on China were often very well trained and knowledgable about the country."

This knowledge and tempering, however, would rarely pass down to the ordinary soldier.)

The historical roots of militarism in Japanese schools stretched back to the Meiji Restoration. In the late nineteenth century the Japanese minister of education declared that schools were run not for the benefit of the students but for the good of the country. Elementary school teachers were trained like military recruits, with student-teachers housed in barracks and subjected to harsh discipline and indoctrination. In 1890 the Imperial Rescript on Education emerged; it laid down a code of ethics to govern not only students and teachers but every Japanese citizen. The Rescript was the civilian equivalent of Japanese military codes, which valued above all obedience to authority and unconditional loyalty to the emperor. In every Japanese school a copy of the Rescript was enshrined with a portrait of the emperor and taken out each morning to be read. It was reputed that more than one teacher who accidentally stumbled over the words committed suicide to atone for the insult to the sacred document.

By the 1930s the Japanese educational system had become regimented and robotic. A visitor to one of its elementary schools expressed pleasant surprise at seeing thousands of children waving flags and marching in unison in perfect lines; quite clearly the visitor had seen the discipline and order but not the abuse required to establish and maintain it. It was commonplace for teachers to behave like sadistic drill sergeants, slapping children across the cheeks, hitting them with their fists, or bludgeoning them with bamboo or wooden swords. Students were forced to hold heavy objects, sit on their knees, stand barefoot in the snow, or run around the playground until they collapsed from exhaustion. There were certainly few visits to the schools by indignant or even concerned parents.

The pressure to conform to authority intensified if the schoolboy decided to become a soldier. Vicious hazing and a relentless pecking order usually squelched any residual spirit of individualism in him. Obedience was touted as a supreme virtue, and a sense of individual self-worth was replaced by a sense of value as a small cog in the larger scheme of things. To establish this sublimation of individuality to the common good, superior officers or older soldiers slapped recruits for almost no reason at all or beat them severely with heavy wooden rods. According to the author Iritani Toshio, officers often justified unauthorized punishment by saying, "I do not beat you because I hate you. I beat you because I care for you. Do you think I perform these acts with hands swollen and bloody in a state of madness?" Some youths died under such brutal physical conditions; others committed suicide; the majority became tempered vessels into which the military could pour a new set of life goals.

Training was no less grueling a process for aspiring officers. In the 1920s all army cadets had to pass through the Military Academy at Ichigaya. With its overcrowded barracks, unheated study rooms, and inadequate food, the place bore a greater resemblance to a prison than a school. The intensity of the training in Japan surpassed that of most Western military academies: in England an officer was commissioned after some 1,372 hours of classwork and 245 hours of private study, but in Japan the standards were 3,382 hours of classwork and 2,765 hours of private study. The cadets endured a punishing daily regimen of physical exercise and classes in history, geography, foreign languages, mathematics, science, logic, drawing, and penmanship. Everything in the curriculum was bent toward the goal of perfection and triumph. Above all the Japanese cadets were to adopt "a will which knows no defeat." So terrified were the cadets of any hint of failure that examination results were kept secret, to minimize the risk of suicide.

The academy was like an island to itself, sealed off from the rest of the world. The Japanese cadet enjoyed neither privacy nor any opportunity to exercise individual leadership skills. His reading material was carefully censored, and leisure time was nonexistent. History and science were distorted to project an image of the Japanese as a superrace. "During these impressionable years they have been walled off from all outside pleasures, interests or influences," one Western writer observed of the Japanese officers. "The atmosphere of the narrow groove along which they have moved has been saturated with a special national and a special military propaganda. Already from a race psychologically far removed from us, they have been removed still further."

In the summer of 1937 Japan finally succeeded in provoking a full-scale war with China. In July a Japanese regiment, garrisoned by treaty in the Chinese city of Tientsin, had been conducting night maneuvers near the ancient Marco Polo Bridge. During a break several shots were fired at the Japanese in the darkness, and a Japanese soldier failed to appear during roll call. Using this incident as an excuse to exercise Japan's power in the region, Japanese troops advanced upon the Chinese fort of Wanping near the bridge and demanded that its gates be opened so that they could search for the soldier. When the Chinese commander refused, the Japanese shelled the fort.

By the end of July, Japan had tightened its grasp on the entire Tientsin-Peking region and by August the Japanese had invaded Shanghai. The second Sino-Japanese War was no longer reversible.

But conquering China proved to be a more difficult task than the Japanese anticipated. In Shanghai alone Chinese forces outnumbered the Japanese marines ten to one, and Chiang Kai-shek, leader of the Nationalist government, had reserved his best troops for the battle. That August, while attempting to land thirty-five thousand fresh troops on the docks of Shanghai, the Japanese encountered their first setback. A hidden Chinese artillery emplacement opened fire and killed several hundred men, including a cousin of the Empress Nagako. For months the Chinese defended the metropolis with extraordinary valor. To the chagrin of the Japanese, the battle of Shanghai proceeded slowly, street by street, barricade by barricade.

In the 1930s, Japanese military leaders had boasted—and seriously believed—that Japan could conquer all of mainland China within three months. But when a battle in a single Chinese city alone dragged from summer to fall, and then from fall to winter, it shattered Japanese fantasies of an easy victory. Here, this primitive people, illiterate in military science and poorly trained, had managed to fight the superior Japanese to a standstill. When Shanghai finally fell in November, the mood of the imperial troops had turned ugly, and many, it was said, lusted for revenge as they marched toward Nanking.

2

SIX WEEKS OF TERROR

THE RACE TO NANKING

THE JAPANESE strategy for Nanking was simple. The imperial army exploited the fact that the city was blocked by water in two directions. The ancient capital lay south of a bend in the Yangtze River that first coursed northward and then turned to flow east. By converging upon Nanking in a semicircular front from the southeast, the Japanese could use the natural barrier of the river to complete the encirclement of the capital and cut off all escape.

In late November, three parallel Japanese troops rushed toward Nanking. One force traveled west under the southern bank of the Yangtze River. Its troops poured into the Yangtze Delta, through the Paimou Inlet northwest of Shanghai, and along the Nanking–Shanghai railway, where the Japanese air force had already blasted away most of the bridges. These troops were led by Nakajima Kesago, who had worked as a

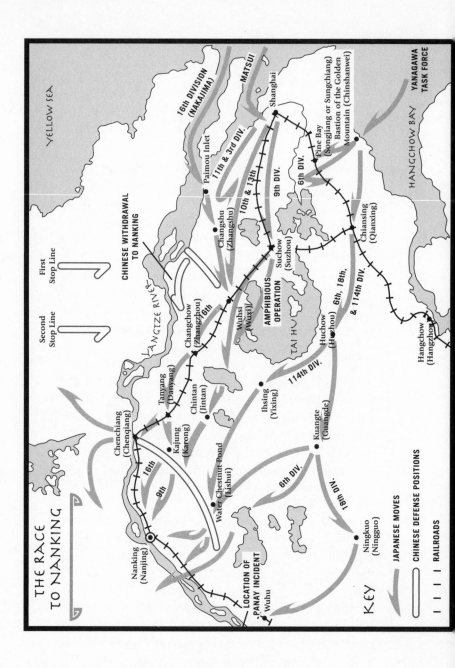

THE RACE TO NANKING

member of Japanese army intelligence in France and later as chief of the Japanese secret police for Emperor Hirohito. Not much has been written about Nakajima, but what has been written is overwhelmingly negative. David Bergamini, author of *Japan's Imperial Conspiracy*, called him a "small Himmler of a man, a specialist in thought control, intimidation and torture" and quoted others describing Nakajima as a sadist who packed for his journey to Nanking special oil for burning bodies. Even his biographer, Kimura Kuninori, mentioned that Nakajima had been described as "a beast" and "a violent man."

Another force readied itself for a bold amphibious assault across Tai Hu, a lake situated halfway between Shanghai and Nanking. This force moved west from Shanghai in a route south of Nakajima's troops. Directing the movement was General Matsui Iwane, a frail, slight, tubercular man with a tiny mustache. Unlike Nakajima, Matsui was a devout Buddhist from a scholarly family. He was also the commander-in-chief of the Japanese imperial army for the entire Shanghai-Nanking region.

A third force traveled further south of Matsui's men and swerved northwest toward Nanking. Heading this force was Lieutenant General Yanagawa Heisuke, a bald, short man with literary interests. Perhaps to a greater degree than most other Japanese involved in the Rape of Nanking, his life during the invasion is veiled in mystery. According to his biographer, Sugawara Yutaka, the fascist clique that took control of the Japanese military had expelled Yanagawa from their ranks because he attempted to stop their 1932 coup. After his marginalization and demotion to the reserves, Yanagawa served as a commanding officer in China and performed "great military achievements . . . including the surrounding of Nanking," but the military withheld his name and photograph from publication at the time. Thus Yanagawa was known to many in Japan as "the masked shogun."

Little was spared on the path to Nanking. Japanese veterans remember raiding tiny farm communities, where they clubbed or bayoneted everyone in sight. But small villages were not the only casualties; entire cities were razed to the ground. Consider the example of Suchow (now called Suzhou), a city on the east bank of Tai Hu Lake. One of the oldest cities of China, it was prized for its delicate silk embroidery, palaces, and temples. Its canals and ancient bridges had earned the city its Western nickname as "the Venice of China." On November 19, on a morning of pouring rain, a Japanese advance guard marched through the gates of Suchow, wearing hoods that prevented Chinese sentries from recognizing them. Once inside, the Japanese murdered and plundered the city for days, burning down ancient landmarks and abducting thousands of Chinese women for sexual slavery. The invasion, according to the *China Weekly Review,* caused the population of the city to drop from 350,000 to less than 500.

A British correspondent had the opportunity to record what was left of Pine River, (Sungchiang, a suburban city of Shanghai), nine weeks after the Japanese had passed through it. "There is hardly a building standing which has not been gutted by fire," he wrote. "Smoldering ruins and deserted streets present an eerie spectacle, the only living creatures being dogs unnaturally fattened by feasting on corpses. In the whole of Sungchiang, which should contain a densely packed population of approximately 100,000, I saw only five Chinese, who were old men, hiding in a French mission compound in tears."

ASAKA TAKES COMMAND

But the worst was still to come.

On December 7, as the Japanese troops zeroed in on Nanking, General Matsui grew feverishly ill in his field headquarters at Suchow—another flare-up of his chronic tuberculosis. The illness struck Matsui right when power shifted from his command to that of a member of the imperial family. Only five days earlier Emperor Hirohito had promoted Matsui out of the action while dispatching his own uncle, Prince Asaka Yasuhiko, to the front to replace him. Under the new order, Matsui would be in charge of the entire central China theater, while Asaka, a lieutenant general with a thirty-year tenure in the military, would take responsibility as the new commander-in-chief of the army around Nanking. As a member of the royal family, Asaka possessed power that would override all other authority on the Nanking front. He was also closer to Lieutenant General Nakajima and General Yanagawa than to Matsui because he had spent three years in Paris with them as a military intelligence officer.

Little is known as to why Hirohito chose at this critical moment to give Asaka this position, though Bergamini believes it was done to test Asaka, who had sided with the emperor's brother Chichibu against Hirohito on a political issue during the February 1936 army mutiny. On the palace rolls, Hirohito had singled out Asaka as the one member of the royal family who possessed an attitude that was "not good" and apparently gave his uncle the appointment at Nanking as an opportunity to redeem himself.

At the time it seemed like a trivial change, but later, for the lives of hundreds of thousands of Chinese, it would prove to be a critical one.

It is hard to describe what really happened behind the scenes in the Japanese army because many of the details were given by Matsui and his colleagues years later at their war crimes trial, or by sources who may be unreliable, and they are therefore cited with caution. But if their testimony can be believed, this is what we learn. Wary of the imperial newcomer and the potential for abuse of power, Matsui issued a set of moral commandments for the invasion of Nanking. He ordered his armies to regroup a few kilometers outside the city walls, to enter the Chinese capital with only a few well-disciplined battalions, and to complete the occupation so that the army would "sparkle before the eyes of the Chinese and make them place confidence in Japan." He also called a meeting of staff officers before his sickbed and proclaimed:

> The entry of the Imperial Army into a foreign capital is a great event in our history . . . attracting the attention of the world. Therefore let no unit enter the city in a disorderly fashion. . . . Let them know beforehand the matters to be remembered and the position of foreign rights and interests in the walled city. Let them be absolutely free from plunder. Dispose sentries

as needed. Plundering and causing fires, even carelessly, shall be punished severely. Together with the troops let many military police and auxiliary military police enter the walled city and thereby prevent unlawful conduct.

But events were brewing elsewhere over which Matsui had no control. On December 5, the story goes, Prince Asaka left Tokyo by plane and arrived on the front three days later. In an abandoned country villa near field headquarters some ten miles southeast of Nanking, Prince Asaka met with General Nakajima, his colleague from his Paris days, who was now recovering from a flesh wound in his left buttock. Nakajima told Asaka that the Japanese were about to surround three hundred thousand Chinese troops in the vicinity of Nanking and that preliminary negotiations revealed that they were ready to surrender.

After Asaka heard this report, it was said that his headquarters sent out a set of orders, under his personal seal, marked "Secret, to be destroyed." We now know that the clear message of these orders was: "KILL ALL CAPTIVES." What is not clear is whether Asaka himself issued the orders.*

----

* Taisa Isamo, Asaka's staff officer for intelligence, later confessed to friends that on his own initiative he had forged the order. Another Japanese officer, Tanaka Ryukichi, said that in April 1938, Chou, then the head of the 74th wing of the Japanese army, told him an interesting tale. Chou told him that when his troops landed at Hangchow (or Hangzhou) Bay and pushed inland, nearly 300,000 Chinese troops were cut off from retreat, so they threw away their weapons and surrendered to the Japanese. "To arrange for so many prisoners, to feed them, was a huge problem," Chou reportedly said.

As the story goes, Chou seized upon a quick-fix solution to eliminate the food problem: "I immediately issued orders to all troops: 'We must entirely massacre these prisoners!' Using the name of the military commander, I sent these orders by telegram. The wording of the order was to annihilate."

We will never know if this story is true, but it must be noted that even if Chou had indeed forged the kill order on his own, this does not absolve Prince Asaka of responsibility for the massacre. Asaka could have issued an order to cancel the massacre once it started and court-martialed his intelligence officer.

By the time Japanese troops entered Nanking, an order to eliminate all Chinese captives had been not only committed to paper but distributed to lower-echelon officers. On December 13, 1937, the Japanese 66th Battalion received the following command:

BATTALION BATTLE REPORTER, AT 2:00 RECEIVED ORDER FROM THE REGIMENT COMMANDER: TO COMPLY WITH ORDERS FROM BRIGADE COMMANDING HEADQUARTERS, ALL PRISONERS OF WAR ARE TO BE EXECUTED. METHOD OF EXECUTION: DIVIDE THE PRISONERS INTO GROUPS OF A DOZEN. SHOOT TO KILL SEPARATELY.

3:30 P.M. A MEETING IS CALLED TO GATHER COMPANY COMMANDERS TO EXCHANGE OPINIONS ON HOW TO DISPOSE OF POWS. FROM THE DISCUSSION IT IS DECIDED THAT THE PRISONERS ARE TO BE DIVIDED EVENLY AMONG EACH COMPANY (1ST, 2ND AND 4TH COMPANY) AND TO BE BROUGHT OUT FROM THEIR IMPRISONMENT IN GROUPS OF 50 TO BE EXECUTED. 1ST COMPANY IS TO TAKE ACTION IN THE GRAIN FIELD SOUTH OF THE GARRISON; 2ND COMPANY TAKES ACTION IN THE DEPRESSION SOUTHWEST OF THE GARRISON; AND 4TH COMPANY TAKES ACTION IN THE GRAIN FIELD SOUTHEAST OF THE GARRISON.

THE VICINITY OF THE IMPRISONMENT MUST BE HEAVILY GUARDED. OUR INTENTIONS ARE ABSOLUTELY NOT TO BE DETECTED BY THE PRISONERS.

EVERY COMPANY IS TO COMPLETE PREPARATION BEFORE 5:00. EXECUTIONS ARE TO START BY 5:00 AND ACTION IS TO BE FINISHED BY 7:30.

There was a ruthless logic to the order. The captives could not be fed, so they had to be destroyed. Killing them would not only eliminate the food problem but diminish the possibility of retaliation. Moreover, dead enemies could not form up into guerrilla forces.

But executing the order was another matter. When the Japanese troops smashed through the walls in the early predawn hours of December 13, they entered a city in which they were vastly outnumbered. Historians later estimated that more than half a million civilians and ninety thousand Chinese troops were trapped in Nanking, compared to the fifty thousand Japanese soldiers who assaulted the city. General Nakajima knew that killing tens of thousands of Chinese captives was a formidable task: "To deal with crowds of a thousand, five thousand, or ten thousand, it is tremendously difficult even just to disarm them. . . . It would be disastrous if they were to make any trouble."

KILLING THE PRISONERS OF WAR

Because of their limited manpower, the Japanese relied heavily on deception. The strategy for mass butchery involved several steps: promising the Chinese fair treatment in return for an end to resistance, coaxing them into surrendering themselves to their Japanese conquerors, dividing them into groups of one to two hundred men, and then luring them to different areas near Nanking to be killed. Nakajima hoped that faced with the impossibility of further resistance, most of the captives would lose heart and comply with whatever directions the Japanese gave them.

All this was easier to achieve than the Japanese had anticipated. Resistance was sporadic; indeed, it was practically nonexistent. Having thrown away their arms when attempting to flee the city as the Japanese closed in, many Chinese soldiers simply turned themselves in, hoping for better treatment. Once the men surrendered and permitted their hands to be bound, the rest was easy.

Perhaps nowhere is the passivity of the Chinese soldiers better illustrated than in the diary of the former Japanese soldier Azuma Shiro, who described the surrender of thousands of Chinese troops shortly after the fall of Nanking. His own troops were assigning sentry and billet in a city square when they suddenly received an order to round up about 20,000 prisoners of war.

Azuma and his countrymen walked some nine or ten miles in search of the prisoners. Night fell, and the Japanese finally heard a rumbling, froglike noise. They also saw numerous cigarette lights blinking in the darkness. "It was a magnificent view," Azuma wrote. "Seven thousand prisoners all in one place, gathering around the two white flags attached to a dead branch, which flew in the night sky." The prisoners were a ragged assortment of men wearing blue cotton military uniforms, blue cotton overcoats, and caps. Some covered their heads with blankets, some carried mat-rush sacks, and some carried futons on their backs. The Japanese lined the prisoners up into four columns, with the white flag at the head. This group of thousands of Chinese soldiers had waited patiently for the Japanese to fetch them and direct them to the next step in the surrender process.

The reluctance of the Chinese army to fight back stunned Azuma. To a man who came from a military culture in which pilots were given swords instead of parachutes, and in which suicide was infinitely preferable to capture, it was incomprehensible that the Chinese would not fight an enemy to the death. His contempt for the Chinese deepened when he discovered that the prisoners' numbers exceeded those of the captors.

"It was funny yet pitiable when I imagined how they gathered whatever white cloth they could find, attached it to a dead twig, and marched forward just to surrender," Azuma wrote.

> I thought, how could they become prisoners, with the kind of force they had—more than two battalions—and without even trying to show any resistance. There must have been a considerable number of officers for this many troops, but not a single one remained, all of them having slipped away and escaped, I thought. Although we had two companies, and those seven thousand prisoners had already been disarmed, our troops could have been annihilated had they decided to rise up and revolt.

A welter of emotions filled Azuma. He felt sorry for the Chinese soldiers, thirsty and frightened men who constantly asked for water and reassurance that they would not be killed. But at the same time their cowardice disgusted him. Azuma suddenly felt ashamed for ever having been secretly afraid of the Chinese in previous battles, and his automatic impulse was to dehumanize the prisoners by comparing them to insects and animals.

> They all walked in droves, like ants crawling on the ground. They looked like a bunch of homeless people, with ignorant expressions on their faces.
>
> A herd of ignorant sheep, with no rule or order, marched on in the darkness, whispering to each other.
>
> They hardly looked like the enemy who only yesterday was shooting at and troubling us. It was impossible to believe that they were the enemy soldiers.
>
> It felt quite foolish to think we had been fighting to the death against these ignorant slaves. And some of them were even twelve- or thirteen-year-old boys.

The Japanese led the prisoners to a nearby village. Azuma recalled that when some of the Chinese were herded into a large house, they hesitated to enter, looking upon the place as if it were "a slaughter house." But finally they gave in and filed through the gate. Some of the prisoners struggled with the Japanese only when the latter tried to take away their blankets and bedding. The next morning Azuma and his comrades received an order to patrol another area; they later learned that while they were on patrol the Chinese prisoners had been assigned to companies in groups of two to three hundred, then killed.

Probably the single largest mass execution of prisoners of war during the Rape of Nanking took place near Mufu Mountain. The mountain lay directly north of Nanking, between the city and the south bank of the Yangtze River; an estimated fifty-seven thousand civilians and former soldiers were executed.

The killing proceeded in stealth and in stages. On December 16, the *Asahi Shimbun* newspaper correspondent Yokoto reported that the Japanese had captured 14,777 soldiers near the artillery forts of Wulong Mountain and Mufu Mountain and that the sheer number of the prisoners posed problems. "The [Japanese] army encountered great difficulties since this was the first time that such a huge number of POWs were captured," Yokoto wrote. "There were not enough men to handle them."

According to Kurihara Riichi, a former Japanese army corporal who kept diaries and notes of the event, the Japanese disarmed thousands of prisoners, stripped them of everything but their clothes and blankets, and escorted them to a row of straw-roofed temporary buildings. When the Japanese military received orders on December 17 to kill the prisoners, they proceeded with extra caution. That morning the Japanese announced that they were going to transport the Chinese prisoners to Baguazhou, a small island in the middle of the Yangtze River. They explained to the captives that they needed to take special precautions for the move and bound the captives' hands behind their backs—a task that took all morning and most of the afternoon.

Sometime between 4:00 and 6:00 P.M., the Japanese divided the prisoners into four columns and marched them to the west, skirting the hills and stopping at the riverbank. "After three or four hours waiting and not knowing what was going on, the prisoners could not see any preparations for crossing the river," the corporal wrote. "It was then growing dark. They did not know . . . that Japanese soldiers already encircled them in a crescent formation along the river and they were in the sights of many machine guns."

By the time the executions began, it was too late for the Chinese to escape. "Suddenly all kinds of guns fired at once," Kurihara Riichi wrote. "The sounds of these firearms mingled with desperate yelling and screams." For an hour the Chinese struggled and thrashed about desperately, until there were few sounds still coming from the group. From evening until dawn the Japanese bayoneted the bodies, one by one.

Body disposal posed a mammoth problem for the Japanese. Only a fraction of the total number of men who perished in and around Nanking were slaughtered at Mufu Mountain, yet the cleanup there took days. Burial was one method of disposal, but General Nakajima complained in his diary that it was hard to locate ditches large enough to bury heaps of seven to eight thousand corpses. Cremation was another, but the Japanese often lacked sufficient fuel to do a proper job. After the Mufu Mountain massacre, for instance, the Japanese poured large drums of gasoline on the bodies to burn them, but the drums ran out before fires could reduce the remains to ashes. "The result was a mountain of charred corpses," a Japanese corporal wrote.

Many bodies were simply dumped into the Yangtze River.

THE MURDER OF CIVILIANS

After the soldiers surrendered en masse, there was virtually no one left to protect the citizens of the city. Knowing this, the Japanese poured into Nanking on December 13, 1937, occupying government buildings, banks, and warehouses, shooting people randomly in the streets, many of them in the back as they ran away. Using machine guns, revolvers, and rifles, the Japanese fired at the crowds of wounded soldiers, elderly women, and children who gathered in the North Chungshan and Central roads and nearby alleys. They also killed Chinese civilians in every section of the city: tiny lanes, major boulevards, mud dugouts, government buildings, city squares. As victims toppled to the ground, moaning and screaming, the streets, alleys, and ditches of the fallen capital ran rivers of blood, much of it coming from people barely alive, with no strength left to run away.

The Japanese systematically killed the city dwellers as they conducted house-to-house searches for Chinese soldiers in Nanking. But they also massacred the Chinese in the nearby suburbs and countryside. Corpses piled up outside the city walls, along the river (which had literally turned red with blood), by ponds and lakes, and on hills and mountains. In villages near Nanking, the Japanese shot down any young man who passed, under the presumption that he was likely to be a former Chinese soldier. But they also murdered people who could not possibly be Chinese soldiers—elderly men and women, for instance—if they hesitated or even if they failed to understand orders, delivered in the Japanese language, to move this way or that.

During the last ten days of December, Japanese motorcycle brigades patrolled Nanking while Japanese soldiers shouldering loaded rifles guarded the entrances to all the streets, avenues, and alleys. Troops went from door to door, demanding that the doors be opened to welcome the victorious armies. The moment the shopkeepers complied, the Japanese opened fire on them. The imperial army massacred thousands of people in this manner and then systematically looted the stores and burned whatever they had no use for.

THE JAPANESE JOURNALISTS

These atrocities shocked many of the Japanese correspondents who had followed the troops to Nanking. A horrified *Mainichi Shimbun* reporter watched the Japanese line up Chinese prisoners on top of the wall near Chungshan Gate and charge at them with bayonets fixed on rifles. "One by one the prisoners fell down to the outside of the wall," the reporter wrote. "Blood splattered everywhere. The chilling atmosphere made one's hair stand on end and limbs tremble with fear. I stood there at a total loss and did not know what to do."

He was not alone in his reaction. Many other reporters—even seasoned war correspondents—recoiled at the orgy of violence, and their exclamations found their way into print. From Imai Masatake, a Japanese military correspondent:

> On Hsiakwan wharves, there was the dark silhouette of a mountain made of dead bodies. About fifty to one hundred people were toiling there, dragging bodies from the mountain of corpses and throwing them into the Yangtze River. The bodies dripped blood, some of them still alive and moaning

weakly, their limbs twitching. The laborers were busy working in total silence, as in a pantomime. In the dark one could barely see the opposite bank of the river. On the pier was a field of glistening mud under the moon's dim light. Wow! That's all blood!

After a while, the coolies had done their job of dragging corpses and the soldiers lined them up along the river. Rat-tat-tat machine-gun fire could be heard. The coolies fell backwards into the river and were swallowed by the raging currents. The pantomime was over.

A Japanese officer at the scene estimated that 20,000 persons had been executed.

From the Japanese military correspondent Omata Yukio, who saw Chinese prisoners brought to Hsiakwan and lined up along the river:

> Those in the first row were beheaded, those in the second row were forced to dump the severed bodies into the river before they themselves were beheaded. The killing went on non-stop, from morning until night, but they were only able to kill 2,000 persons in this way. The next day, tired of killing in this fashion, they set up machine guns. Two of them raked a cross-fire at the lined-up prisoners. Rat-tat-tat-tat. Triggers were pulled. The prisoners fled into the water, but no one was able to make it to the other shore.

From the Japanese photojournalist Kawano Hiroki:

> Before the "Ceremony of Entering the City," I saw fifty to one hundred bodies drifting down the Yangtze River. Did they die in battle, or were they killed after being taken prisoner? Or were they slaughtered civilians?
>
> I remember there was a pond just outside Nanking. It looked like a sea of blood—with splendid colors. If only I had color film . . . what a shocking shot that would have been!

Sasaki Motomasa, a Japanese military correspondent at Nanking, observed, "I've seen piled-up bodies in the Great Quake in Tokyo, but nothing can be compared to this."

The Rape of Nanking

Next, the Japanese turned their attention to the women.

"Women suffered most," Takokoro Kozo, a former soldier in the 114th Division of the Japanese army in Nanking, recalled. "No matter how young or old, they all could not escape the fate of being raped. We sent out coal trucks from Hsiakwan to the city streets and villages to seize a lot of women. And then each of them was allocated to 15 to 20 soldiers for sexual intercourse and abuse."

Surviving Japanese veterans claim that the army had officially outlawed the rape of enemy women. But rape remained so deeply embedded in Japanese military culture and superstition that no one took the rule seriously. Many believed that raping virgins would make them more powerful in battle. Soldiers were even known to wear amulets made from the pubic hair of such victims, believing that they possessed magical powers against injury.

The military policy forbidding rape only encouraged soldiers to kill their victims afterwards. During an interview for the documentary *In the Name of the Emperor*, Azuma Shiro, a former Japanese soldier, spoke candidly about the process of rape and murder in Nanking:

> At first we used some kinky words like *Pikankan*. *Pi* means "hip," *kankan* means "look." *Pikankan* means, "Let's see a woman open up her legs." Chinese women didn't wear underpants. Instead, they wore trousers tied with a string. There was no belt. As we pulled the string, the buttocks were exposed. We "pikankan." We looked. After a while we would say something like, "It's my day to take a bath," and we took turns raping them. It would be all right if we only raped them. I shouldn't say all right. But we always stabbed and killed them. Because dead bodies don't talk.

Takokoro Kozo shared Azuma's bluntness in discussing the issue. "After raping, we would also kill them," he recalled. "Those women would start to flee once we let them go. Then we would 'bang!' shoot them in the back to finish them up."

According to surviving veterans, many of the soldiers felt remarkably little guilt about this. "Perhaps when we were raping her, we looked at her as a woman," Azuma wrote, "but when we killed her, we just thought of her as something like a pig."

This behavior was not restricted to soldiers. Officers at all levels indulged in the orgy. (Even Tani Hisao, the senior general and commander of the Japanese 6th Division, was later found guilty of raping some twenty women in Nanking.) Some not only urged soldiers to commit gang rape in the city but warned them to dispose of the women afterwards to eliminate evidence of the crime. "Either pay them money or kill them in some out-of-the-way place after you have finished," one officer told his underlings.

THE ARRIVAL OF MATSUI IWANE

The killing and raping subsided when Matsui Iwane, still weak from his illness, entered the city on the morning of December 17 for a ceremonial parade. After recovering from his bout of tuberculosis, he traveled upriver on a naval launch and rode by car to the triple archway of the Mountain Gate on the east side of Nanking. There he mounted a chestnut horse, wheeled it to face the direction of the imperial palace in Tokyo, and led a triple banzai for the emperor for Japan's national radio broadcasting company: "Great Field Marshal on the Steps of Heaven—banzai—ten thousand years of life!" He rode down a boulevard that was carefully cleared of dead bodies and flanked by tens of thousands of cheering soldiers and arrived at the Metropolitan Hotel in the northern part of town, which held a banquet for Matsui that evening.

It was sometime during this banquet, the record suggests, that Matsui suspected that something had gone terribly amiss at Nanking. That evening he called a staff conference and ordered all unnecessary troops transferred out of the city. The next day the Western news media reported that the Japanese army was engaged in a giant conspiracy of silence against Matsui to prevent him from knowing the full truth of the Nanking atrocities.

When Matsui began to comprehend the full extent of the rape, murder, and looting in the city, he showed every sign of dismay. On December 18, 1937, he told one of his civilian aides: "I now realize that we have unknowingly wrought a most grievous effect on this city. When I think of the feelings and sentiments of many of my Chinese friends who have fled from Nanking and of the future of the two countries, I cannot but feel depressed. I am very lonely and can never get in a mood to rejoice about this victory." He even let a tinge of regret flavor the statement he released to the press that morning: "I personally feel sorry for the tragedies to the people, but the Army must continue unless China repents. Now, in the winter, the season gives time to reflect. I offer my sympathy, with deep emotion, to a million innocent people."

Later that day, when the Japanese command held a burial service for the Japanese soldiers who died during the invasion, Matsui rebuked the three hundred officers, regimental commanders, and others on the grounds for the orgy of violence in the city. "Never before," Matsumoto, a Japanese correspondent wrote, "had a superior given his officers such a scathing reprimand. The military was incredulous at Matsui's behavior because one of the officers present was a prince of Imperial descent."

By Sunday, December 19, Matsui was moved to Asaka's headquarters outside the city and put on a destroyer the following day to be sent back to Shanghai. But once there he made an even more shocking move, one perhaps driven by desperation: he confided his worries to the *New York Times* and even told an American foreign correspondent that "the Japanese army is probably the most undisciplined army in the world today." That month he also sent a bold message to Prince Asaka's chief of staff. "It is rumored that unlawful acts continue," he wrote. "Especially because Prince Asaka is our commander, military discipline and morals must be that much more strictly maintained. Anyone who misconducts himself must be severely punished."

On New Year's Day, Matsui was still upset about the behavior of the Japanese soldiers at Nanking. Over a toast he confided to a Japanese diplomat: "My men have done something very wrong and extremely regrettable."

But the raping went on, and the killing went on. Matsui seemed incapable of stopping it. If one can believe the story Matsui told years later, his brief visit to Nanking even reduced him to tears in front of his colleagues. "Immediately after the memorial services, I assembled the higher officers and wept tears of anger before them," Matsui told his Buddhist confessor before his hanging in 1948. "Both Prince Asaka and Lieutenant General Yanagawa . . . were there. I told them everything had been lost in one moment through the brutalities of the soldiers. And can you imagine it, even after that, those soldiers laughed at me."

THE COMFORT WOMEN: THE LEGACY OF NANKING

One of the most bizarre consequences of the wholesale rape that took place at Nanking was the response of the Japanese government to the massive outcry from Western nations. Rather than stifle or punish the soldiers responsible, the Japanese high command made plans to create a giant underground system of military prostitution—one that would draw into its web hundreds of thousands of women across Asia. "The Japanese Expeditionary Force in Central China issued an order to set up comfort houses during this period of time," Yoshimi Yoshiaki, a prominent history professor at Chuo University, observes, "because Japan was afraid of criticism from China, the United States of America and Europe following the cases of massive rapes between battles in Shanghai and Nanking."

The plan was straightforward. By luring, purchasing, or kidnapping between eighty thousand and two hundred thousand women—most of them from the Japanese colony of Korea but many also from China, Taiwan, the Philippines, and Indonesia—the Japanese military hoped to reduce the incidence of random rape of local women (thereby diminishing the opportunity for international criticism), to contain sexually transmitted diseases through the use of condoms, and to reward soldiers for fighting on the battlefront for long stretches of time. Later, of course, when the world learned of this plan, the Japanese government refused to acknowledge responsibility, insisting for decades afterwards that private entrepreneurs, not the imperial government, ran the wartime military brothels. But in 1991 Yoshimi Yoshiaki unearthed from the Japanese Defense Agency's archives a document entitled "Regarding the Recruitment of Women for Military Brothels." The document bore the personal stamps of leaders from the Japanese high command and contained orders for the immediate construction of "facilities of sexual comfort" to stop troops from raping women in regions they controlled in China.

The first official comfort house opened near Nanking in 1938. To use the word *comfort* in regard to either the women or the "houses" in which they lived is ludicrous, for it conjures up spa images of beautiful geisha girls strumming lutes, washing men, and giving them shiatsu massages. In reality, the conditions of these brothels were sordid beyond the imagination of most civilized people. Untold numbers of these women (whom the Japanese called "public toilets") took their own lives when they learned their destiny; others died from disease or murder. Those who survived suffered a lifetime of shame and isolation, sterility, or ruined health. Because most of the victims came from cultures that idealized chastity in women, even those who survived rarely spoke after the war—most not until very recently—about their experiences for fear of facing more shame and derision. Asian Confucianism—particularly Korean Confucianism—upheld female purity as a virtue greater than life and perpetuated the belief that any woman who could live through such a degrading experience and not commit suicide was herself an affront to society. Hence, half a century passed before a few of the comfort women found the courage to break their silence and to seek financial compensation from the Japanese government for their suffering.

THE MOTIVES BEHIND NANKING

Now we come to the most disturbing question of all—the state of the Japanese mind in Nanking. What was inside the mind of the teenage soldier handed a rifle and bayonet that propelled him to commit such atrocities?

Many scholars have wrestled with this question and found it almost impossible to answer. Theodore Cook, who coauthored the book *Japan at War: An Oral History* with his wife Haruko Taya Cook, admits that the brutality of the Rape of Nanking baffles him. He finds no parallels in the history of civil war in Japan; rather, systematic destruction and mass slaughter of urban populations appear to be part of Mongol rather than Japanese history. Trying to examine the mind-set of the Japanese at Nanking, he said, was like peering into "a black hole."

Many find it difficult to reconcile the barbarism of Nanking with the exquisite politeness and good manners for which the Japanese are renowned. But certain military experts believe that these two seemingly separate behaviors are in reality entwined. They point to the awesome status of the ancient samurai, who for centuries possessed the power to lop off the head of a peasant if he failed to give the warrior a polite answer to his questions. "To this day," an American naval intelligence officer wrote of Japanese culture during World War II, "the Japanese idea of a polite answer is one satisfactory to the questioner. Is it surprising that good manners are a national trait with the Japanese?"

Other experts have attributed Japanese wartime atrocities to Japanese culture itself. In her book *The Chrysanthemum and the Sword*, the American anthropologist Ruth Benedict wrote that because moral obligations in Japanese society were not universal but local and particularized, they could be easily broken on foreign soil. Other experts blame the non-Christian nature of Japanese religion, claiming that while Christianity puts forth the idea that all humans are brothers—indeed, that all things were created in God's image—Shintoism in Japan purports that only the emperor and his descendants were created in God's image. Citing such differences, these experts have concluded that some cultures, however sophisticated they become, remain at their core tribal, in that the obligations the individual owes to others within the tribe are very different from those owed to outsiders.

There is an inherent danger in this assumption, for it has two implications: one, that the Japanese, by virtue of their religion, are naturally less humane than Western cultures and must be judged by different standards (an implication I find both irresponsible and condescending), and two, that Judeo-Christian cultures are somehow less capable of perpetrating atrocities like the Rape of Nanking. Certainly Nazis in Germany, a devoutly Christian country, found a way in the 1930s and 1940s to dehumanize the German psyche and even demonize peoples they had declared to be enemies of the Germans. What resulted were some of the worst crimes against humanity this planet has ever seen.

Looking back upon millennia of history, it appears clear that no race or culture has a monopoly on wartime cruelty. The veneer of civilization seems to be exceedingly thin—one that can be easily stripped away, especially by the stresses of war.

How then do we explain the raw brutality carried out day after day after day in the city of Nanking? Unlike their Nazi counterparts, who have mostly perished in prisons and before execution squads or, if alive, are spending their remaining days as fugitives from the law, many of the Japanese war criminals are still alive, living in peace and comfort, protected by the Japanese government. They are therefore some of the few people on this planet who, without concern for retaliation in a court of international law, can give authors and journalists a glimpse of their thoughts and feelings while committing World War II atrocities.

Here is what we learn. The Japanese soldier was not simply hardened for battle in China; he was hardened for the task of murdering Chinese combatants and noncombatants alike. Indeed, various games and exercises were set up by the Japanese military to numb its men to the human instinct against killing people who are not attacking.

For example, on their way to the capital, Japanese soldiers

were made to participate in killing competitions, which were avidly covered by the Japanese media like sporting events. The most notorious one appeared in the December 7 issue of the *Japan Advertiser* under the headline "Sub-Lieutenants in Race to Fell 100 Chinese Running Close Contest."

> Sub-Lieutenant Mukai Toshiaki and Sub-Lieutenant Noda Takeshi, both of the Katagiri unit at Kuyung, in a friendly contest to see which of them will first fell 100 Chinese in individual sword combat before the Japanese forces completely occupy Nanking, are well in the final phase of their race, running almost neck to neck. On Sunday [December 5] . . . the "score," according to the Asahi, was: Sub-Lieutenant Mukai, 89, and Sub-Lieutenant Noda, 78.

A week later the paper reported that neither man could decide who had passed the 100 mark first, so they upped the goal to 150. "Mukai's blade was slightly damaged in the competition," the *Japan Advertiser* reported. "He explained that this was the result of cutting a Chinese in half, helmet and all. The contest was 'fun' he declared."

Such atrocities were not unique to the Nanking area. Rather, they were typical of the desensitization exercises practiced by the Japanese across China during the entire war. The following testimony by a Japanese private named Tajima is not unusual:

> One day Second Lieutenant Ono said to us, "You have never killed anyone yet, so today we shall have some killing practice. You must not consider the Chinese as a human being, but only as something of rather less value than a dog or cat. Be brave! Now, those who wish to volunteer for killing practice, step forward."
>
> No one moved. The lieutenant lost his temper.
>
> "You cowards!" he shouted. "Not one of you is fit to call himself a Japanese soldier. So no one will volunteer? Well then, I'll order you." And he began to call out names, "Otani— Furukawa—Ueno—Tajima!" (My God—me too!)
>
> I raised my bayoneted gun with trembling hands, and— directed by the lieutenant's almost hysterical cursing—I walked slowly towards the terror-stricken Chinese standing beside the

pit—the grave he had helped to dig. In my heart, I begged his pardon, and—with my eyes shut and the lieutenant's curses in my ears—I plunged the bayonet into the petrified Chinese. When I opened my eyes again, he had slumped down into the pit. "Murderer! Criminal!" I called myself.

For new soldiers, horror was a natural impulse. One Japanese wartime memoir describes how a group of green Japanese recruits failed to conceal their shock when they witnessed seasoned soldiers torture a group of civilians to death. Their commander expected this reaction and wrote in his diary: "All new recruits are like this, but soon they will be doing the same things themselves."

But new officers also required desensitization. A veteran officer named Tominaga Shozo recalled vividly his own transformation from innocent youth to killing machine. Tominaga had been a fresh second lieutenant from a military academy when assigned to the 232nd Regiment of the 39th Division from Hiroshima. When he was introduced to the men under his command, Tominaga was stunned. "They had evil eyes," he remembered. "They weren't human eyes, but the eyes of leopards or tigers."

On the front Tominaga and other new candidate officers underwent intensive training to stiffen their endurance for war. In the program an instructor had pointed to a thin, emaciated Chinese in a detention center and told the officers: "These are the raw materials for your trial of courage." Day after day the instructor taught them to how to cut off heads and bayonet living prisoners.

On the final day, we were taken out to the site of our trial. Twenty-four prisoners were squatting there with their hands tied behind their backs. They were blindfolded. A big hole had been dug—ten meters long, two meters wide, and more than three meters deep. The regimental commander, the battalion commanders, and the company commanders all took the seats arranged for them. Second Lieutenant Tanaka bowed to the regimental commander and reported, "We shall now begin." He ordered a soldier on fatigue duty to haul one of the prisoners to the edge of the pit; the prisoner was kicked when he resisted. The soldiers finally dragged him over and forced him to his knees. Tanaka turned toward us and looked into each of our faces in turn. "Heads should be cut off like this," he said, unsheathing his army sword. He scooped water from a bucket with a dipper, then poured it over both sides of the blade. Swishing off the water, he raised his sword in a long arc. Standing behind the prisoner, Tanaka steadied himself, legs spread apart, and cut off the man's head with a shout, "Yo!" The head flew more than a meter away. Blood spurted up in two fountains from the body and sprayed into the hole.

The scene was so appalling that I felt I couldn't breathe.

But gradually, Tominaga Shozo learned to kill. And as he grew more adept at it, he no longer felt that his men's eyes were evil. For him, atrocities became routine, almost banal. Looking back on his experience, he wrote: "We made them like this. Good sons, good daddies, good elder brothers at home were brought to the front to kill each other. Human beings turned into murdering demons. Everyone became a demon within three months."

Some Japanese soldiers admitted it was easy for them to kill because they had been taught that next to the emperor, all individual life—even their own—was valueless. Azuma Shiro, the Japanese soldier who witnessed a series of atrocities in Nanking, made an excellent point about his comrades' behavior in his letter to me. During his two years of military training in the 20th Infantry Regiment of Kyoto-fu Fukuchi-yama, he was taught that "loyalty is heavier than a mountain, and our life is lighter than a feather." He recalled that the highest honor a soldier could achieve during war was to come back dead: to die for the emperor was the greatest glory, to be caught alive by the enemy the greatest shame. "If my life was not important," Azuma wrote to me, "an enemy's life became inevitably much less important. . . . This philosophy led us to look down on the enemy and eventually to the mass murder and ill treatment of the captives."

In interview after interview, Japanese veterans from the Nanking massacre reported honestly that they experienced a complete lack of remorse or sense of wrongdoing, even when torturing helpless civilians. Nagatomi Hakudo spoke candidly about his emotions in the fallen capital:

> I remember being driven in a truck along a path that had been cleared through piles of thousands and thousands of slaughtered bodies. Wild dogs were gnawing at the dead flesh as we stopped and pulled a group of Chinese prisoners out of the back. Then the Japanese officer proposed a test of my courage. He unsheathed his sword, spat on it, and with a sudden mighty swing he brought it down on the neck of a Chinese boy cowering before us. The head was cut clean off and tumbled away on the group as the body slumped forward, blood spurting in two great gushing fountains from the neck. The officer suggested I take the head home as a souvenir. I remember smiling proudly as I took his sword and began killing people.

After almost sixty years of soul-searching, Nagatomi is a changed man. A doctor in Japan, he has built a shrine of remorse in his waiting room. Patients can watch videotapes of his trial in Nanking and a full confession of his crimes. The gentle and hospitable demeanor of the doctor belies the horror of his past, making it almost impossible for one to imagine that he had once been a ruthless murderer.

"Few know that soldiers impaled babies on bayonets and tossed them still alive into pots of boiling water," Nagatomi said. "They gang-raped women from the ages of twelve to eighty and then killed them when they could no longer satisfy sexual requirements. I beheaded people, starved them to death, burned them, and buried them alive, over two hundred in all. It is terrible that I could turn into an animal and do these things. There are really no words to explain what I was doing. I was truly a devil."

3

THE FALL OF NANKING

NANKING. A city long celebrated as one of China's greatest literary, artistic, and political centers, a city that served as the ancient capital of China from the third century to the sixth, and then intermittently after the fourteenth century. It was in Nanking that the canons of Chinese calligraphy and painting were set, that the four-tone system of the Chinese language was established, that some of the most famous Buddhist scriptures were edited and transcribed, and from which the classic "Six Dynasties" essay style (a blending of Chinese poetry and prose) emerged. It was in Nanking in 1842 that the treaty ending the Opium Wars was signed, opening China to foreign trade. And it was in Nanking in 1911 that the Nationalist leader Sun Yat-sen became the first provisional president of his nascent Republic of China. Today it proudly holds his tomb.

Mention the name Nanking to any Chinese, and he or she will draw you a picture of a city filled with ancient imperial palaces, lavish tombs, museums, and memorials. The picture would include the intricately carved stone statues of warriors and animals built during the Ming dynasty, the famous Drum Tower (Marco Polo saw the original one seven hundred years ago—the modern version was built three centuries later by a military leader who beat a huge drum from the tower to signal his soldiers), and the scenery on the outskirts of Nanking—temples perched on nearby mountains and hills, tea pavilions and lotus blossoms on its lakes, a massive bridge spanning the Yangtze River.

For centuries, water and mountain provided not only beauty for Nanking but military protection. The Yangtze River to the west and the Purple Mountain to the east shielded the city "like a coiling dragon and a crouching tiger," to borrow an ancient phrase describing Nanking's natural strength.

But sadly, three times Nanking has been an invaded city.

The first invasion occurred more than a millennium ago, at the end of the sixth century, when barbarian hordes demolished every important building in the city and even plowed up the land inside the walls. The second came more than one thousand years later, between 1853 and 1864, when the Taiping rebels captured the city. They were led by the fanatical leader Hong Xiuquan, who, after failing scholarly examinations that would have guaranteed him a place in the nation's elite, convinced himself and others that he was the younger brother of Jesus Christ. The attempt he then spearheaded to overthrow the Qing dynasty eventually killed some twenty million Chinese over thirteen years. The rebels used Nanking as their capital for more than a decade until they were driven out, at which time they reduced the city to smoldering ruins and even smashed the Porcelain Pagoda, a multicolored tower of glazed tiles considered the most beautiful structure of its kind in China.

For the remainder of the nineteenth century, Nanking slumbered in peace and obscurity. When the Manchu emperors resumed their reign of China from the northern city of Peking, Nanking became nothing more than a cultural relic. It would not regain its importance until the Nationalists overthrew the

Qing and anointed Nanking as China's capital, which it officially became in 1928.

By 1937, the year of the Rape, the old Nanking, the Nanking of the Quing dynasty, was competing with the new Nanking of the Nationalists. Vestiges of the old China remained in the streets of the capital: the restaurant vendors balancing tiny rice bowls and teapots on baskets from poles, the hand weavers hunching over looms of silk in open-air factories, the noodle-shop workers stretching pasta by hand, the tinsmiths jangling their tin wares through the streets, the cobblers mending shoes before the doors of their customers, the candy made before the eyes of eager children clutching copper coins with square holes in the middle, the men with squeaking wheelbarrows piled so high with reeds that one could see neither the wheelbarrow nor the man. Yet the new was everywhere—in the asphalt roads that gradually replaced dirt and cobblestone paths, in the electric and neon lamps that replaced the last of the flickering gaslight, candle, and oil lamps, in the water that flowed from taps instead of being sold on the streets by the casketful. Honking buses and automobiles filled with military officials, bureaucrats, and foreign diplomats wove their way past ricksha pullers, mule carts laden with vegetables, and ambling crowds of pedestrians and animals—dogs, cats, horses, donkeys, even the occasional water buffalo or camel.

But part of the old seemed as if it would never change. Encircling the city was an ancient, immense stone wall built during the Ming dynasty, a wall that one missionary called one of the greatest wonders of the world. Surely, he proclaimed, if one were permitted to drive on top of it, that person would see one of the most spectacular views in China. From atop the wall at the southern tip of the city, one could see beyond crenellated gray battlements, the dust-gray brick of the working-class districts, the red and blue tile roofs of some of the more affluent homes, then, peering northward, some of the taller, modern buildings of the government district: the ministries and embassies built in Western-style architecture.

Gazing toward the northeast, one might detect the glistening white Sun Yat-sen mausoleum against the darker sweep of

Purple Mountain and dots of country villas owned by the wealthiest and most powerful citizens of Nanking. Then, looking to the northwest, one might catch glimpses of the industrial activity on the waterfront: the fingers of smoke from the factories, the inky smudge of the coal port, the steamships and gunboats near the dock, the tracks of the North China railway and the Shanghai-Nanking railway slashing across the city and horizon to intersect at the station in Hsiakwan, a northern suburb. Along the horizon one might see the giant, brawling, khaki-colored waters of the Yangtze River, curving west and north beyond the walls of Nanking.

In the summer of 1937 all these lustrous, cacophonous parts of Nanking lay under a blanket of somnolence. The air, soggy with humidity, had long earned the capital its title as one of "the three furnaces of China." The heat, mingled with the pungent odor of the night soil of nearby fields, drove many of the rich out of the city during the worst of the summer heat to seaside resorts. For those who remained, summer was a time of frequent naps, of lazy swishes of reed or bamboo fans, of houses draped with bamboo matting to shade them from the sun. In the evenings neighbors fled from the ovens of their homes by pulling lawn chairs into the streets to gossip the night away and then to sleep in the open air.

Few could predict that within months war would march by their very doorsteps—leaving their homes in flames and their streets drenched with blood.

On August 15, Chang Siao-sung, an instructor of psychology at Ginling College, had just lain back in bed for a nap when she heard the shriek of a siren. "Are they giving us an air-raid practice?" she thought. "Why didn't I see an announcement in the morning papers?"

When fighting had broken out between Chinese and Japanese forces in Shanghai earlier that month, forcing the Nanking government to ready itself for possible enemy attacks elsewhere as well, Chinese officials not only held practice air-raid drills in the city but ordered residents to camouflage their houses and create bomb shelters. Across Nanking men painted black the red rooftops and white walls of their houses or dug holes in the ground to hide in. It was as if the city were preparing for a "funeral on a large scale," remembers Chang eerily.

So on August 15, when she heard a second signal, Chang took notice. But her friends in the house convinced her that it was just another practice, and so she again went back to bed, until she heard a dull rumbling sound, like that of a cannon. "Oh, it is thunder," one friend said and went back to reading her novel. Chang returned to bed, ashamed of being overly excited, until she heard the unmistakable sounds of machine-gun fire and airplanes overhead. Nanking was experiencing its first aerial bombardment in history.

For the next few months Nanking would endure dozens of Japanese air raids, forcing residents to hide in basements, trenches, and dugouts in the ground. Japanese pilots bombed the capital indiscriminately, hitting schools, hospitals, power plants, and government buildings and prompting thousands of people both rich and poor to flee the city.

Frank Xing, now a practitioner of Oriental medicine in San Francisco, recalls the hectic, nightmarish conditions under which he and his parents left Nanking during the autumn of 1937. Then a boy of eleven, he packed his precious collection of slingshots and marbles for the journey while his grandmother gave his father, a railway mechanic, bracelets of jade and silver to pawn in the event of future emergency. The train that bore his family to Hankow was so packed that hundreds of refugees unable to get seats sat on top of the compartments, while others also unable to get seats literally strapped themselves underneath the train, their bodies hanging only inches above the tracks. Throughout the journey Xing heard rumors that people had fallen off the train or rolled under the wheels. Xing himself barely survived the trip when Japanese bombers attacked the train, forcing his family to jump out and hide in a cemetery.

My own grandparents nearly separated forever during the evacuations from Nanking. In the autumn of 1937 my grandfather Chang Tien-Chun, a poet and journalist, was working for the Chinese government to instruct officials in Nationalist Party philosophy. The Japanese bombardment of the capital forced him and his family to hide repeatedly in ditches covered by wooden planks and sandbags. By October he had decided it was unsafe for my grandmother (then a pregnant young woman in her early twenties) and my aunt (a one-year-old infant) to remain in Nanking. Both returned to my grandmother's home village in the countryside, a village near Ihsing, a city on the banks of Tai Hu Lake, between Nanking and Shanghai.

In November, on the anniversary of Sun Yat-sen's death, my grandfather left the city to see his wife and family. Returning to Nanking just a few days later, he found his entire work unit busy packing up in preparation for their evacuation from the city. Told that provisions had been made for the unit to leave by ship from the city of Wuhu, on the banks of the Yangtze River, my grandfather sent word to his family to meet him there immediately.

They almost didn't make it. With aerial bombing, the Japanese had destroyed the railway tracks between my grandmother's village and the city of Wuhu; the only route was by sampan through the intricate network of tiny waterways that laced the entire region.

For four long days my grandfather waited anxiously at the docks scanning boatload after boatload of war refugees. By the fourth day his family still had not arrived, leaving him with a choice that no man should ever be forced to make: board the next and final boat out of Wuhu, in the belief that his wife and daughter were not on their way to Nanking, or stay, in case they were, knowing full well that shortly thereafter the city would be overrun.

In despair, he screamed his beloved's name—"Yi-Pei!"—to the heavens. Then, like an echo from far away, he heard a reply. It came from one last sampan approaching the docks in the distance, a tiny sampan bearing his wife, his daughter, and several of my grandmother's relatives. My mother always told me that their reunion was a miracle.

Unlike my grandparents, many residents of Nanking remained in the city through much of November, some choosing to take a wait-and-see attitude, others staying because they were too old or too poor to do anything else. For them November brought consistently bad news—the battle had not gone well in Shanghai. Long files of Chinese soldiers, many of them mere boys, some no older than twelve, were returning from the battlefront, exhausted, wounded, and demoralized, marching in grim silence or riding in huge trucks draped with the banners of the Red Cross. Those who could took solace from the fact that new units of heavily armed troops could be seen marching through the streets to the waterfront, where they boarded junks towed by tugs on their way to the battlefront. Obviously, the fight was not over. Through rain and howling wind, small modern Chinese tanks rumbled from the capital toward Shanghai, next to lines of pack mules weighed down with cotton uniforms, blankets, rifles, and machine guns.

Later that month the dreaded news finally reached Nanking. Shanghai—"the New York City of China"—had fallen. More than two hundred thousand Japanese troops now stood between the ocean and the capital while some seven hundred thousand Chinese troops fell back in retreat. They brought the news no one wanted to hear. With Shanghai in ruins, the Japanese were now headed for Nanking.

The loss of Shanghai came as a blow to Chiang Kai-shek, the leader of the Nationalists. Faced with the loss of China's largest metropolis, Chiang tried to resolve a difficult dilemma: whether to defend Nanking against the Japanese or move the entire capital to safer ground. In the end the Generalissimo decided to do both. But rather than stay and defend Nanking himself, he shifted the burden to someone else—a subordinate called Tang Sheng-chih.

The relationship between Chiang and Tang Sheng-chih was strange and highly complex. Neither really trusted the other—indeed, at different points in their lives the two men had been partners as well as the deadliest of rivals. During the Northern

Expedition, for example, as the Nationalists tried to unite the country, Tang helped Chiang wage battle against feudal warlords. But Tang had never shown Chiang any particular loyalty, and power struggles between the two men resulted twice in Tang's exile from China—once to Hong Kong and then again to Japan. In 1931, however, when the crisis erupted between the Chinese and Japanese over Manchuria, Chiang summoned Tang back into service in an effort to strengthen Chinese defenses. Tang rose swiftly through the Chinese military hierarchy, and by 1937 he had become Chiang's director of military training.

In November 1937, during several high-level military conferences on the issue of defending or abandoning Nanking, Tang, virtually alone among Chiang's advisers, spoke up in support of providing a strong defense. By defending Nanking, he argued, Chinese troops could simultaneously slow the advance of the Japanese army and give the rest of the Chinese military a chance to rest and reorganize.

But when Chiang asked who would stay and lead the defense, Tang and the other officials were quiet. Singling Tang out, Chiang presented him with an ultimatum: "Either I stay or you stay." In the presence of his peers, Tang undoubtedly felt he had no choice. "How can we let the Generalissimo stay?" Tang asked. He promised that he would remain in Nanking and fight to the death.

The decision to entrust Tang with the defense of Nanking made big news. On November 27, Tang gave a press conference to boost morale. Before reporters he delivered a rousing speech—vowing to live or die with Nanking. His speech was so passionate that when it ended, reporters gave him a big round of applause.

But some reporters noted that Tang also appeared to be extremely agitated. In fact, he had just recovered from a major illness, and in the words of one foreign correspondent, he seemed "dazed if not doped." He sweated so profusely that someone handed him a hot towel to dry his brow.

Perhaps Chiang knew that his adviser was in no shape to do battle with the seasoned Japanese military and had appointed him merely to make it appear as if the Chinese were really going to put up a strong defense. Or perhaps caution told Chiang to be ready with a second plan just in case. What we do know is that during the latter half of November the second plan went into effect. First Chiang ordered most government officials to move to three cities west of Nanking—Changsha, Hankow, and Chungking—stoking rumors among the few officials left behind that they had been abandoned to whatever fate the Japanese planned for them. Within days official-looking cars packed with luggage clogged the streets; then, just as quickly, such cars disappeared altogether. Buses and rickshas also left with the departing government officials, leaving the city with no public municipal transportation. Indeed, soon almost every truck was gone, even those trucks that were used primarily to transport rice from the countryside to Nanking. And then, in mid-November, fifty thousand Chinese troops arrived to take the place of departed government officials. Arriving from upriver ports, they first unloaded boxes and boxes of weapons on the waterfront and then started to occupy empty government buildings of their choosing. By December an estimated ninety thousand Chinese troops populated the Nanking area.

The troops transformed the face of Nanking. Chinese soldiers dug trenches in the streets, laid down underground telephone wire, and strung barbed wire over city intersections—intersections that began to resemble battlefields. The troops also fortified the city wall, installing machine-gun redoubts along the ancient battlements. They shut all gates except three, keeping narrow passageways open only for military transport. Gates were barricaded with sandbags twenty feet deep and reinforced with wood and angle iron. At least one of them was walled up entirely with concrete.

In early December the military also resolved to clear by fire a mile-wide battle zone around the entire circumference of the city walls, regardless of the cost and suffering involved. The cost was incalculable. Along the outskirts of the city, the inferno consumed petrol and ammunition, barracks, agricultural research experimental laboratories, a police training school, and mansions in Mausoleum Park. In the countryside soldiers torched straw huts, farmhouses with thatched roofs, trees, bamboo groves, and underbrush. Not even major Nanking suburbs were spared. Troops herded residents from Hsiakwan and districts around the South Gate into the city walls before incinerating their neighborhoods. People whose houses had been targeted for destruction were told to move out within hours or risk being arrested as spies. The military justified the burning as a strategic move to eliminate any structure of potential use to the invader. But one foreign correspondent pointed out that charred walls could serve the Japanese almost as well as actual buildings for shelter against ammunition. He speculated that the fire was really "an outlet for rage and frustration" for the Chinese—a desire to leave the Japanese with little more than scorched earth.

And so a city prepared for invasion. Anyone and anything with the strength, the judgment, the money, or the opportunity to leave began to get out. Whole museums were packed and carted away. On December 2, hundreds of boxes of Palace Museum treasures—practically the whole of China's cultural heritage—were loaded onto a boat for safe storage outside the city. Six days later, on December 8, Chiang Kai-shek, his wife, and his adviser fled the city by plane. There was no longer any doubt. The Japanese siege of Nanking was about to begin.

For decades one of the mysteries of the Rape of Nanking was how, with so many soldiers in place, the city of Nanking fell in just four days, on the evening of December 12, 1937. The troops, after all, possessed enough ammunition to last through at least five months of siege. As a result, many survivors, journalists, and historians attributed the collapse to a loss of nerve among the Chinese soldiers. They also branded Tang a villain who abandoned his troops when they most needed him.

Later history based on newer documents suggests a somewhat different picture. During the battle of Shanghai, the Japanese air force of almost three thousand planes dwarfed the tiny Chinese air force of three hundred. In other ways the Chinese were no match aerially for the Japanese. During the battle of Shanghai, Italian-trained Chinese pilots wreaked havoc on the city, dropping bombs near Western ships and even on crowded streets and buildings within the international settlement.

But even a bad air force is better than no air force. And that was the situation presented to Tang. On December 8, the day Chiang and his advisers left the city, so too did the entire Chinese air corps. Tang fought the next four days without the benefit of any strategic aerial data on Japanese movements, rendering even the expensive Chinese fort guns on the hills and mountains around Nanking much less effective.

Second, the government officials who moved to Chungking took with them most of the sophisticated communications equipment; thus, one part of the army could not talk to another.

Third, the troops did not come from the same regions and literally had trouble speaking to each other. One paramedic in Nanking recalled that the Chinese military doctors spoke Cantonese while the Chinese soldiers spoke Mandarin, a situation that created endless confusion in the hospitals.

Fourth, many of the "soldiers" in this army became soldiers overnight, having been kidnapped or drafted against their will into the army from the countryside. A substantial number had never held a gun in their hands before Nanking. Because bullets were scarce, few were wasted teaching these recruits how to shoot. Of those soldiers who had previous experience, many had just come back from Shanghai. Tired, hungry, and sick, most were much too exhausted to finish the necessary preparation work of building barricades and digging trenches in the city.

Worst of all, Chinese soldiers felt little sense of cohesiveness or purpose. In a battle report about conditions in Nanking, a Chinese military officer noted that whenever troops occupied an area, they tended to idle about rather than take the initiative to help other troops engaged in nearby battles with the Japanese. The commanding officers, apparently, were no better.

They did not trust each other, the report observed, and for this reason the Japanese were able to move from one area to another, defeating Chinese armies one by one.

On December 9, Japanese airplanes began dropping leaflets near Nanking written by Matsui Iwane, one of the three Japanese generals. The best way to "protect innocent civilians and cultural relics in the city," the message read, was to capitulate. The message promised that the Japanese would be "harsh and relentless to those who resist" but "kind and generous to noncombatants and to Chinese troops who entertain no enmity to Japan." It demanded that the city surrender within twenty-four hours, by noon the next day, "otherwise all the horrors of war will be let loose."

Publicly Tang expressed outrage at the terms of the ultimatum. Throwing the leaflet to the ground, he dictated two orders that were distributed among the troops. The first order forbade the army to retreat. "Our army must fight to defend every inch of the front line," the order read. "If anyone does not follow this order and retreats, he will be punished severely." The second order prohibited any military group from using boats privately to cross the river. If any military units possessed boats, they were required to turn them over to the transportation department. Tang designated the 78th Army as the unit responsible for directing and handling transportation matters and warned that any military personnel found using boats for private purposes would be punished.

Privately, however, Tang negotiated for a truce. Despite his original promise to fight to the last man, he seemed eager to do anything to avoid a showdown in the city. Supporting him in this stance were the few Americans and Europeans still in the city. These selfless individuals, about whom we will learn more later, had decided to remain in Nanking to do what they could to help and had created the International Committee for the Nanking Safety Zone. One of their first steps was to cordon off an area of the city and declare it the Nanking Safety Zone, or the International Safety Zone, with the understanding that anyone within the zone of two and a half square miles, Chinese or non-Chinese, was off-limits to the Japanese. Now, in a final effort to save lives, they offered to try to arrange a truce with the Japanese. Their plan was to suggest a three-day cease-fire, during which the Japanese could keep their present positions and march into Nanking peacefully while the Chinese troops withdrew from the city. Tang agreed to the proposed truce and asked the committee to send a message from him to Chiang Kai-shek through the U.S. embassy. The plan was transmitted by radio on the USS *Panay* gunboat to the Generalissimo. Chiang promptly rejected it.

On December 10, the Japanese waited for the city to surrender. At midday two Japanese staff officers stood outside the Mountain Gate in the eastern wall to see whether the Chinese government would send out a delegation with the flag of truce. When none arrived, the Japanese high command ordered a furious bombardment of the city.

The next few days saw intense fighting between the Chinese and Japanese troops around Nanking. The Japanese dropped bombs on the city and pounded the walls with heavy artillery fire. Tang would later reveal the gravity of the situation near certain landmarks and gates of the city in a long, rambling, and desperate telegram to Chiang Kai-shek:

> From the 9th to the 11th of December the Japanese forced their way through Guanghuamen three times, first the military training corps tried to resist them, then the 156th division bitterly fought back, killing many of the enemy and holding the gate. Starting noon on the 11th, bad news came frequently from the Yuhuatai area, Andemen, Fongtaimen fell to the enemy, ordered immediately the 88th division to shrink the front-line, coordinate with the 74th army, 71st army, rapidly transferred 154th division to help.

But worse news awaited Tang, and this time the bad news would come not from the enemy's successes but from Chiang himself. At noon on December 11, General Gu Zhutong placed a telephone call to Tang's office. Orders had come directly from Chiang, Gu informed Tang, for a massive retreat of Tang's forces. Tang himself was to hurry to Pukow, the site of a ferry and railway terminal that lay across the river from Nanking, where another general would wait to pick him up and bring him to safety.

Tang expressed shock. Aside from the fact that he was being asked to abandon his troops, an unattractive alternative for any leader, he had another very real problem—his troops were at that moment engaged in furious fighting. He informed Gu that the Japanese had already penetrated the troops' front lines; an orderly retreat was not even a possibility. It would readily turn into a rout.

"I can't worry about that," Gu Zhutong said. "Anyhow, you have to retreat by tonight."

When Tang again detailed the likely consequences of a sudden and hasty retreat, Gu reminded him that he, Tang, had been personally ordered by Chiang to "cross the river tonight." Leave a subordinate behind to handle the situation if you have to, Gu told Tang, but "you must cross the river tonight," he repeated.

Impossible, Tang said. The earliest he could cross the Yangtze was the next night. Gu warned him to leave town as soon as possible, for the situation with the enemy had grown urgent.

That afternoon Tang received a telegram from Chiang confirming the order: "Commander-in-Chief Tang, if you cannot maintain the situation you should take the opportunity to retreat in order to preserve and reorganize [the army] for future counterattack. —Kai. 11th." Later that day the distressed Tang received a second telegram from Chiang, again urging retreat.

Unable to hold the line and under pressure, Tang complied. It was a decision that resulted in one of the worst disasters of Chinese military history.

At 3:00 A.M. on December 12, Tang held a predawn meeting at his home. As his vice commanders and top staff gathered before him, Tang told them sadly that the front had fallen, that there was no way for them to defend the gates of the city, and that Chiang Kai-shek had ordered the troops to retreat. He told his subordinates to prepare for the retreat by printing copies of the order and other related documents. That afternoon, at 1:00 P.M., the orders were distributed among the Chinese military.

But then electrifying reports reached Tang. Tang hoped to remove his troops via the Yangtze River. Now he learned that the Japanese navy was minesweeping the river to the east of the island of Baguazhou and steaming its way to Nanking. Its arrival would block that escape route, the last from the city. With the situation dire, Tang again approached the International Committee for the Nanking Safety Zone on 5 Ninghai Road, asking Eduard Sperling, a German businessman, for help in negotiating a truce with the Japanese. Sperling agreed to take a flag and message to the Japanese but later reported to Tang that General Matsui had refused his offer.

That afternoon, just minutes before his commanders gathered for a second meeting, Tang watched from the window of his house as an entire city took flight, the streets jammed with cars, horses, and refugees—the young and the old, the weak and the strong, the rich and the poor. Anyone with half a brain was determined to get out while he still could. At 5:00 P.M. the meeting began. It lasted only ten minutes. Many of the top military officials did not attend because communication between the field commanders and central command had all but collapsed. Others never received notification of the meeting because they had assessed the situation for themselves and run away.

The Japanese, Tang told those gathered in his home, had already broken through the gates of the city and penetrated the wall in three places. "Do you still have any confidence to hold the defense line?" he asked the group. Although he waited several minutes for a response, the room remained silent.

After this pause, Tang calmly discussed strategies for retreat. The evacuation would start within minutes—at 6:00 P.M.—and last until 6:00 A.M. the next day. One portion of the army—the 36th Division and the military police—would cross the river from Hsiakwan and gather at a designated village on the other side. The rest of the army, he announced, would have to force its way out of the Japanese encirclement, with the survivors congregating at the southern region of the Anhwei province. Weapons, ammunition, and communications equipment left behind were to be destroyed, and all roads and bridges in the path of the retreating army burned.

Later in the same meeting, Tang modified his order. He informed his men that if the 87th Division, 88th Division, 74th Army, and military training corps could not break through the Japanese encirclement, then they too should try to cross the river. Tang now gave five divisions the authority to cross the Yangtze River—doubling the original number of men involved in the operation. That evening Tang would himself journey to the docks. It would be a journey he remembered for the rest of his life.

Not surprisingly, the order to retreat threw the Chinese military into an uproar. Some officers ran about the city haphazardly informing anyone they came into contact with to pull out. These soldiers took off. Other officers told no one, not even their own troops. Instead, they saved their own hides. Their soldiers continued to fight the Japanese; thinking they were witnessing a mass desertion when they saw other troops fleeing, they machine-gunned hundreds of their fleeing comrades in an effort to stop them. In the haste and confusion to leave the city, at least one Chinese tank rolled over countless Chinese soldiers in its path, stopping only when blown up by a hand grenade.

Even in the larger, tragic scheme of things, the retreat had its comic moments. As soldiers grew desperate to blend into the populace and thereby elude capture, they broke into shops to steal civilian clothes and undressed in the open. The streets soon filled not only with half-naked soldiers but with half-naked police officers, who had discarded their uniforms to avoid being mistaken as soldiers. One man roamed about wearing nothing but his underwear and a top hat, probably stolen from the home of a wealthy government official. In the early stages of the retreat, when a semblance of order remained, entire sections of the Chinese army were shedding their uniforms, changing into civilian clothes, and marching in formation, simultaneously. But when the retreat turned into a rout, the scramble for clothes grew urgent. Soldiers were actually seen throwing themselves on pedestrians and ripping clothes off their backs.

There was only one way to get out of the city safely without encountering the Japanese, and that was through the northern harbor to the Yangtze River, where a fleet of junks were waiting for those who could get there first. In order to reach the harbor, soldiers had to first move up the main artery of Chungshan Road, and then pass through the northwest gate of the city, called the Ichang, or Water Gate, before they could enter the northern port suburb of Hsiakwan.

But before the gate lay a scene of almost unbelievable congestion. One problem was that thousands of soldiers, many in trucks, cars, and horse-drawn wagons, were trying to squeeze themselves through the narrow seventy-foot tunnel. The trickle of men had turned into a river by 5:00 P.M., and a flood by late evening, as everyone tried to funnel through the tiny opening of the gate. Another problem was that the retreating soldiers had discarded countless armaments and supplies to lighten their load for the journey across the river, and the resulting heaps of hand grenades, buses, machine guns, coats, shoes, and helmets near the gate of the city blocked traffic. A barricade that had been built near the gate also blocked half the road. The area was ripe for disaster.

Tang witnessed much of this chaos from the window of his chauffeured black car on his way to the docks. As the car maneuvered through tangles of people, he heard pedestrians curse him. How can you ride in a car at a time like this? they yelled, unaware that the passenger in the car was Tang Sheng-chih. Tang pretended not to hear and shut his eyes as the car inched turtlelike to its final destination. He was supposed to arrive at the docks by 6:00 P.M., but it was 8:00 P.M. before he finally got there.

Absolute bedlam greeted Tang at the riverfront. Military officers were arguing with each other over which pieces of equipment to destroy and which to ferry across the Yangtze River, while soldiers tried to balance tanks on rows of boats bound together. Much of it capsized and sank anyway.

As the night progressed, the soldiers focused on getting themselves across and abandoned the tanks and equipment. The scene grew violent as boats grew scarce, and in the end some ten thousand men would fight over two or three vessels, struggling to cram themselves aboard or to scare off others by firing shots in the air. Terrified crews tried to ward off the surging mob by swinging axes down on the fingers of soldiers who clung to the sides of their junks and sampans.

Innumerable men died trying to cross the river that night. Many never even made it past the gate. That evening a fire broke out on Chungshan Road, and the flames swept through heaps of ammunition, engulfing houses and vehicles. Horses ensnarled in traffic panicked and reared, heightening the confusion of the mob. The terror-mad soldiers surged forward, their momentum pushing hundreds of men into the flames and hundreds more into the tunnel, where they were trampled underfoot. With the gate blocked and an inferno raging nearby, the soldiers who could break free from the mob made a wild rush to climb over the walls. Hundreds tore their clothing into strips and knotted them with belts and puttees to make rope ladders. One after another, they scaled the battlements and tossed down rifles and machine guns from the parapets. Many fell and plummeted to their deaths.

When the last boats disappeared, soldiers dove into the waters on makeshift flotation devices, hugging or sitting on wooden railroad tracks, logs, boards, buckets, bathtubs, or doors stolen from nearby houses. When the last pieces of wood disappeared, many attempted to swim across, meeting almost certain death.

Tang and two vice commanders boarded a tiny coal-driven launch and waited until 9:00 P.M. for two more military staff members who never arrived. From the launch Tang would have heard the noise and screams of people fighting with each other, mingled with the louder punctuated sounds of Japanese cannon fire. Then there was the sight, the sight of Nanking on fire. The conflagration lit the dark sky bright.

One can only imagine the thoughts of the humiliated Tang as his launch moved across the river. His last glimpse of Nanking was of a city in flames, its people frantically trying to save themselves, his own troops hanging onto driftwood to stay afloat in the dark cold waters of the Yangtze. He would later tell friends that while he had fought in hundreds of battles over twenty years, he had never experienced a day as dark as that one.

4

SIX WEEKS OF HORROR

B Y THE TIME the Japanese passed through the gates of the city, all those residents who possessed any degree of money, power, or foresight had already left for parts unknown. Approximately half the original population departed: before the war, the native population of the city exceeded 1 million people, and by December it had fallen to about half a million. However, the city was swollen with tens of thousands of migrants from the countryside who had left their homes for what they believed would be safety within the city walls. Those who remained after the soldiers departed tended to be the most defenseless: children, the elderly, and all those either too poor or physically weak to secure passage out of the city.

Without protection, without personal resources, without a plan, all these people had was hope that the Japanese would treat them well. Many likely talked themselves into the belief that once the fighting stopped the

Japanese would of course treat them civilly. Some may have even convinced themselves that the Japanese would be better rulers—after all, their own government had clearly abandoned them in their hour of need. Weary of fire, weary of bombardment, and weary of siege, scattered groups of Chinese actually rushed out to welcome the Japanese invaders as they thundered into the city with their tanks, artillery, and trucks. Some people hung Japanese flags from their windows while others even cheered the Japanese columns as they marched through the south and west gates of the city.

But the welcome was short-lived. Eyewitnesses later claimed that the Japanese soldiers, who roamed the city in groups of six to twelve men, fired at anyone in sight as soon as they entered the capital. Old men were found face down on the pavement, apparently shot in the back on whim; civilian Chinese corpses lay sprawled on almost every block—many who had done nothing more provocative than run away as the Japanese approached.

In the war crimes transcripts and Chinese government documentation, story after story of what happened next begins to sound, even in all its horrific dimensions, almost monotonous. With few variations, the story goes something like this:

The Japanese would take any men they found as prisoners, neglect to give them water or food for days, but promise them food and work. After days of such treatment, the Japanese would bind the wrists of their victims securely with wire or rope and herd them out to some isolated area. The men, too tired or dehydrated to rebel, went out eagerly, thinking they would be fed. By the time they saw the machine guns, or the bloodied swords and bayonets wielded by waiting soldiers, or the massive graves, heaped and reeking with the bodies of the men who had preceded them, it was already too late to escape.

The Japanese would later justify their actions by saying that they had to execute POWs to save their own limited food supply and prevent revolts. But nothing can excuse what the Japanese did to hundreds of thousands of helpless Chinese civilians in Nanking. They had no weapons and were in no position to mutiny.

Not all Chinese, of course, submitted easily to extermination in Nanking. The Rape of Nanking is a story not only of mass victimization but of individual strength and courage. There were men who clawed their way out of shallow graves, or clung to reeds for hours in the icy Yangtze River, or lay buried for days under the corpses of friends before dragging their bullet-ridden bodies to the hospital, sustained only by a tenacious will to survive. There were women who hid in holes or in ditches for weeks, or ran through burning houses to rescue their babies.

Many of these survivors later gave their stories to reporters and historians or testified at the war crimes trials held in Nanking and Tokyo after the defeat of Japan. When interviewing several of them during the summer of 1995, I learned that many of the Chinese victims of the Japanese were apparently murdered for no other reason than pleasure. Such was the observation of Tang Shunsan, now in his eighties, a Nanking resident who had miraculously survived a Japanese killing contest back in 1937.

THE KILLING CONTESTS

Unlike thousands of hapless civilians who were bombed out of their homes and stranded on the streets of Nanking, Tang had actually secured a haven during the massacre. Then a twenty-five-year-old shoemaker's apprentice, Tang hid in the home of two fellow apprentices on Xiaomenkou, a tiny street in the northern part of the city. His friends (known to Tang as "Big Monk" and "Little Monk") had camouflaged the doorway of their house by removing the door and filling the open space with bricks so that it resembled, from the outside, a smooth, unbroken wall. For hours they sat on the dirt floor of the house, listening to the screams and gunshots outside.

Tang's problem began when he experienced a sudden urge to see a Japanese soldier with his own eyes. All his life he had heard that the Japanese looked like the Chinese, but never having been to Japan, he had been unable to verify this. Here was a golden opportunity to see for himself. Tang tried to suppress his curiosity but finally succumbed to it. He asked his friends to remove the bricks from the doorway to let him out.

Not surprisingly, his friends pleaded with Tang not to go, warning him that the Japanese would kill him if they caught him wandering around outdoors. But Tang was not so easily dissuaded. Big Monk and Little Monk argued with him at length but finally gave up trying to change his mind. Risking their own safety, they removed the bricks from the door and let Tang out.

As soon as Tang stepped outside, he began to regret it. A scene of almost surreal horror gripped him. He saw the bodies of men and women—even the bodies of small children and the elderly—crumpled before him in the streets. Most had been stabbed or bayoneted to death. "Blood was splattered everywhere," Tang recalled of that horrible afternoon, "as if the heavens had been raining blood."

Then Tang saw another Chinese person in the street and, behind him, a group of eight or nine Japanese approaching in the distance. Instinctively, Tang and the stranger jumped into a nearby rubbish bin, heaping straw and paper over their heads. They shivered from cold and fear, causing the sides of the bin to shiver with them.

Suddenly the straw was knocked away. A Japanese soldier hovered overhead, glaring at them, and before Tang quite knew what was happening the soldier had decapitated the person next to him with his sword. Blood gushed from the victim's neck as the soldier reached down and seized the head as a trophy. "I was too frightened to even move or think," Tang remembered. "I thought of my family and knew that if I died here, they would never know what happened to me."

Then a Chinese voice ordered Tang out. "*Gun chu lai!* (Roll out!)," exclaimed a Chinese man whom Tang suspected was a traitor for the Japanese. "*Gun chu lai*, or I'll kill you!"

Tang crawled out of the trash bin. Seeing a ditch by the road, he wondered whether he should fling himself into it and attempt an escape but found that he was too frightened even to move his legs. Then he saw a group of Japanese soldiers herding hundreds of Chinese people down the street. Tang was ordered to join them. As he marched next to the other prisoners, he saw corpses sprawled on both sides of the streets, something that made him feel so wretched he almost welcomed death.

Before long Tang found himself standing near a pond and a freshly dug, rectangular pit filled with some sixty Chinese corpses. "As soon as I saw the newly dug pit, I thought they might either bury us alive or kill us on the spot. I was too frightened to move so I stood there motionless. It suddenly occurred to me to jump into the pit but then I saw two Japanese military wolf dogs eating the corpses."

The Japanese ordered Tang and the other prisoners to line up in rows on each side of the mass grave. He stood in one closest to the edge. Nine Japanese soldiers waited nearby, soldiers who presented an imposing sight to Tang with their yellow uniforms, star-studded caps, and shiny bayonets and rifles. At such proximity, Tang could see that Japanese men really *did* resemble Chinese men, although at this point he was too frightened to care.

Then, to Tang's horror, a competition began among the soldiers—a competition to determine who could kill the fastest. As one soldier stood sentinel with a machine gun, ready to mow down anyone who tried to bolt, the eight other soldiers split up into pairs to form four separate teams. In each team, one soldier beheaded prisoners with a sword while the other picked up heads and tossed them aside in a pile. The prisoners stood frozen in silence and terror as their countrymen dropped, one by one. "Kill and count! Kill and count!" Tang said, remembering the speed of the slaughter. The Japanese were laughing; one even took photographs. "There was no sign of remorse at all."

A deep sorrow filled Tang. "There was no place to run. I was prepared to die." It saddened him to think that his family and loved ones would never find out what happened to him.

Lost in such thoughts, Tang snapped back to reality when the commotion started. Two rows up from him a pregnant woman began to fight for her life, clawing desperately at a soldier who tried to drag her away from the group to rape her. Nobody helped her, and in the end the soldier killed her, ripping open her belly with his bayonet and jerking out not only her intestines but a squirming fetus. That, Tang believes, should have been the moment for them all to rebel, to do *something*, to fight back and try to kill the soldiers even if they all died in the process. But even though the Chinese prisoners greatly outnumbered their Japanese tormentors and might have been able to overwhelm them, no one moved. Everyone remained eerily docile. Sad to say, of all the people around the pit, Tang remembers only the pregnant woman showing the slightest bit of courage.

Soon a sword-wielding Japanese soldier worked his way closer to Tang, until he was only one row up from him. Then Tang had a stroke of luck, which was nothing short of a miracle. When the soldier decapitated the man directly in front of Tang, the victim's body fell against Tang's shoulder. In keeping with the corpse's momentum, Tang also toppled backwards and dropped, together with the body, into the pit. No one noticed.

Tang ducked his head under the corpse's clothing. His ploy would have never worked had the Japanese stuck with their original game of decapitation. In the beginning the soldiers used the heads of their victims to keep score. But later, to save time, they killed prisoners not by lopping off heads but by slashing throats. That is what saved Tang—the fact that dozens of bodies were piling up in the pit with their heads intact.

The killing spree lasted for about an hour. While Tang lay still, feigning death, the Japanese pushed the rest of the bodies on top of him. Then, as Tang recalls, most of the soldiers left the scene except for one who thrust his bayonet into the mass grave repeatedly to make sure everyone was dead. Tang suffered five bayonet wounds without a scream, and then fainted.

Later that afternoon, at about 5:00 P.M., Tang's fellow apprentices Big Monk and Small Monk came to the pit, hoping to retrieve his corpse. Through a crack in the brick wall of their house, they had seen the Japanese herd Tang and the others away and assumed that he was now dead with all the others.

But when they found Tang moving under the heap of bodies, they pulled him out immediately and ushered him back to the house.

Out of the hundreds of people killed that day during the competition, Tang was the only survivor.

Torture

The torture that the Japanese inflicted upon the native population at Nanking almost surpasses the limits of human comprehension. Here are only a few examples:

—*Live burials:* The Japanese directed burial operations with the precision and efficiency of an assembly line. Soldiers would force one group of Chinese captives to dig a grave, a second group to bury the first, and then a third group to bury the second and so on. Some victims were partially buried to their chests or necks so that they would endure further agony, such as being hacked to pieces by swords or run over by horses and tanks.

—*Mutilation:* The Japanese not only disemboweled, decapitated, and dismembered victims but performed more excruciating varieties of torture. Throughout the city they nailed prisoners to wooden boards and ran over them with tanks, crucified them to trees and electrical posts, carved long strips of flesh from them, and used them for bayonet practice. At least one hundred men reportedly had their eyes gouged out and their noses and ears hacked off before being set on fire. Another group of two hundred Chinese soldiers and civilians were stripped naked, tied to columns and doors of a school, and then stabbed by *zhuizi*—special needles with handles on them—in hundreds of points along their bodies, including their mouths, throats, and eyes.

—*Death by fire:* The Japanese subjected large crowds of victims to mass incineration. In Hsiakwan a Japanese soldier bound Chinese captives together, ten at a time, and pushed them into a pit, where they were sprayed with gasoline and ignited. On Taiping Road, the Japanese ordered a large number of shop clerks to extinguish a fire, then bound them together with rope and threw them into the blaze. Japanese soldiers even devised games with fire. One method of entertainment was to drive mobs of Chinese to the top stories or roofs of buildings, tear down the stairs, and set the bottom floors on fire. Many such victims committed suicide by jumping out windows or off rooftops. Another form of amusement involved dousing victims with fuel, shooting them, and watching them explode into flame. In one infamous incident, Japanese soldiers forced hundreds of men, women, and children into a square, soaked them with gasoline, and then fired on them with machine guns.

—*Death by ice:* Thousands of victims were intentionally frozen to death during the Rape of Nanking. For instance, Japanese soldiers forced hundreds of Chinese prisoners to march to the edge of a frozen pond, where they were ordered to strip naked, break the ice, and plunge into the water to go "fishing." Their bodies hardened into floating targets that were immediately riddled with Japanese bullets. In another incident, the Japanese tied up a group of refugees, flung them into a shallow pond, and bombarded them with hand grenades, causing "an explosive shower of blood and flesh."

—*Death by dogs:* One diabolical means of torture was to bury victims to their waist and watch them get ripped apart by German shepherds. Witnesses saw Japanese soldiers strip a victim naked and direct German shepherds to bite the sensitive areas of his body. The dogs not only ripped open his belly but jerked out his intestines along the ground for a distance.

The incidents mentioned above are only a fraction of the methods that the Japanese used to torment their victims. The Japanese saturated victims in acid, impaled babies with bayonets, hung people by their tongues. One Japanese reporter who later investigated the Rape of Nanking learned that at least one Japanese soldier tore the heart and liver out of a Chinese victim to eat them. Even genitals, apparently, were consumed: a Chinese soldier who escaped from Japanese custody saw several dead people in the streets with their penises cut off. He was later told that the penises were sold to Japanese customers who believed that eating them would increase virility.

THE RAPES

If the scale and nature of the executions in Nanking are difficult for us to comprehend, so are the scale and nature of the rapes.

Certainly it was one of the greatest mass rapes in world history. Susan Brownmiller, author of the landmark book *Against Our Will: Men, Women and Rape*, believes that the Rape of Nanking was probably the single worst instance of wartime rape inflicted on a civilian population with the sole exception of the treatment of Bengali women by Pakistani soldiers in 1971. (An estimated 200,000–400,000 women were raped in Bangladesh during a nine-month reign of terror following a failed rebellion.) Brownmiller suspects that the Rape of Nanking surpasses in scale even the raping of women in the former Yugoslavia, though it is difficult for her to say for certain because of the unreliability of Bosnian rape statistics.

It is impossible to determine the exact number of women raped in Nanking. Estimates range from as low as twenty thousand to as high as eighty thousand. But what the Japanese did to the women of Nanking cannot be computed in a tally sheet of statistics. We will never know the full psychic toll, because many of the women who survived the ordeal found themselves pregnant, and the subject of Chinese women impregnated by Japanese rapists in Nanking is so sensitive that it has never been completely studied. To my knowledge and to the knowledge of the Chinese historians and officials at the memorial hall erected in memory of the Nanking massacre, not a single Chinese woman has to this day come forward to admit that her child was the result of rape. Many such children were secretly killed; according to an American sociologist in the city at the time of the massacre, numerous half-Japanese children were choked or drowned at birth. One can only guess at the guilt, shame, and self-loathing that Chinese women endured when they faced the choice of raising a child they could not love or committing infanticide. No doubt many women could not make that choice. Between 1937 and 1938 a German diplomat reported that "uncounted" Chinese women were taking their own lives by flinging themselves into the Yangtze River.

We do know, however, that it was very easy to be a rape victim in Nanking. The Japanese raped Nanking women from all classes: farm wives, students, teachers, white-collar and blue-collar workers, wives of YMCA employees, university professors, even Buddhist nuns, some of whom were gang-raped to death. And they were systematic in their recruitment of women. In Nanking Japanese soldiers searched for them constantly as they looted homes and dragged men off for execution. Some actually conducted door-to-door searches, demanding money and *hua gu niang*—young girls.

This posed a terrible dilemma for the city's young women, who were not sure whether to remain at home or to seek refuge in the International Safety Zone—the neutral territory guarded by Americans and Europeans. If they stayed in their houses, they ran the risk of being raped in front of their families. But if they left home in search of the Safety Zone, they ran the risk of being captured by the Japanese in the streets. Traps lay everywhere for the Nanking women. For instance, the Japanese army fabricated stories about markets where women could exchange bags of rice and flour for chickens and ducks. But when women arrived on the scene prepared to trade, they found platoons of soldiers waiting for them. Some soldiers employed Chinese traitors to seek out prospective candidates for rape. Even in the Safety Zone, the Japanese staged incidents to lure foreigners away from the refugee camps, leaving women vulnerable to kidnapping raids.

Chinese women were raped in all locations and at all hours. An estimated one-third of all rapes occurred during the day. Survivors even remember soldiers prying open the legs of victims to rape them in broad daylight, in the middle of the street, and in front of crowds of witnesses. No place was too sacred for rape. The Japanese attacked women in nunneries, churches, and Bible training schools. Seventeen soldiers raped one woman in succession in a seminary compound. "Every day, twenty-four hours a day," the *Dagong Daily* newspaper testified of the great Rape of Nanking, "there was not one hour when an innocent woman was not being dragged off somewhere by a Japanese soldier."

Old age was no concern to the Japanese. Matrons, grandmothers, and great-grandmothers endured repeated sexual assaults. A Japanese soldier who raped a woman of sixty was ordered to "clean the penis by her mouth." When a woman of sixty-two protested to soldiers that she was too old for sex, they "rammed a stick up her instead." Many women in their eighties were raped to death, and at least one woman in that age group was shot and killed because she refused a Japanese soldier's advances.

If the Japanese treatment of old women was terrible, their treatment of young children was unthinkable. Little girls were raped so brutally that some could not walk for weeks afterwards. Many required surgery; others died. Chinese witnesses saw Japanese rape girls under ten years of age in the streets and then slash them in half by sword. In some cases, the Japanese sliced open the vaginas of preteen girls in order to ravish them more effectively.

Even advanced stages of pregnancy did not render women immune to assault. The Japanese violated many who were about to go into labor, were in labor, or who had given birth only a few days earlier. One victim who was nine months pregnant when raped suffered not only stillbirth but a complete mental collapse. At least one pregnant woman was kicked to death. Still more gruesome was the treatment allotted to some of the unborn children of these women. After gang rape, Japanese soldiers sometimes slashed open the bellies of pregnant women and ripped out the fetuses for amusement.

The rape of women frequently accompanied the slaughter of entire families.

One of the most notorious stories of such a slaughter was recorded in detail by American and European missionaries in

Nanking. On December 13, 1937, thirty Japanese soldiers came to the Chinese home at 5 Hsing Lu Kao in the southeastern part of Nanking. They killed the landlord when he opened the door, and then Mr. Hsia, a tenant who had fallen to his knees to beg them not to kill anyone else. When the landlord's wife asked why they murdered her husband, they shot her dead. The Japanese then dragged Mrs. Hsia from under a table in the guest hall where she had tried to hide with her one-year-old baby. They stripped her, raped her, then bayoneted her in the chest when they were finished. The soldiers thrust a perfume bottle in her vagina and also killed the baby by bayonet. Then they went into the next room, where they found Mrs. Hsia's parents and two teenage daughters. The grandmother, who tried to protect the girls from rape, was shot by revolver; the grandfather clasped the body of his wife and was killed immediately.

The soldiers then stripped the girls and took turns raping them: the sixteen-year-old by two or three men, the fourteen-year-old by three. The Japanese not only stabbed the older girl to death after raping her but rammed a bamboo cane into her vagina. The younger one was simply bayoneted and "spared the horrible treatment meted out to her sister and mother," a foreigner later wrote of the scene. The soldiers also bayoneted another sister, aged eight, when she hid with her four-year-old sister under the blankets of a bed. The four-year-old remained under the blankets so long she nearly suffocated. She was to endure brain damage for the rest of her life from the lack of oxygen.

Before leaving, the soldiers murdered the landlord's two children, aged four and two; they bayoneted the older child and split the head of the younger one with a sword. When it was safe to emerge, the eight-year-old survivor, who had been hiding under the blankets, crawled to the next room where she lay beside the body of her mother. Together with her four-year-old sister, they lived for fourteen days on rice crusts that their mother had prepared before the siege. When a member of the International Committee arrived at the house weeks after the slaughter, he saw that one young girl had been raped on the table. "While I was there," he testified later, "the blood on the table [was] not all dry yet."

A similar story, no less grisly, involves a fifteen-year-old Chinese girl whose family was murdered before her eyes. The Japanese first killed her brother, whom they wrongly accused of being a Chinese soldier, then her brother's wife and her older sister because they both resisted rape, and finally her mother and father, who knelt on the floor begging the Japanese to spare the lives of their children. Before they died under the thrusts of Japanese bayonets, their last words urged the young girl to do whatever the enemy soldiers wanted from her.

The girl fainted. She revived to find herself naked on the floor in a strange, locked room. Someone had raped her while she had been unconscious. Her clothes had been taken from her, as they had been taken from other girls in the building. Her room was on the second floor of a building converted into barracks for two hundred Japanese soldiers. The women inside consisted of two groups: prostitutes, who were given their freedom and treated well, and respectable girls who had been kidnapped into sexual slavery. Of the latter group, at least one girl attempted suicide. For a month and a half the fifteen-year-old was raped two or three times a day. Eventually she became so diseased the Japanese left her alone. One day a kind Japanese officer who spoke Chinese approached her and asked why she was weeping. After hearing her story, he took her to Nanking by car, set her free inside the South Gate, and wrote down the name of Ginling College for her on a piece of paper. The girl was too sick to walk to Ginling the first day and took refuge in a Chinese house. Only on the second day did she reach Ginling, where International Committee members immediately rushed her to the hospital.

That girl was considered fortunate. Many other girls, tied naked to chairs, beds, or poles as permanent fixtures for rape, did not survive such treatment. Chinese witnesses described the body of an eleven-year-old girl who died after she was raped continuously for two days: "According to eyewitness reports, the blood-stained, swollen and ruptured area between the girl's legs created a disgusting scene difficult for anyone to look at directly."

During the mass rape the Japanese destroyed children and infants, often because they were in the way. Eyewitness reports describe children and babies suffocating from clothes stuffed in their mouths or bayoneted to death because they wept as their mothers were being raped. American and European observers of the Rape of Nanking recorded numerous entries like this one: "415. February 3, about 5 P.M. at Chang Su Hsiang (near Ta Chung Chiao) three soldiers came and forced a woman to throw away her baby and after raping her they went away laughing."

Countless men died trying to protect their loved ones from rape. When the Japanese dragged away one woman from a mat shed and her husband intervened, they "stuck a wire through his nose and tied the other end of the wire to a tree just like one would tie up a bull." There they bayoneted him repeatedly despite the pleas of his mother, who rolled around on the ground, crying hysterically. The Japanese ordered the mother to go into the house or they would kill her. The son died from the wounds on the spot.

There seemed to be no limit to the Japanese capacity for human degradation and sexual perversion in Nanking. Just as some soldiers invented killing contests to break the monotony of murder, so did some invent games of recreational rape and torture when wearied by the glut of sex.

Perhaps one of the most brutal forms of Japanese entertainment was the impalement of vaginas. In the streets of Nanking, corpses of women lay with their legs splayed open, their orifices pierced by wooden rods, twigs, and weeds. It is painful, almost mind-numbing, to contemplate some of the other objects that were used to torment the Nanking women, who suffered almost unendurable ordeals. For instance, one Japanese soldier who raped a young woman thrust a beer bottle into her and shot her. Another rape victim was found with a golf stick rammed into her. And on December 22, in a neighborhood near the gate of Tongjimen, the Japanese raped a barber's wife and then stuck a firecracker in her vagina. It blew up and killed her.

But not all of the victims were women. Chinese men were often sodomized or forced to perform a variety of repulsive sexual acts in front of laughing Japanese soldiers. At least one Chinese man was murdered because he refused to commit necrophilia with the corpse of a woman in the snow. The Japanese also delighted in trying to coerce men who had taken lifetime vows of celibacy to engage in sexual intercourse. A Chinese woman had tried to disguise herself as a man to pass through one of the gates of Nanking, but Japanese guards, who systematically searched all passing pedestrians by groping at their crotches, discovered her true sex. Gang rape followed, at which time a Buddhist monk had the misfortune to venture near the scene. The Japanese tried to force him to have sex with the woman they had just raped. When the monk protested, they castrated him, causing the poor man to bleed to death.

Some of the most sordid instances of sexual torture involved the degradation of entire families. The Japanese drew sadistic pleasure in forcing Chinese men to commit incest—fathers to rape their own daughters, brothers their sisters, sons their mothers. Guo Qi, a Chinese battalion commander stranded in Nanking for three months after the city fell, saw or heard of at least four or five instances in which the Japanese ordered sons to rape their mothers; those who refused were killed on the spot. His report is substantiated by the testimony of a German diplomat, who reported that one Chinese man who refused to rape his own mother was killed with saber strokes and that his mother committed suicide shortly afterwards.

Some families openly embraced death rather than participate in their own destruction. One such family was crossing the Yangtze River when two Japanese soldiers stopped them and demanded an inspection. Upon seeing the young women and girls in the boat, the soldiers raped them right in front of their parents and husbands. This was horrifying enough, but what the soldiers demanded next of the family devastated them. The soldiers wanted the old man of the family to rape the women as well. Rather than obey, the entire family jumped into the river and drowned.

Once women were caught by Japanese soldiers, there was little hope for them, for most were killed immediately after rape.

But not all women submitted easily. Many were able to hide from the Japanese for months—in fuel stacks, under piles of grass or straw, in pig pens, on boats, in deserted houses. In the countryside women hid in covered holes in the earth—holes that Japanese soldiers tried to discover by stamping on the ground. One Buddhist nun and a little girl avoided rape and murder because they lay still in a ditch filled with bodies and feigned death for five days.

Women eluded rape using a variety of methods. Some used disguise—rubbing soot on their faces to appear old and diseased or shaving their heads to pass themselves off as men. (One clever young woman disguised herself as an old woman, hobbling about on a cane and even borrowing a little boy of six to carry on her back until she safely entered the Safety Zone at Ginling College.) Others feigned sickness, such as the woman who told Japanese soldiers she had given birth to a dead child four days before. Another woman took the advice of a Chinese captive to force her finger down her throat and vomit several times. (Her Japanese captors hastily expelled her from the building.) Some escaped by sheer quickness, ducking in and out of crowds, climbing over walls, with the Japanese in hot pursuit. One girl barely avoided assault by tripping up a Japanese soldier on the third floor of a house and sliding down a bamboo pole that a Chinese man propped up for her from the garden.

Once caught, women who struggled faced the possibility of torture as a warning to others who dared to resist the Japanese. Those who defied the Japanese were often found later with their eyes torn out, or their noses, ears, or breasts cut off. Few women dared fight their assailants, but there were scattered accounts of resistance. A schoolteacher gunned down five Japanese soldiers before being shot to death. The most famous story involves Li Xouying, a woman who not only suffered thirty-seven bayonet wounds during her struggle against the Japanese but survived and remained robust enough to narrate and play-act the story almost sixty years later.

In 1937, eighteen-year-old Li Xouying was the bride of a military technician. When the government evacuated the capital, her husband left Nanking on the top of a train packed with Chinese soldiers. Li stayed behind because she was six to seven months pregnant and believed it was dangerous in her condition to board a crowded train.

Like many other Chinese civilians in Nanking, Li and her father fled into the foreign-run Safety Zone. They hid in the basement of an elementary school that had been converted into a refugee camp. But this camp, like others in the zone, was subject to repeated Japanese inspections and invasions. On December 18, a group of Japanese soldiers broke in and dragged the young men out of the school. The following morning they returned for the women. Fearful of what the Japanese would do to a pregnant housewife, Li made an impulsive decision. She tried to kill herself by slamming her head against the basement wall.

When she regained consciousness, she found herself lying on a small canvas cot on the floor of the basement. The Japanese were gone, but they had taken several young women with them. Wild thoughts raced through Li's head while she lay in a daze on the cot. If she ran out of the building, she might be throwing herself at Japanese rapists. But if she did nothing and waited, they would probably come back for her. Li decided to stay. If the Japanese did not return, all would be well and good, but if they did, she would fight them to the death. She would rather die, she told herself, than be raped by the Japanese.

Soon she heard the heavy footsteps of three Japanese soldiers coming down the stairs. Two of them seized a couple of women and dragged them screaming out of the room. The one who remained eyed Li intently as she lay immobile on the cot. Someone told him Li was sick, and he responded by kicking all the other people out of the room into the corridor.

Slowly the soldier walked back and forth, appraising her. Suddenly—before he quite realized what was happening—she made her move. She jumped from the cot, snatched his bayonet from his belt and flung her back against the wall. "He panicked," Li recalled. "He never thought a woman would fight back." He seized her wrist that held the bayonet, but Li clutched his collar with her free hand and bit his arms with all her might. Even though the soldier wore full battle gear and Li wore only a cotton *chipao*, which impeded movement, she put up a good fight. The two of them grappled and kicked until the soldier found himself overwhelmed and screamed for help.

The other soldiers ran in, no doubt incredulous at what they saw. They lunged toward her with their bayonets but failed to stab her effectively because their comrade was in the way. Because her opponent was so short and small, Li was able to jerk him completely off his feet and use him like a shield to parry their thrusts. But then the soldiers aimed their bayonets at her head, slashing her face with their blades and knocking out her teeth. Her mouth filled with blood, which she spit into their eyes. "Blood was on the walls, on the bed, on the floor, everywhere," Li remembered. "I had no fear in my mind. I was furious. My only thought was to fight and kill them." Finally a soldier plunged his bayonet into her belly and everything went black for her.

The soldiers left her for dead. When Li's body was brought before her father, he could not sense any breath coming from her and assumed the worst. He asked someone to carry her behind the school and to dig a pit for her grave. Fortunately, someone noticed before the burial that Li was still breathing and that bubbles of blood foamed from her mouth. Friends immediately rushed Li to Nanking University Hospital, where doctors stitched up her thirty-seven bayonet wounds. While unconscious, she miscarried that evening.

Word of Li's fight somehow reached her husband, who immediately asked the military for three months' leave and borrowed money to get back to Nanking. In August 1938, he returned and found his wife with her face swollen and crosshatched with scars and her newly shorn hair growing from her head like bristles.

Li would suffer both pain and embarrassment from her wounds for the rest of her life. Mucus leaked from a gaping hole on the side of her nose, and tears ran down her eyes during bad weather or bouts of illness. (Miraculously, although the Japanese had stabbed the whites of her eyes with their bayonets, Li did not go blind). Every time she looked in a mirror, she saw the scars that reminded her of that terrible day, December 19, 1938. "Now, after fifty-eight years, the wrinkles have covered the scars," she told me during my visit to her apartment in Nanking. "But when I was young, the scars on my face were obvious and terrible."

Li believes it was the combination of her personality and unique family background that gave her the will to fight back. Unlike other Chinese women, typically taught at an early age to be submissive, she came from a family completely devoid of feminine influence. Her mother died when she was only thirteen, forcing Li to grow up among men in a tough military family. Her father, brother, and uncles were either soldiers or policemen, and under their influence she became a tomboy. As a young girl, she also possessed a temper so short that her father dared not teach her kung fu, no doubt out of fear that she would terrorize the other kids on the block. Almost sixty years later, surrounded by her numerous children and grandchildren, Li had retained her health and passion for life—even her reputation for being ill-tempered. Her one regret, she said, was not learning kung fu from her father; otherwise, she might have enjoyed the pleasure of killing all three of the Japanese soldiers that day.

THE DEATH TOLL

How many people died during the Rape of Nanking? When Miner Searle Bates, a history professor at Nanking University, was asked during the International Military Tribunal of the Far East (IMTFE) to give an estimate of the deaths, he answered:

"The question is so big, I don't know where to begin. . . . The total spread of this killing was so extensive that no one can give a complete picture of it."

The Chinese military specialist Liu Fang-chu proposed the figure of 430,000. Officials at the Memorial Hall of the Victims of the Nanking Massacre by Japanese Invaders and the procurator of the District Court of Nanking in 1946 claimed at least 300,000 were killed. The IMTFE judges concluded that more than 260,000 people were killed in Nanking. Fujiwara Akira, a Japanese historian, gives the figure of approximately 200,000. John Rabe, who never conducted a systematic count and left Nanking in February, before the slaughter ended, estimated that only 50,000–60,000 were killed. The Japanese author Hata Ikuhiko claims that the number was between 38,000 and 42,000. Still others in Japan place the number as low as 3,000. In 1994 archival evidence emerged from a former Japanese-owned railway company in Manchuria to reveal that one burial squad alone disposed of more than 30,000 bodies in Nanking between January and March 1938.

Perhaps no one has made a more thorough study of the statistics than Sun Zhaiwei, a historian at the Jiangsu Academy of Social Sciences. In a 1990 scholarly paper entitled "The Nanking Massacre and the Nanking Population," he reports that, according to census reports, the population in Nanking in 1937 exceeded 1 million before hostilities broke out between Japan and China. Using Chinese archival material, memoirs from Chinese military officials, and reports of the Nanking branch of the Red Cross, Sun determined that at the time of Japanese occupation there were at least half a million long-term residents in the city (the rest had already left the city), plus 90,000 Chinese soldiers and tens of thousands of migrants—a total of approximately 600,000 people in Nanking, perhaps even 700,000.

Sun gives his estimate in a second paper. The Nanking city archives and the No. 2 National Archives of China contained burial records submitted by private families, local charitable organizations, and the *Nanjing zizhi weiyuanhui*—the Chinese puppet government under the Japanese. After carefully examining these records, Sun found that charitable organizations in Nanking buried at least 185,000 bodies, private individuals at least 35,000, and the Japanese-controlled local government more than 7,400. (Some of the burial records are so detailed they include categories for even the sex of the victims and the location of the disposal.) Using Chinese burial records alone, Sun calculated that the number of dead from the Rape of Nanking exceeded the figure of 227,400.

However, this statistic balloons still larger if one factors in a stunning confession made by a Japanese prisoner almost four decades before Sun's paper was written. In 1954, while awaiting trial at the Fuxuan war criminal camp in the northeastern province of Liaoning, Ohta Hisao, a Japanese imperial army major, submitted a forty-four-page report in which he confessed that the Japanese army burned, dumped, or buried bodies in a massive disposal effort. Most of the bodies came from Hsiakwan, the area near the river northwest of Nanking. On the waterfront the Japanese piled fifty bodies onto each waiting boat, then took them to the middle of the river to dump overboard. Trucks carried bodies to other areas where they were burned and buried to eliminate evidence of the massacre. For three days starting on December 15, 1937, Ohta's army unit dumped 19,000 bodies of Chinese victims into the Nanking River, while a neighboring unit disposed of 81,000 bodies and other units got rid of 50,000—a total of some 150,000 bodies. By adding Ohta's figure to his tally of Chinese burial record statistics, Sun concluded that the total number of corpses amounted to a staggering 377,400—a figure that surpasses the death toll for the atomic blasts at Hiroshima and Nagasaki combined.

Even if skeptics dismiss Ohta's confession as a lie, one should keep in mind that even without his testimony the burial records at Nanking offer convincing evidence that the death toll of the massacre was, at the very least, in the 200,000 range. Sun's research is corroborated by court exhibits that I unearthed from IMTFE records (see table on page 102). By adding together the burial estimates of charitable organizations (later mentioned in Sun's paper) and the body counts made by other individuals (not mentioned in Sun's paper), the tribunal concluded that approximately 260,000 people were killed during the Nanking massacre. It is important to remember that the IMTFE number does not include Japanese burial statistics of the Chinese dead, which could push the figure into the 300,000 or even 400,000 range.

ESTIMATED NUMBER OF VICTIMS OF
JAPANESE MASSACRE IN NANKING

Tsun-shan-tang	112,266
Red Swastika Society	43,071
Shia Kwan District (sic)	26,100
Stated by Mr. Lu Su	57,400
Stated by Messrs. Jui, Chang, and Young	7,000 or more
Stated by Mr. Wu	2,000 or more
Stated on the Tomb of the Unknown Victims	3,000 or more
TOTAL (approximately)	260,000

SOURCE: Document no. 1702, box 134, IMTFE records, court exhibits, 1948, World War II War Crimes Records Collection, entry 14, record group 238, National Archives.

In recent years other scholars have bolstered Sun's study and given credence to the argument that the death toll at Nanking may have surpassed 300,000 people. For instance, in his paper "Let the Whole World Know the Nanking Massacre," Wu Tienwei, professor emeritus of history at Southern Illinois University, estimates that the population of the city before its fall was approximately 630,000 people, a figure he concedes is far from exact but may be relatively close to the actual figure. After providing a detailed historiography of the body count research and examining the numbers carefully, he concludes that the death toll of the massacre exceeded 300,000 people—probably 340,000 people, of which 190,000 were killed collectively and 150,000 individually.

The authors James Yin and Shi Young obtained a number on the same scale—approximately 355,000—after conducting their own investigation. Although their figure already represents the high end of the spectrum of death toll estimates, Yin and Young believe that the actual number of people killed in Nanking far exceeds the number they have been able to unearth from the records. They dismiss arguments from other experts who believe that considerable overlap may exist between death statistics and who suggest, for instance, that many of the bodies the Japanese dumped in the river were washed onshore, reburied, and tallied twice in the body count. Any corpse that washed up on land, they contend, would have been buried next to the river rather than in some remote location far from the river, but according to their research, most of the burial grounds were miles away from the banks of the Yangtze. It defies common sense, they argue, that the corpses, in advanced stages of decay from exposure, would be transported up hills or mountains or across fields for burial. Moreover, Yin and Young discovered through interviews with survivors that family members of rape-and-murder victims usually buried their dead immediately and neglected to report the burials to the authorities. Since their study tabulates numbers only from the reports of mass killings—rather than individual, random murders—Yin and Young believe that the total number of deaths from the Nanking massacre lies well in the 400,000 range.

There is even compelling evidence that the Japanese themselves believed at the time of the massacre that the death toll at Nanking may have been as high as 300,000. The evidence is significant because not only was it generated by the Japanese themselves but it was done so during the first month of the massacre, when the killing was far from over. On January 17, 1938, Foreign Minister Hirota Koki in Tokyo relayed the following message to his contacts in Washington, D.C., a message that American intelligence intercepted, deciphered, and later translated into English on February 1, 1938 (parentheses in the original):

> Since return (to) Shanghai a few days ago I investigated reported atrocities committed by Japanese army in Nanking and elsewhere. Verbal accounts (of) reliable eye-witnesses and letters from individuals whose credibility (is) beyond question afford convincing proof (that) Japanese Army behaved and (is) continuing (to) behave in (a) fashion reminiscent (of) Attila (and) his Huns. (Not) less than three hundred thousand Chinese civilians slaughtered, many cases (in) cold blood.

It is tempting to suggest that if Chiang Kai-shek had pulled out his armies during the mass government evacuation from Nanking in November and left behind a defenseless city, perhaps wholesale massacre could have been averted. But a minute's thought shows the weakness in that argument. The Japanese, after all, had spent the preceding few months systematically destroying entire villages and cities on their warpath to Nanking and committing similar atrocities elsewhere. Clearly they needed no provocation from the Chinese for their actions. All we can say for certain is that a city devoid of Chinese soldiers would have—at the very least—taken away the Japanese excuse that serial executions were necessary to eliminate the soldiers hiding among the civilian population. But there is no evidence to suggest that it would have changed their actions.

It is also tempting to suggest that if Chiang had refrained from ordering a senseless last-minute withdrawal from Nanking and had instead fought to the last man to save the city, the city's fate would have been different. But here again we must be careful. Head-to-head combat would certainly not have worked. The Japanese were much better armed and trained and would surely have overcome the Chinese forces sooner or later. But a lengthy, drawn-out struggle using guerrilla-style tactics might have demoralized the Japanese and elevated the Chinese. If nothing else, many more Japanese soldiers would have died fighting the Chinese and their arrogance toward the Chinese soldier would have been muted by a fierce resistance.

5

THE NANKING
SAFETY ZONE

I N THE HISTORY of every war, there are always a few rare individuals who emerge as beacons of hope for the persecuted. In the United States the Quakers freed their own slaves and helped establish the Underground Railroad. In Europe during World War II, Oskar Schindler, a Nazi, expended his fortune to save twelve hundred Jews from the Auschwitz gas chambers, and Raoul Wallenberg, a Swedish diplomat, saved more than one hundred thousand Jews by giving them false passports. Who can forget Mies Giep, the Austrian woman who together with others hid the young Anne Frank and her family in an Amsterdam attic?

Dark times paralyze most people, but some very few, for reasons most of us will never understand, are able to set aside all caution and do things even they could not imagine themselves doing in ordinary times.

It is hard to talk about a bright spot in the horror that is the Rape of Nanking, but if one can, it is surely to shine a light on the actions of a small band of Americans and Europeans who risked their lives to defy the Japanese invaders and rescue hundreds of thousands of Chinese refugees from almost certain extermination. These courageous men and women created the International Committee for the Nanking Safety Zone. This is their story.

The decision to create a safety zone in the city of Nanking arose almost spontaneously, within weeks of the collapse of Shanghai. In November 1937, Father Jacquinot de Bessage, a French priest, established a neutral area in Shanghai to shelter 450,000 Chinese refugees whose homes had been destroyed by the invading Japanese soldiers. When the Presbyterian missionary W. Plumer Mills learned of Bessage's project, he suggested to his friends that a similar zone be created in Nanking. Mills and some two dozen other people (mostly American, but also German, Danish, Russian, and Chinese) ultimately designated a region slightly west of the center of the city as a safety zone. Within the zone were situated Nanking University, Ginling Women's Arts and Science College, the American embassy, and various Chinese government buildings. In setting up the zone, the committee sought to offer refuge for noncombatants caught in the cross-fire between the Japanese and Chinese militaries. The foreigners had every intention of shutting the zone down a few days or weeks after the city passed safely into Japanese hands.

The idea was not universally accepted at first. The Japanese, for one, flatly refused to honor it. And as enemy troops approached the city, the zone committee heard urgent pleas not only from friends and family but from Chinese, Japanese, and Western officials to abandon the project at once and flee for their lives. In early December the American embassy staff insisted that the zone leaders join them onboard the USS *Panay*, a gunboat packed with diplomats, journalists, and Western and Chinese refugees as it prepared to move upriver away from Nanking. But the zone leaders politely declined the offer, and after giving them a final warning, the diplomats on the *Panay* sailed away on December 9, 1937, leaving the remaining foreigners to their fate.

Interestingly enough, the *Panay* would later be bombed and machine-gunned by Japanese aviators. On the afternoon of December 12, Japanese aviators sank the gunboat without warning, killing two people and wounding numerous others, even circling over the area repeatedly as if they planned to exterminate the survivors, who hid under a thicket of riverbank reeds. The reasons for the attack were unclear. The Japanese later claimed that their aviators lost their cool judgment in the heat of battle and that fog or smoke prevented them from seeing the American flags on the *Panay*, but this claim was later proven to be demonstrably false. (Not only was the day of the bombing sunny and cloudless, but the Japanese aviators had received explicit orders to bomb the *Panay*, orders the aviators carried out reluctantly only after vehement protests and arguments.) Today some suspect that the bombing was a test to see how the Americans would react, while others believe it was the result of internal politics within the Japanese high command. But whatever the reason behind the attack, the city of Nanking turned out to be a safer place for the remaining foreigners than the *Panay*.

The first refugees to enter the Nanking Safety Zone were those who had lost their homes to aerial bombardments or had abandoned homes on the outskirts of the city in the face of the approaching Japanese army. Soon these first refugees packed the camps so densely that it was said that many had to stand without sleeping for several days until new camps were added. Once the city fell, the zone housed not just thousands but hundreds of thousands of people. For the next six weeks the committee had to find a way to provide these refugees with the bare necessities of survival—food, shelter, and medical care. The committee members also had to protect them from physical harm. Often this required on-the-spot intervention to prevent the Japanese military from proceeding with some threatened action. And through it all, though no one asked them to do so, they documented and broadcasted Japanese outrages to the world. In doing so, they left a written record for posterity of what they had witnessed.

In retrospect, it seems almost miraculous that some two dozen foreigners managed to do everything they did while fifty thousand Japanese soldiers ripped apart the city. Remember, by occupation these men and women were missionaries, doctors, professors, and executives—not seasoned military officers. Their lifestyles had been sheltered and leisurely. "We were not rich," one woman said of that period, "but a little foreign money went a long way in China." Many were ensconced in luxurious mansions, surrounded by teams of servants.

Strangely, because of an incident in Nanking a decade earlier, most expected to have more trouble with the Chinese than the Japanese. Those who had been in Nanking in 1927 remembered that during the Nationalist invasion of the city, Chinese troops recklessly killed foreigners and besieged a group of them, including the American consul and his wife, in a house on top of Socony Hill. ("Would they kill us?" one woman wrote of that horrible time. "Would they torture us as in the Boxer? Would they do worse? Torture the children before our eyes? I did not let my mind touch what they might do to us as women.") Indeed, one of the foreign eyewitnesses of the 1937 massacre admitted: "We were more prepared for excesses from the fleeing Chinese . . . but never, never from the Japanese. On the contrary, we had expected that with the appearance of the Japanese the return of peace, quiet and prosperity would occur."

The heroic efforts of the Americans and Europeans during this period are so numerous (their diaries run for thousands of pages) that it is impossible to narrate all of their deeds here. For this reason, I have decided to concentrate on the activities of three individuals—a German businessman, an American surgeon, and an American missionary professor—before describing the committee's achievements as a whole. On the surface, the three could not have been more different.

THE NAZI WHO SAVED NANKING

Perhaps the most fascinating character to emerge from the history of the Rape of Nanking is the German businessman John Rabe. To most of the Chinese in the city, he was a hero, "the living Buddha of Nanking," the legendary head of the International Safety Zone who saved hundreds of thousands of Chinese lives. But to the Japanese, Rabe was a strange and unlikely savior. For he was not only a German national—a citizen of a country allied with Japan—but the leader of the Nazi Party in Nanking.

In 1996 I began an investigation into the life of John Rabe and eventually unearthed thousands of pages of diaries that he and other Nazis kept during the Rape. These diaries led me to conclude that John Rabe was "the Oskar Schindler of China."

Prior to the Rape, Rabe had led a relatively peaceful though well-traveled life. The son of a sea captain, he was born in Hamburg, Germany, on November 23, 1882. After completing his apprenticeship in Hamburg he worked a few years in Africa and then in 1908 moved to China, where he found employment at the Peking office of the Siemens China Company. In 1931 he transferred to the Nanking office, selling telephones and electrical equipment to the Chinese government. Bald and bespectacled, dressed in conservative suits and bow ties, he looked like a typical, middle-aged Western businessman in the city. Soon he became a pillar of the German community in Nanking, administering his own German school for elementary and junior high school students.

As the years went by, Rabe became a staunch supporter of Nazism and the representative town leader for the Nazi Party in Nanking. In 1938 he would tell German audiences that "I believe not only in the correctness of our political system but, as an organizer of the party, I am behind the system 100 percent."

Decades later his granddaughter, Ursula Reinhardt, insists that Rabe saw the Nazi Party primarily as a socialist organization and did not support the persecution of Jews and other ethnic groups in Germany. This may well be true. During his visits to various ministries in Nanking, Rabe repeatedly summed up his Nazi philosophy in socialist terms: "We are soldiers of work, we are a government of workers, we are friends to the worker, we will never leave the worker's side in times of crisis."

When most of his fellow German nationals, on the advice of friends and embassy officials, departed China long before the Japanese military reached the gates of the city, Rabe chose to stay and was soon elected the head of the Safety Zone. In fact, even when Japanese embassy officials met with him and suggested more strongly that he leave, he remained. Dispatched by his superiors to protect Rabe during the fall of Nanking, Japanese Major Oka asked him: "Why in the devil did you stay? Why do you want to involve yourself in our military affairs? What does all this matter to you? You haven't lost anything here!"

Rabe paused for a moment, then gave Oka his answer. "I have been living here in China for over thirty years," Rabe said. "My kids and grandchildren were born here, and I am happy and successful here. I have always been treated well by the Chinese people, even during the war. If I had spent thirty years in Japan and were treated just as well by the Japanese people, you can be assured that, in a time of emergency, such as the situation China faces now, I would not leave the side of the people in Japan."

This answer satisfied the Japanese major, who respected the concept of loyalty. "He took a step back, mumbled some words about Samurai obligations, and bowed deeply," Rabe wrote of the incident.

But Rabe had an even more personal reason not to walk away and protect himself—he felt responsible for the safety of his Chinese employees, a team of Siemens mechanics who maintained the turbines in the city's main power plant, the telephones and clocks in every ministry, the alarms in the police stations and the banks, and an enormous X-ray machine at the central hospital. "What I only had a premonition of then," Rabe wrote, "—but what I now know—is that all of them would have been killed or severely injured if I had left their side."

Earlier that year Rabe had endured countless air raids in Nanking with scarcely more than a foxhole and a few planks of wood for protection. Clothing was also scarce, especially after Rabe made the mistake around late September of storing his entire wardrobe on the *Kutwo*, a ship used to transport German nationals out of Nanking, for safekeeping. Upon its arrival at Hankow, the *Kutwo* dumped its unclaimed luggage, leaving Rabe with only two suits, one of which he gave to a Chinese refugee whom he believed needed it more than he did.

But his biggest concern was not for his own personal safety or well-being but for the establishment of the Safety Zone. The committee members wanted the zone to be free of all military activity, but the Japanese army refused to recognize it as neutral territory, and the committee found it next to impossible to dislodge Chinese General Tang Sheng-chih's men from the area—especially because Tang's own villa stood within it. For Rabe the final straw came when the Chinese army not only refused to evacuate the area but erected its gun turrets on streets inside the zone. Losing his patience, Rabe threatened to quit his position as head of the Safety Zone and tell the world the reason why unless Tang evacuated his troops from the area immediately. "They promised me that my wishes would be respected," Rabe said, "but the fulfillment itself took a bit longer."

Rabe sensed the need to call on higher authorities for help. On November 25, he wired Adolf Hitler to request the fuehrer's "kindly intercession in asking that the Japanese government grant the building of a neutral zone for those who are not fighting to battle for Nanking." At the same time Rabe also sent a telegram to his friend General Counsel Mr. Kriebel: "Asking cordially for support of my request of the Fuehrer . . . which otherwise would make a terrible bloodbath unavoidable. Heil Hitler! Rabe—Siemens representative and head of the International Committee in Nanking."

Neither Hitler nor Kriebel replied, but Rabe soon noticed

something unusual in the Japanese bombing pattern in the city. Before he sent the telegrams, Japanese planes bombed areas within Nanking indiscriminately; afterwards they attacked only military targets, such as military schools, airstrips, and arsenals. Wrote Rabe, "This . . . was the goal of my telegram and it made quite a lasting impression on my American colleagues."

But his triumph was short-lived as one crisis loomed after another. Originally Rabe and his colleagues hoped to reserve the empty buildings in the zone for the poorest citizens of Nanking. To avoid a rush of people, the committee had pasted posters all over the city, urging refugees to rent housing from friends. But so many people surged into the area of two and a half square miles that Rabe soon found himself with fifty thousand more residents than he had expected even in the worst-case scenario. The refugees not only packed the buildings but spilled forth onto lawns, trenches, and bomb dugouts. Entire families slept in the open streets, while hundreds of mat dwellings mushroomed next to the American embassy. By the time the city fell, the Safety Zone—its borders lined by white flags and sheets marked with the red cross symbol within a red circle—was a swarming "human beehive" of 250,000 refugees.

Sanitation soon posed another nightmare. The filth in the camps—especially the toilets—enraged Rabe, and it took a tirade on his part to get the refugee center on the Siemens grounds in acceptable order. Afterwards, when Rabe inspected the Siemens camp, he found not only were the toilets in better shape but every wall on the Siemens grounds had been repaired. "Nobody would tell me where the beautiful new bricks came from," Rabe wrote. "I determined later on that many of the newer buildings in the area were considerably shorter than before."

But the shortage of food created the worst headache of all for the zone leaders. In early December the mayor of Nanking gave the International Committee thirty thousand *tan* (or two thousand tons) of rice and ten thousand bags of flour to feed the population. But the food was stored outside of the city, and the committee lacked the necessary trucks to bring it into the zone. The Chinese military had already commandeered most of the vehicles in the area to transport twenty thousand men and five thousand cases of Peking Palace treasures out of the capital; desperate civilians and individual soldiers had stolen virtually all the rest. With no alternative open to them, Rabe and the remaining foreigners drove frantically through Nanking, using their own automobiles to haul as much rice as possible into the zone. As the Japanese bombarded the city, the foreigners continued the deliveries; one driver actually lost an eye from flying shrapnel. In the end the zone leaders secured only a fraction of the total food available—ten thousand *tan* of rice and one thousand bags of flour—but the food went far to stave off hunger for many of the refugees in the zone.

On December 9, recognizing the dire situation ahead, the committee tried to negotiate a three-day cease-fire (see chapter 3), during which the Japanese could keep their positions and the Chinese could withdraw peacefully from the walled city. However, Chiang Kai-shek did not agree to the cease-fire, prompting the Japanese to begin a furious bombardment of Nanking the following day. On December 12, the committee was again approached by the Chinese military, this time to negotiate a surrender, but again the plan fell through.

From that point on, there was little Rabe could do that day but watch and wait for the inevitable. He recorded the events as they enfolded, hour by hour. At 6:30 P.M. on December 12 he wrote: "The cannons on the Purple Mountain fire continuously—there is lighting and thunder all around it. Suddenly, the entire mountain is in flames—some houses and munitions depots are also on fire." At that moment Rabe recalled an ancient Chinese saying that portended the city's doom: "When the Purple Mountain burns . . . then Nanking is lost."

At 8:00 P.M., Rabe watched as the skies to the south of the city glowed red with flames. Then he heard frantic knocking on both gates of his house: Chinese women and children were begging for entrance, men were scaling the garden wall behind his German school, and people were cramming themselves into the foxholes in his garden, even ducking under the giant German flag he had used to warn pilots from bombing his property. The cries and knocking increased until Rabe could bear it no longer. He flung open the gates to let the crowd in. But the noise only intensified as the night wore on. Exasperated, Rabe donned a steel helmet and ran through his garden, yelling at everyone to shut up.

At 11:30 P.M., Rabe received a surprise visitor. It was Christian Kröger, a fellow Nazi Party member in his midthirties who worked for the German engineering firm of Carlowitz & Company. The tall, blond engineer had come to China to oversee the construction of a large steel mill but found himself, like Rabe, in the midst of Nanking's insanity. The International Committee had appointed Kröger its treasurer.

Kröger had stopped by to tell Rabe that Chungshan Road was littered with weapons and supplies that the Chinese military had left behind during its retreat. Someone had even abandoned a bus, offering it for sale for twenty dollars.

"Do you think someone will take it?" Kröger asked.

"But Christian, how can they?" Rabe said.

"Na. I ordered the man to come into my office in the morning."

Finally, the din around his house began to diminish. The exhausted Rabe, who had not had time even to change clothes for two days, lay back in bed, trying to relax as the society he knew and loved collapsed around him. He knew that the Ministry of Communication building was burning down and that the city would fall any minute. Rabe reassured himself that things would only get better, not worse, from this point on. "You don't have to be scared of the Japanese," his Chinese colleagues had told him. "As soon as they have taken over the city, peace and order will prevail—the rail connections with Shanghai will be quickly rebuilt and the stores will return to their normal functions." Before he fell asleep, Rabe thought, "Thank God that the worst has been overcome!"

The next morning Rabe awoke to the sound of yet another air raid. Apparently not all of the Chinese army had been forced from of the city, he thought. It was only 5:00 A.M., so he lay down again. Like most people in the city, Rabe had become so jaded by air raids that the blasts no longer bothered him.

Later that morning Rabe explored the city to check out the extent of the damage. In the streets lay numerous Chinese corpses, many of them civilians who had been shot in the back. He watched a group of Japanese soldiers push their way into a German coffeehouse. When Rabe chastised them for stealing, pointing to the German flags on the house, an English-speaking Japanese soldier snapped: "We are hungry! If you want to complain, go to the Japanese embassy. They will pay for it!" The Japanese soldiers also told Rabe that their supply column had not arrived, and they could not count on the column for any nourishment even if it did arrive. Later Rabe learned that the soldiers looted the coffeehouse, then set it afire.

Worse was to come. In the distance, Rabe saw Japanese soldiers marching north from the south side of Nanking to occupy the rest of the city. To avoid them, he immediately drove north and reached the main street of the city, Chungshan Road, stopping at the Red Cross hospital in the Foreign Ministry. The Chinese staff had fled the premises, and bodies were everywhere—clogging the rooms, corridors, and even the exits from the hospital.

That day Rabe encountered the remains of the Chinese army—hungry and exhausted stragglers who had failed to cross the Yangtze River to safety. Driving through Shansi Road Circle, he met four hundred Chinese troops, all of them still armed, marching in the direction of the advancing Japanese army. It was then that Rabe had a sudden "humanitarian impulse" that was to haunt his conscience for months, if not years, afterwards. Warning them about the Japanese troops to the south, Rabe advised the Chinese soldiers to throw away their machine guns and join the refugees in the Safety Zone. After a short discussion, they agreed and followed Rabe into the zone.

Similarly, when hundreds of Chinese soldiers found themselves trapped on the northern side of the city, unable to secure passage across the river, many broke into the Safety Zone, begging the American and European administrators to save their lives. The committee members were uncertain as to whether they should help them. After all, they had created the zone as a sanctuary for civilians, not soldiers. The committee tried to resolve the dilemma by addressing the issue with Japanese army headquarters but got no further than a captain on Han Chung Road.

Moved by the plight of the soldiers, the committee eventually caved in to their pleas. Like Rabe, they told the soldiers that if they laid down their arms, the Japanese might treat them mercifully. Then they helped the soldiers disarm and housed them in various buildings within the neutral area. In the confusion, many of the soldiers stripped off their uniforms and mingled with the civilians in the zone.

The next day John Rabe wrote a long letter explaining the situation to a Japanese military commander. He begged the Japanese to exercise mercy toward the former soldiers and to treat them humanely according to the recognized laws of war. To Rabe's great relief, a Japanese officer promised him that the lives of the Chinese soldiers would be spared.

But relief turned into horror when the Japanese betrayed Rabe and seized the disarmed soldiers for execution. If Rabe had hoped that the Japanese would not be able to separate the troops from the hundreds of thousands of civilians, he was sorely mistaken. The Japanese detected virtually every one of the former soldiers by examining their hands, knowing that the daily use of guns caused calluses on certain areas on the fingers of soldiers. They also examined shoulders for backpack marks, foreheads and hair for indentations from military caps, and even feet for blisters caused from months of marching.

During a staff conference the night of December 14, the committee learned that the Japanese had rounded up thirteen hundred men in a Safety Zone camp near the headquarters to shoot them. "We knew that there were a number of ex-soldiers among them, but Rabe had been promised by an officer that afternoon that their lives would be spared," George Fitch, the

YMCA representative, wrote in his diary of the incident. "It was now all too obvious what they were going to do. The men were lined up and roped together in groups of about 100 by soldiers with bayonets fixed; those who had hats had them roughly torn off and thrown to the ground—and then by the lights of our headlights we watched them marched away to their doom."

"Did I have the right to act that way?" Rabe wrote later of his decision to quarter the soldiers in the zone. "Did I handle that correctly?"

For the next few days Rabe watched helplessly as the Japanese dragged thousands more soldiers from the zone and executed them. The Japanese killed thousands of innocent men who happened to have calluses on their fingers, foreheads, or feet—men who were ricksha coolies, manual laborers, and police officers. Rabe later witnessed the Red Swastika Society, a charitable Buddhist organization in the city, pull more than 120 corpses from a single pond. (In a later report, Rabe pointed out that several ponds in Nanking actually disappeared because they were so filled with corpses.)

As both head of the International Committee and local head of the Nazi Party, a position that was certain to carry some weight with the Japanese authorities, Rabe wrote letter after letter to the Japanese embassy. At first he was unfailingly polite, toning down his anger because of his perceived obligation, as a German citizen and Nazi leader, to maintain the relationship between the two embassies. He asked the American members of the committee to let him review their letters to the Japanese embassy so that he could "put some honey" into them as well. He maintained his polite tone in his personal visits to the embassy.

In turn, the Japanese diplomats received Rabe's letters and visits with gracious smiles and official courtesy, but in the end he always received the same answer: "We shall inform the military authorities." As days passed, each bringing its own unrelenting onslaught of fresh atrocities, Rabe's written communication to the Japanese grew increasingly hostile, punctuated with exclamations of outrage:

> All 27 Westerners in the city at that time and our Chinese population were totally surprised by the reign of robbery, rapine, and killing initiated by your soldiers on the 14th!

> We did not find a single Japanese patrol either in the Zone or at the entrances!

> Yesterday, in broad daylight, several women at the Seminary were raped right in the middle of a large room filled with men, women and children! We 22 Westerners cannot feed 200,000 Chinese civilians and protect them night and day. That is the duty of the Japanese authorities. If you can give them protection, we can help feed them!

> If this process of terrorism continues, it will be next to impossible to locate workers to get the essential services started.

Gradually Rabe and the rest of the International Committee begin to read the real message in the diplomat's answers—it was the military, not embassy, calling the shots. Fukuda Tokuyasu, secretary of the Japanese embassy, told Rabe as much by saying: "The Japanese army wants to make it very bad for the town, but we, the embassy, will try to prevent it." During the great Rape some Japanese embassy officials actually suggested that the International Committee seek publicity in Japan directly so that public opinion would force the Japanese government to take action. But at the same time another embassy official urged Rabe to remain silent, warning him that "if you tell the newspaper reporters anything bad, you will have the entire Japanese army against you."

Finally, with only his status as an official of an allied nation for protection, Rabe did what now seems the unthinkable: he began to roam about the city, trying to prevent atrocities himself.

Whenever he drove through Nanking, some man would inevitably leap out and stop the car to beg Rabe to stop a rape in progress—a rape that usually involved a sister, a wife, or a daughter. Rabe would then let the man climb into the car and direct him to the scene of the rape. Once there, he would chase Japanese soldiers away from their prey, on one occasion even bodily lifting a soldier sprawled on top of a young girl. He knew these expeditions were highly dangerous ("The Japanese had pistols and bayonets and I . . . had only party symbols and my swastika armband," Rabe wrote in his report to Hitler), but nothing could deter him from making them—not even the risk of death.

His diary entry on January 1, 1938, is typical: "The mother of a young attractive girl called out to me, and throwing herself on her knees, crying, said I should help her. Upon entering [the house] I saw a Japanese soldier lying completely naked on a young girl, who was crying hysterically. I yelled at this swine, in any language it would be understood, 'Happy New Year!' and he fled from there, naked and with his pants in his hand."

Rabe was appalled by the rape in the city. In the streets he passed scores of female corpses, raped and mutilated, next to the charred remains of their homes. "Groups of 3 to 10 marauding soldiers would begin by traveling through the city and robbing whatever there was to steal," Rabe wrote in his report to Hitler.

> They would continue by raping the women and girls and killing anything and anyone that offered any resistance, attempted to run away from them or simply happened to be in the wrong place at the wrong time. There were girls under the age of 8 and women over the age of 70 who were raped and then, in the most brutal way possible, knocked down and beat up. We found corpses of women on beer glasses and others who had been lanced by bamboo shoots. I saw the victims with my own eyes—I talked to some of them right before their deaths and had their bodies brought to the morgue at the Kulo hospital so that I could be personally convinced that all of these reports had touched on the truth.

As he walked through the burning wreckage of his beloved city, Rabe could read, on almost every street corner, beautiful

Japanese posters that proclaimed: "Trust Our Japanese Army—They Will Protect and Feed You."

Determined to save Chinese lives, Rabe sheltered as many people as he could, turning his house and office into sanctuaries for Siemens employees and their families. Rabe also harbored hundreds of Chinese women on his property, permitting them to live in tiny straw huts in his backyard. With these women Rabe developed a warning system to protect them from Japanese rapists. Whenever Japanese soldiers scaled the wall of his yard, the women would blow a whistle and send Rabe running out into the yard to chase the offenders away. This happened so frequently that Rabe rarely left his home at night, fearful that Japanese intruders would commit an orgy of rape in his absence. He complained about the situation to Japanese military officers, but they failed to take the matter seriously. Even when Rabe caught a Japanese soldier raping a woman in one of the backyard straw huts, a military officer did nothing to punish the rapist except slap him across the face.

If Rabe was frustrated by the futility of the situation—by the limitations of what he and some twenty other individuals could accomplish to protect hundreds of thousands of civilians from more than fifty thousand Japanese soldiers—he did not show it. He knew it was crucial to hide any sign of weakness from the Japanese and to overwhelm them with "a domineering presence and energy."

Fortunately, his status as a Nazi caused several Japanese soldiers to hesitate before committing further mayhem—at least in his presence. George Fitch, the local YMCA secretary, wrote that "when any of them objects [Rabe] thrusts his Nazi armband in their face and points to his Nazi decoration, the highest in the country, and asks them if they know what that means. It always works!" The Japanese soldiers appeared to respect—at times even fear—the Nazis of Nanking. While the Japanese privates did not hesitate to beat up the Americans, charge at them with bayonets, or even to push one American missionary down a flight of stairs, they exercised considerable restraint in their dealings with Rabe and his countrymen. Once, when four Japanese soldiers in the midst of raping and looting saw Eduard Sperling's swastika armband, they screamed "Deutsche! Deutsche!" and ran away. On another occasion, the swastika probably saved Rabe's life. One evening Japanese soldiers broke into his property, and Rabe confronted them with his flashlight. One of them reached for his pistol, as if to shoot Rabe, but stopped when he realized it would be "bad business to shoot a German subject."

If the Japanese respected Rabe, the Chinese refugee community revered him. To them he was the man who rescued daughters from sexual slavery and sons from machine-gun fire. Rabe's very presence sometimes touched off riots in Safety Zone camps. During one of his visits to the zone, thousands of Chinese women flung themselves to the ground before him, weeping and begging for protection, declaring they would rather commit suicide on the spot than leave the zone to be raped and tortured.

Rabe tried to keep hope alive for his refugees in the midst of their terror. He hosted little birthday celebrations for the children born to refugee women living in his backyard. Each newborn received a gift: $10 for baby boys and $9.50 for baby girls. (As Rabe explained in his report to Hitler—"Girls in China aren't worth as much as boys.") Typically, when a boy was born, he received Rabe's name, and if a girl was born, she received his wife's name, Dora.

Rabe's courage and generosity ultimately won the respect of the other members of the International Committee, even those fundamentally opposed to Nazism. George Fitch wrote to his friends that he would "almost wear a Nazi badge" to keep fellowship with Rabe and the other Germans in Nanking. Even Dr. Robert Wilson, a man thoroughly repulsed by Nazism, sang Rabe's praises in letters to his family: "He is well up in Nazi circles and after coming into such close contact with him as we have for the past few weeks and discover[ing] what a splendid man he is and what a tremendous heart he has, it is hard to reconcile his personality with his adulation of 'Der Fuhrer.' "

THE ONLY SURGEON IN NANKING

It is not surprising that Robert Wilson stayed in Nanking when virtually every other surgeon left, for Nanking, the city of his birth and boyhood, had always commanded a special place in his heart. Born in 1904, Wilson was reared by a family of Methodist missionaries who had shaped many of Nanking's educational institutions. His uncle, John Ferguson, founded the University of Nanking. His father worked as an ordained minister and middle-school instructor in the city, while his mother, a college-educated Greek scholar who spoke several languages fluently, ran her own school for missionary children. As a teenager, Robert Wilson even learned geometry from Pearl Buck, who would later win the Nobel Prize in Literature for her novels about China. Thriving in this environment, and displaying exceptional intellectual promise, Wilson won, at age seventeen, a scholarship to Princeton University. Upon graduation from college, he taught Latin and mathematics for two years at a high school in Connecticut, enrolled in Harvard Medical School, and then served as an intern at St. Luke's Hospital in New York, where he courted and married the head nurse. But rather than pursue a career in the United States, Wilson decided that his future lay in his hometown of Nanking, and taking his bride with him, he returned in 1935 to practice medicine at the University of Nanking Hospital.

The first two years for the Wilsons were perhaps the most idyllic of their lives. Time was marked by a slow-paced charm—dinners with other missionary couples, elegant teas and receptions at foreign embassies, parties at sprawling country villas staffed with private cooks and coolies. In the evenings he read ancient Chinese in its original text and studied under a private tutor to expand his knowledge of the language. He also took every Wednesday afternoon off to play tennis. Sometimes he and his wife would go to the lake together and have dinner on a boat, inhaling the perfumed air as they drifted through watery lanes of red lotus blossom.

War, however, shattered forever the timeless serenity the Wilsons had enjoyed in Nanking. After the Marco Polo Bridge incident in July, the people of Nanking began to carry gas masks in the street, along with chemical solution and layers of gauze, fearing a Japanese poison-gas attack. By August 1937, when the Japanese started to bomb the capital, his wife Marjorie had boarded a gunboat with their infant daughter Elizabeth and arrived safely at Kuling. But Wilson, fearing his wife and child would starve to death if the war continued, insisted that they return to the United States. Mrs. Wilson complied with his wishes and went back to work at St. Luke's in New York while her mother cared for the baby. But there was no question that Dr. Wilson himself would stay in Nanking. "He saw this as his duty," his wife recalled, almost sixty years later. "The Chinese were his people."

No doubt to dispel loneliness that autumn, Wilson moved into the house of J. Lossing Buck, the former husband of Pearl Buck, and the house soon filled up with his friends: the surgeon Richard Brady, the United Christian missionary James McCallum, and other people who would later serve as members of the International Committee for the Nanking Safety Zone. Like Wilson, many of these men had sent their wives and children away from Nanking.

When he wasn't busy with patients, Wilson often wrote letters home to his family. Most contained gruesome descriptions of the victims of Japanese bombs, such as the girl who had crouched with her back to an explosion, only to have her buttocks ripped off. From the casualties of war he dug out a growing heap of shrapnel and bullets—enough, he wrote cynically, to open "a respectable museum" before the war was over.

Even though he knew that the Japanese had no qualms about bombing hospitals, Wilson continued to go to work. On September 25, in one of the worst air raids Nanking had ever experienced, the Japanese aimed two 1,000-pound bombs at the Central Hospital and Ministry of Health, despite the presence of a large red cross clearly painted on one of the roofs. The bombs landed only fifty feet away from a dugout where one hundred doctors and nurses were hiding.

Wilson did everything possible in the hospital to minimize the risk of attracting Japanese bombs. Heavy black curtains were drawn over the windows to hide lit rooms from Japanese aviators. But the city crawled with rumors of spies guiding pilots to key targets with red and green lanterns at night. During one raid a stranger crept into the hospital with a red-shielded flashlight instead of a green- or black-shielded one and aroused suspicions when he tried to open a window that had been securely shut to prevent the seepage of poison gas. He raised even more eyebrows when he asked a Chinese aviator patient a number of unusual questions about the flying height and range of Chinese bombers.

As autumn drew to a close, Wilson found himself tremendously overworked. More people needed medical attention than ever before—not only civilian victims of Japanese bombs but veterans from Shanghai. There were approximately one hundred thousand wounded Chinese veterans in hospitals between Shanghai and the city of Wuhu. Trainload after trainload dumped them off at the station in Hsiakwan, the northern Nanking suburb. Some lay dying on the floor of the station, while others limped aimlessly through the capital. Soldiers who healed were returned to the front, but those who lost arms or legs, those crippled beyond hope, were simply turned loose with two-dollar compensations and instructions to go home. Home was far away for most soldiers. Few had the money or physical energy to get there. Abandoned by their leaders, stranded in the Shanghai-Nanking area, thousands of Chinese veterans—blind, lame, rotting away from wounds and infections—were reduced to begging in the streets.

As the situation worsened, the staff at the hospital shrank. Chinese doctors and nurses fled the city, joining the hundreds of thousands of Nanking residents in their westward migration. Wilson did all he could to dissuade his medical staff from leaving, insisting that under martial law they would have nothing to fear after the city fell. Ultimately, however, he was unable to convince them to stay. By the end of the first week of December there were only three doctors at the University of Nanking Hospital: Robert Wilson, C. S. Trimmer, and a Chinese physician. When Richard Brady, the only other American surgeon in the city, left Nanking because his little girl was seriously ill in Kuling, Wilson was the only person left to perform the hourly amputations. "It is quite a sensation," he wrote on December 7, "to be the only surgeon in a big war-torn city."

A week later, Wilson nearly lost his life. On the afternoon of December 13, he had decided to perform a delicate operation on a patient who had suffered severe eye injury from a bomb. Wilson had to remove what was left of the eye in order to save the other one. The eyeball was halfway out when a shell landed fifty yards away from Wilson and exploded, shattering the windows and spraying the room with shrapnel. No one was killed or injured, but Wilson noted that the nurses were "naturally pretty shaky" and wanted to know whether they should continue the operation. "There was obviously nothing else to do," Wilson wrote, "but I don't think any eyes have come out that fast."

By nightfall of December 13, the Japanese had seized complete control of the ancient capital. Wilson saw Japanese flags fluttering all over town. The following day the conquering army began to take over the hospitals in the city. They broke into the main hospital of the Chinese army—located within the Ministry of Foreign Affairs and run by Safety Zone members who had organized themselves as a chapter of the Red Cross—and trapped hundreds of Chinese soldiers inside. The Japanese forbade doctors to enter the hospital or send food to the wounded soldiers, who were later marched out and systematically shot. After three out of four Red Cross hospitals fell in this manner to the Japanese, the International Committee concentrated its efforts on the University of Nanking Hospital.

During the first few days of occupation, Wilson watched the Japanese soldiers loot and burn the city. He saw them rob the University of Nanking Hospital and, frustrated that he could not stop all of the thefts, mentally aimed a "swift kick" at a soldier who tried to steal a camera from a nurse. He also watched soldiers burn a heap of musical instruments in the street and wondered whether the destruction of property was a Japanese plot to compel the people of Nanking to buy Japanese goods later.

Wilson even witnessed the ransacking of his own home. Venturing to his house to survey possible damage, he caught

red-handed three Japanese soldiers in the process of looting it.
They had broken into the attic, opened up a big trunk, and
strewn its contents all over the floor. One of them was peering
into a microscope when Wilson walked in. Upon seeing him,
all three soldiers ran down the stairs and out the door. "The
crowning insult was on the second floor where one had just
finished depositing his calling card on the floor of the toilet
within a foot of the toilet bowl," Wilson wrote. "He had covered it with a clean towel which had been left hanging in the
room."

But nothing of the looting could compare to the rape and
murder that he witnessed in the city. Even Wilson, now a jaded
war surgeon, found the intensity of the atrocities shocking.

> *December 15:* The slaughter of civilians is appalling. I could go
> on for pages telling of cases of rape and brutality almost be-
> yond belief.

> *December 18:* Today marks the 6th day of modern Dante's In-
> ferno, written in huge letters with blood and rape. Murder by
> the wholesale and rape by the thousands of cases. There seems
> to be no stop to the ferocity, lust and stavism of the brutes. At
> first I tried to be pleasant to them to avoid arousing their ire,
> but the smile has gradually worn off and my stare is fully as
> cool and fishy as theirs.

> *December 19:* All the food is being stolen from the poor people
> and they are in a state of terror-stricken, hysterical panic. When
> will it stop!

> *Christmas Eve:* Now they tell us that there are twenty thousand
> soldiers still in the Zone (where they get their figures no one
> knows), and that they are going to hunt them out and shoot
> them all. That will mean every able-bodied male between the
> ages of 18 and 50 that is now in the city. How can they ever
> look anybody in the face again?

By the end of the year his letters carried a fatalistic air. "The
only consolation is that it can't be worse," he wrote on Decem-

ber 30. "They can't kill as many people as there aren't any more to kill."

Frequently Wilson and the others saw the Japanese round up Chinese soldiers, shoot them, and stuff the bodies in dirt air-raid shelters that doubled as mass graves. But Wilson heard that many Chinese people were executed not because they posed any threat to the Japanese army but because their bodies served a practical purpose. After the fall of Nanking, the big trenches that the Chinese had built for tank traps were filled to the brim by the Japanese with the bodies of dead and wounded soldiers. When the Japanese failed to find enough bodies of dead soldiers so tanks could pass over them, they shot nearby residents and threw them in the trenches as well. The witness who told Wilson the story borrowed a camera so that he could take pictures to confirm his statements.

There was very little Wilson could do to prevent these murders. The Japanese soldiers he confronted often made a point of conspicuously playing with their weapons—loading and unloading them—in order to intimidate him and other foreigners. Wilson fully expected to be shot in the back at any moment.

One of the worst scenes Wilson saw in Nanking—a scene he would remember for the rest of his life—was a massive gang rape of teenage girls in the street. A group of young women between the ages of fifteen and eighteen were lined up by the Japanese and then raped in the dirt, one after another, by an entire regiment. Some hemorrhaged and died, while others killed themselves shortly afterwards.

But the scenes in the hospitals were even more horrifying than those in the streets. Wilson was mortified by the women who came to the emergency room with their bellies ripped open, by the charred and horribly disfigured men whom the Japanese tried to burn alive, and by numerous other horrors he barely had time to describe on paper. He told his wife that he would never forget the woman whose head was nearly cut off, teetering from a point on her neck. "This morning came another woman in a sad plight and with a horrible story," a hospital volunteer wrote of this woman in his diary on January 3, 1938.

She was one of the five women whom the Japanese soldiers had taken to one of their medical units—to wash their clothes by day, to be raped by night. Two of them were forced to satisfy from 15 to 20 men and the prettiest one as many as 40 each night. This one who came to us had been called off by three soldiers into an isolated place where they attempted to cut off her head. The muscles of the neck had been cut but they failed to sever the spinal cord. She feigned death but dragged herself to the hospital—another of the many to bear witness to the brutality of soldiers.

Yet in the midst of their pain and suffering, Wilson was amazed by the willpower of some of his patients. In a letter to his family dated New Year's Day 1938, he told an incredible account of survival. Chinese soldiers burned down the home of a twenty-nine-year-old woman in a tiny village south of Nanking, forcing her to head for the capital by foot with her five small children. Before nightfall a Japanese airplane dove down at them, strafing the family with machine-gun fire and sending a bullet through the mother's right eye and out her neck. She fainted in shock but awoke the next morning, lying in a pool of blood next to her crying children. Too weak to carry her youngest child, a three-month-old baby, she left it behind in an empty house. Yet she somehow found the strength to struggle on to Nanking with her four remaining children, making her way successfully to the hospital.

Wilson and other volunteers stayed in the hospital until they wavered on the verge of collapse. The International Committee could have used medical help from outside the city, but the Japanese would not permit doctors or medical volunteers to enter Nanking. So the burden of caring for the sick and administering the zone fell on this tiny beleaguered committee of no more than some twenty individuals. They worked in shifts to ensure that the hospital was guarded from the Japanese by at least one foreigner twenty-four hours a day. Some of them became so overworked that they succumbed to colds, flu, and various other illnesses. During the massacre the only other Western doctor in the city, C. S. Trimmer, struggled with a fever of 102 degrees.

The University of Nanking Hospital swiftly became another refugee camp because Wilson refused to discharge patients who had no place to go. Patients who did leave the hospital were accompanied by foreigners to ensure that they returned home safely. James McCallum acted as the hospital chauffeur, driving patients about town in unpainted, patched-up ambulances. Survivors of the massacre remember that the exhausted McCallum pressed cold towels against his face to stay awake as he drove patients home. But when even cold towels failed to keep his eyes open, McCallum resorted to chewing his tongue until it bled.

Few people in Nanking pushed themselves as hard as Wilson did in the hospital. When the massacre and rapes gradually subsided, several of the other physicians went to Shanghai every weekend to recover from the strain. But Wilson continued to operate on patients relentlessly, day and night, around the clock. His selflessness was remembered almost sixty years later by survivors who spoke of Wilson with great reverence, at least one of them discussing in detail the preparation and successful result of his operation under Wilson's hands. He operated for free, because few patients had money to pay him, but the surgeries exacted a terrible price from his own health. In the end, his family believes that only his faith as a devout Methodist, combined with his love for China, gave him the courage to survive the Rape of Nanking.

THE LIVING GODDESS OF NANKING

Wilhelmina Vautrin (or Minnie Vautrin, as most people called her), by occupation head of the Education Department and dean of studies at Ginling Women's Arts and Science College, was one of the few Western women in the city during the first few weeks of the Nanking massacre. Years later she would be remembered not only for her courage in protecting thousands of women from Japanese soldiers but also for the diary she kept, a diary that some historians believe will eventually be recognized, much like the diary of Anne Frank, for its importance in illuminating the spirit of a single witness during a holocaust of war.

Vautrin, the daughter of a blacksmith, was fifty-one years old in 1937. Raised in the tiny farming community of Secor, Illinois, she was sent to live with neighbors when her mother died six years later. In their homes Vautrin was often treated little better than a servant or field hand, and she found herself herding cattle during the bleakest months of winter. Despite the impoverishment of her childhood, she was able to work her way through school, graduating with honors in 1912 from the University of Illinois at Urbana-Champaign.

Tall and handsome in her youth, with long dark hair, she was a vivacious and popular woman who attracted numerous suitors. But by the time she graduated from the University of Illinois, she had made up her mind to forgo marriage. Instead, she joined the United Christian Missionary Association and moved to Hofei, a city in the Anhwei province of China, where she worked for seven years as the principal of a girls' school and learned to speak Chinese. Then Vautrin moved to Nanking, to the position she held at the time of the massacre.

Vautrin was clearly very happy in Nanking. On visits to her hometown in Illinois, she talked incessantly of China—its culture, its people, and its history. She gave her family silkworm cocoons and taught them how to cook and eat Chinese food. In her diary, she never ceased to marvel at the beauty of the Nanking landscape. An avid gardener, she planted roses and chrysanthemums at Ginling College, visiting greenhouses at Sun Yat-sen Memorial Park, walking down the fragrant lanes of plum and peach trees near the Ming Tombs.

In the summer of 1937, while vacationing with friends in the seaside summer resort of Tsingtao, Vautrin heard that a Japanese soldier had disappeared a few miles south of Peking. The disappearance triggered several battles between the Chinese and Japanese in the area, prompting a friend of hers to comment darkly that the assassination of only two people in Sarajevo in 1914 had eventually culminated in the deaths of more than 11 million people.

Still, Vautrin refused to join the other Americans evacuating

Nanking, and so the American embassy lent her a new nine-foot American flag to lay flat on the center of the grassy quadrangle of Ginling College to protect the campus against Japanese pilots. The embassy staff also gave her and the other International Committee members lengths of rope to knot into ladders and told them that once the *Panay* departed with the American embassy officials, and the Chinese military slammed all the gates shut, their only hope of escape would be over the city walls.

But Vautrin hardly had time to think about running away. With most of the faculty gone from Nanking (most had abandoned their homes to flee to cities like Shanghai and Chengtu), Vautrin was now the acting head of the institution. She labored to prepare the campus for female refugees and to evacuate wounded soldiers from the area. To disguise their identities, she burned their military papers and garments in the college incinerator. Under her direction, furniture was moved into attics, safes were emptied, dorms were cleaned, and valuables were wrapped in oil paper and hidden. Meanwhile, posters, signs, and armbands for the Nanking Safety Zone were created and distributed among volunteers. Vautrin also commissioned the sewing of a second American flag, this one twenty-seven feet long, but the Chinese tailor who put it together accidentally sewed the blue field with the stars on the lower, left-hand corner instead of the upper.

By the second week of December the gates of Ginling opened for women and children. Thousands of people poured in. Refugees were passing through the city at the rate of one thousand a day. Many of them, exhausted, bewildered, and hungry, came into the Safety Zone camps with only the clothing on their backs. "From 8:30 this morning until 6 this evening, excepting for the noon meal, I have stood at the front gate while the refugees poured in," she continued. "There is terror in the faces of many of the women—last night was a terrible night in the city and many young women were taken from their homes by the Japanese soldiers."

Vautrin allowed the women and children to come in freely but implored older women to stay home to leave space for the younger ones. Few women took her suggestion, and most begged just for a place to sit on the lawn. By the night of December 15, the population of the camps at Ginling had swelled to more than three thousand people.

The next day Japanese soldiers stormed the college. At 10:00 A.M. on December 16, more than one hundred Japanese troops burst onto the Ginling campus to inspect the buildings for hidden Chinese soldiers. They demanded that every door be opened, and if a key was not forthcoming, a Japanese soldier stood ready with an ax to break down the door by force. Vautrin's heart sank at the thought of the Japanese finding the hundreds of padded garments stored in the Geography Department office upstairs, but fortunately an attic packed with two hundred Chinese women and children diverted the Japanese soldiers' attention. (Vautrin later buried the garments to hide them from the Japanese.)

Twice that day the Japanese seized servants on campus and started to drag them away. They certainly would have been killed if Vautrin had not rescued them with cries of "No soldier—coolie!" Only later did she learn that the Japanese had trained at least six machine guns on the campus, with many more soldiers on guard outside, ready to shoot anyone who attempted to run away.

That evening Vautrin saw women being carted away in the streets and heard their desperate pleas. A truck went by with eight to ten girls, and as it passed she heard them scream, "Jiu Ming! Jiu Ming! (Save our lives!)"

The following day, December 17, 1937, was even worse. The migration of women into Ginling only intensified as Japanese soldiers flooded the city. "What a heartbreaking sight!" Vautrin wrote. "Weary women, frightened girls, trudging with children and bedding and small packages of clothes." If only someone had time to write the story of each refugee who came in, she thought—especially the stories of the girls who had blackened their faces and cut their hair. As she accommodated the stream of "wild-eyed women," she heard stories of the Japanese raping girls as young as twelve and women as elderly as sixty, or raping pregnant women at bayonet point. The harried Vautrin spent the entire day trying to secure food for the refugees, direct Chinese men to other camps in the Safety Zone, and run to areas on campus where Japanese soldiers had been sighted.

But nothing prepared Vautrin for the encounter that awaited her that evening. Two Japanese soldiers were pulling at the door of the Central Building, demanding that Vautrin open it immediately, but when she insisted that she had no key and that no soldiers were hiding inside, a Japanese soldier slapped her in the face and also struck the Chinese man next to her. Then she saw two Japanese soldiers lead away three bound servants from the college. She followed them to the front gate, where the Japanese had forced a large group of Chinese to kneel beside the road. The Japanese demanded to speak to the master of the institution and, learning that it was Vautrin, ordered her to identify every kneeling person. One man in the party spoke up to help Vautrin, and for this he was slapped severely.

In the midst of this ordeal, three committee members drove up: the YMCA secretary George Fitch, the Nanking University sociology professor Lewis Smythe, and the Presbyterian missionary W. Plumer Mills. The soldiers forced the three men to stand in line and frisked them for pistols. Suddenly they heard screams and cries and saw the Japanese dragging women out of the side gate. It was only then that Vautrin realized that the entire interrogation was a ploy to keep the foreigners at the front gate while other Japanese soldiers searched the campus for women to rape. "Never shall I forget that scene," she wrote, remembering her rage and helplessness: "The people kneeling at side of road, Mary, Mrs. Tsen and I standing, the dried leaves rattling, the moaning of the wind, the cry of women being led out."

For the next few months, Vautrin often found herself one of the sole defenders of the refugee camps at Ginling College. Japanese soldiers constantly harassed the refugees there by rounding up men for execution or women for military brothels. Sometimes their recruitment tactics were brazen. On at least one occasion Japanese soldiers drove up to campus with a

truck and asked for girls. Most of the time, however, the kidnapping of women for rape was done covertly. Soldiers
jumped over bamboo fences at night or broke open the side
or back gates to seize random women in the darkness—
expeditions that began to be known throughout the populace
as "the lottery."

On New Year's Day 1938, Vautrin rescued a girl whom a soldier had dragged into a bamboo grove north of the library. On
several occasions her heroism nearly cost Vautrin her life.
Many of the soldiers were "fierce and unreasonable" toward
her, brandishing bayonets reddened with fresh bloodstains.
Vautrin wrote that "in some cases they are defiant and look at
me with a dagger in their eyes, and sometimes a dagger in their
hands." One time, when she tried to stop Japanese soldiers
from looting, one of them aimed a gun at her.

Sometimes in her dealings with the Japanese, Vautrin made
mistakes. Just as Rabe and the other committee members had
been duped by the Japanese into handing over men for execution, Vautrin appears to have been duped into delivering innocent women into the arms of Japanese soldiers. On December
24, Vautrin was summoned to her office to meet with a high
Japanese military officer and an elderly Chinese interpreter,
who discussed with her the Japanese army's need for prostitutes. "The request was that they be allowed to pick out the
prostitute women from our ten thousand refugees," Vautrin
later wrote of the meeting in her diary. "They said they wanted
one hundred. They feel if they can start a regular licensed place
for the soldiers then they will not molest innocent and decent
women."

Strangely enough, Vautrin granted the request. Perhaps she
had no choice in the matter, or perhaps she actually believed
that once the Japanese left with the prostitutes for their military brothel they would stop bothering the virgins and respectable matrons in the refugee camps. Whatever the reasons
behind her decision, it is safe to assume that Vautrin made it
under pressure. She waited while the Japanese conducted their
search and after a long time they finally secured twenty-one
women. How the Japanese were able to distinguish these

women as prostitutes Vautrin does not say, but she did mention that the Japanese were dissatisfied with the result because they were convinced that more prostitutes were hiding somewhere in the zone. "Group after group of girls have asked me if they will select the other seventy-nine from among the decent girls—and all I can answer is that they will not do so if it is in my power to prevent it," she wrote.

A week after the city fell, the Japanese began a systematic effort to regulate activity within the zone. The commander of the military police of the Japanese army made a proclamation, effective December 24, dictating that all civilians obtain passports (also called "good citizen's papers") from the issuing office of the Japanese army. No one was allowed to get a passport for someone else, and those without passports would not be allowed to live within the Nanking city walls. The military posted bulletins in the streets notifying people to register or face the risk of being executed.

On December 28, registration of the men began. At Ginling College they formed lines of four, received copies of forms, and marched to a house at the northeast corner of the campus where the Japanese recorded their names, ages, and occupations. Vautrin noticed that the men who arrived for registration were mainly old or maimed because most of the young men had already fled the city or been killed. Among those who showed up, more men were taken away as ex-soldiers, leaving behind old men and women who wept and kneeled before the Safety Zone leaders, begging them to secure the release of their husbands and sons. In a few cases the zone leaders were successful, but they noticed that the Japanese military officials were growing increasingly resentful of their interference.

When the turnout of men for registration disappointed the Japanese, they tried to intimidate the populace into compliance. On December 30, they announced that all who had not been registered by 2:00 P.M. the following day would be shot. "This proved to be a bluff," one missionary wrote of the incident, "but it frightened the people." The next morning huge crowds of people dutifully appeared at the registration areas, many of whom had risen before 3:00 A.M. to ensure their place in line. The Draconian threats of the Japanese had instilled such fear that by January 14 the authorities succeeded in registering at least 160,000 people.

Then registration began for the women. At 9:00 A.M. on December 31, thousands of Chinese women gathered in front of the Central Building of Ginling College, where a Japanese military official lectured to them. Speeches were given first in Japanese, then translated into Chinese by an interpreter: "You must follow the old customs of marriage," Vautrin recalled them saying. "You must not study English or go to theatres. China and Japan must be one." The women were then marched single file in two lines through frames set up for selling rice, where they were given tickets. Vautrin observed that the Japanese soldiers seemed to get a great deal of amusement herding the women about like cattle, sometimes putting the stamp on their cheeks. The soldiers also forced the women to smile and look happy for Japanese newsmen and photographers, even though the mere prospect of registration had made some women literally ill with fear.

At times the Japanese registration of Chinese women seemed to Vautrin nothing less than a full-scale inspection of the most attractive candidates for rape. On the very first day of female registration, the Japanese scrutinized certain women in the zone and tried to take them away. They had singled out twenty girls, no doubt for prostitution, because they had curled hair or dressed too well. But all were released, Vautrin later wrote, "because a mother or some other person could vouch for them."

After registration, the Japanese tried to eliminate the zone itself. In late January the Japanese announced that they wanted everyone out of the camps and back into their homes by the end of the month. February 4 was given as the deadline for evacuation. When the deadline arrived, Japanese soldiers inspected Ginling College and ordered the remaining girls and women to leave. When Vautrin told the inspectors that they could not leave because they were from other cities or their homes had burned down, the Japanese announced that the military police would assume the responsibility of protecting them. Vautrin was wary of these promises, and even the Chinese interpreter who came with the Japanese to deliver their messages whispered to Vautrin that he felt the young women were not safe and should continue to stay where they were.

The sheer number of refugees eventually overwhelmed Vautrin. Hundreds of women crammed themselves into verandas and covered ways head to feet, and many more women slept outside on the grass at night. The attic of Ginling's Science Hall housed more than one thousand women, and a friend of Vautrin's noted that women "slept shoulder to shoulder on the cement floor for weeks on end during the cold winter months! Each cement step in the building was the home of one person—and those steps are not more than four feet long! Some were happy to have a resting place on the chemistry lab tables, the water pipes and other paraphernalia not interfering at all."

The Rape of Nanking wore down Vautrin physically, but the mental torture she endured daily was far worse than her physical deterioration. "Oh, God, control the cruel beastliness of the soldiers in Nanking tonight . . . " she wrote in her diary. "How ashamed the women of Japan would be if they knew these tales of horror."

Under such pressure, it is remarkable that Vautrin still found the spirit to comfort others and give them a renewed sense of patriotism. When an old lady went to the Red Cross kitchen at Ginling College to fetch a bowl of rice porridge, she learned that there was no porridge left. Vautrin immediately gave her the porridge she had been eating and said to her: "Don't you people worry. Japan will fail. China will not perish." Another time, when she saw a boy wearing an armband marked with the Japanese symbol of the rising sun to ensure his safety, Vautrin scolded him and said: "You do not need to wear this rising sun emblem. You are a Chinese and your country has not perished. You should remember the date you wear this thing, and you should never forget." Again and again, Vautrin urged the Chinese refugees on campus never to lose faith in their future. "China has not perished," she told them. "China will never perish. And Japan will definitely fail in the end."

Others could see how hard she was working. "She didn't sleep from morning till night," one Chinese survivor recalled. "She kept watching and if Japanese soldiers came . . . she would try her best to push them out and went out to their officials to pray them not to do so much evil things to the Chinese women and children." "It was said that once she was slapped several times by beastly Japanese soldiers," another wrote in his eyewitness account of the Nanking massacre. "Everyone was worried about her. Everyone tried to comfort her. She still fought for the cause of protecting Chinese women with courage and determination from beginning to end."

The work of running the zone was not only physically taxing but psychologically debilitating. Christian Kröger, a Nazi member of the International Committee, claimed that he saw so many corpses in the streets that he soon suffered nightmares about them. But in the end, under unbelievable circumstances, the zone saved lives. Here are some startling facts:

—Looting and arson made food so scarce that some Chinese refugees ate the Michaelmas daisies and goldenrod growing on the Ginling College campus or subsisted on mushrooms found in the city. Even the zone leaders went hungry from lack of meals. They not only provided free rice to the refugees through soup kitchens but delivered some of it directly to refugee compounds, because many Chinese in the zone were too scared to leave their buildings.

—Bookish and genteel, most of the zone leaders had little experience in handling a horde of rapists, murderers, and street brawlers. Yet they acted as bodyguards for even the Chinese police in the city and somehow, like warriors, found the physical energy and raw courage to throw themselves in the line of fire—wrestling Chinese men away from execution sites, knocking

Japanese soldiers off of women, even jumping in front of cannons and machine guns to prevent the Japanese from firing.

—In the process, many zone leaders came close to being shot, and some received blows or cuts from Japanese soldiers wielding bayonets and swords. For example: Charles Riggs, a University of Nanking professor of agricultural engineering, was struck by an officer when he tried to prevent him from taking away a group of Chinese civilians mistaken as soldiers. The infuriated Japanese officer "threatened Riggs with his sword three times and finally hit him hard over the heart twice with his fist." A Japanese soldier also threatened Professor Miner Searle Bates with a pistol. Another soldier pulled a gun on Robert Wilson when he tried to kick out of the hospital a soldier who had crawled into bed with three girls. Still another soldier fired a rifle at James McCallum and C. S. Trimmer but missed. When Miner Searle Bates visited the headquarters of the Japanese military police to learn the fate of a University Middle School student who had been tied up and carried off by soldiers, the Japanese shoved Bates down a flight of stairs. Even the swastikas the Nazis carried about like amulets occasionally failed to protect them from assault. On December 22, John Rabe wrote that Christian Kröger and another German named Hatz were attacked when they tried to save a Chinese man who had been wounded in the throat by a drunken Japanese soldier. Hatz defended himself with a chair, but Kröger apparently ended up being tied and beaten.

—The zone eventually accommodated some 200,000–300,000 refugees—almost half the Chinese population left in the city.

The last is a chilling statistic when placed in the context of later studies of the Nanking massacre. Half the original inhabitants of Nanking left before the massacre. About half of those who stayed (350,000 people out of the 600,000–700,000 Chinese refugees, native residents, and soldiers in the city when it fell) were killed.

If half of the population of Nanking fled into the Safety Zone during the worst of the massacre, then the other half—almost everyone who did not make it to the zone—probably died at the hands of the Japanese.

PART II

6

WHAT THE
WORLD KNEW

THE WORLD was not kept in the dark about the Rape of Nanking; news of the massacre continuously reached the global public while events unfolded. For months before the fall of Nanking, numerous foreign correspondents lived in the capital to cover its aerial bombardment by Japanese aviators. As the Japanese army neared the doomed capital in early December, reporters provided vivid and almost daily coverage of battles, fires, last-minute evacuations, and the creation of the International Safety Zone. Amazingly, when the massacre began, Japanese newspapers ran photographs of Chinese men being rounded up for execution, heaps of bodies waiting for disposal by the riverside, the killing contests among the Japanese soldiers, and even the shocked commentary of the reporters themselves.

Apparently, before international opinion

kicked in, the first few days of the massacre were a source of tremendous pride to the Japanese government. Celebrations broke out across Japan when the people heard the news of Nanking's defeat. Special meals of Nanking noodles were prepared in Tokyo, and children across Japan carried globe-shaped, candle-lit paper lanterns in evening parades to symbolize the ascendancy of the rising sun. It was only later, after news of the sinking of the *Panay* and the butchering of Nanking citizens had met with international condemnation, that the Japanese government quickly tried to hide what its army had done and replaced the news with propaganda. Thanks to the efforts of a few American journalists, the Japanese as a nation soon faced a scandal of gargantuan proportions.

THE AMERICAN JOURNALISTS

The journalists who had the greatest influence on Western foreign opinion at the time were three American foreign correspondents: Frank Tillman Durdin of the *New York Times*, Archibald Steele of the *Chicago Daily News*, and C. Yates McDaniel of the Associated Press. An adventurous streak ran through all three men. Durdin, a twenty-nine-year-old reporter from Houston, had spent time mopping decks and cleaning winches on a freighter to secure free passage from the United States to China. Once in Shanghai, he worked for a daily English-language newspaper and soon moved on to the *Times* to cover the Sino-Japanese War. Steele was an older correspondent who had reported on the Japanese occupation of Manchuria and the expanding Asian war. McDaniel was perhaps the most daring of the three: before the massacre he had driven through battle lines in the countryside, barely escaping death from exploding shells during his quest "to find the war."

Durdin, Steele, and McDaniel left only a few days after the massacre began, but in the brief time they were in Nanking they made an enormous impact. Not only did they write riveting stories that were splashed across the biggest and most pres-

Nanking fell to the Japanese on December 13, 1937. Here the ecstatic Japanese celebrate by cheering on the walls of the city (Photo courtesy of *Pictorial History of Sino-Japanese War*).

Japanese tanks rumbled through Nanking on the morning of December 13, 1937 (New China News Agency).

On December 12, the Japanese navy bombed and sank the USS *Panay*, an American gunboat, on the Yangtze River near the city of Nanking, even though it was packed with diplomats, journalists, businessmen, and refugees from Western countries (UPI/Corbis-Bettman).

General Matsui Iwane salutes his victorious troops as he enters the walled city of Nanking (UPI/Bettmann).

An example of Japanese propaganda. The Japanese pasted this image all over Nanking—a poster displaying a kindly Japanese solder holding a Chinese baby while giving food to his grateful parents. The posters urged the citizens, "Return to your homes! We will give you rice to eat! Trust and rely on the Japanese army, you can get help!" Many of these posters were found near homes in which atrocities had occurred. Japanese army planes also dropped leaflets promising, "All good Chinese who return to their homes will be fed and clothed. Japan wants to be a good neighbor to those Chinese not fooled by monsters who are Chiang Kai-shek's soldiers." After such drops, thousands of Nanking citizens left the Safety Zone to return to their homes (John Rabe Collection, Yale Divinity School Library).

As the Japanese moved across China, they rounded up thousands of women. Many of them were gang raped or forced into military prostitution (Politburo of Military Committee, Taipei).

The Japanese bound the wrists of young men in the city and loaded many of them onto trucks, where they were transported to the outskirts of Nanking for mass execution (*Mainchi Shimbun*).

December 16, 1937. Seventeen Japanese military police officers inspecting a large crowd of Chinese civilians so terrorized by the mass murder in the city that none dare raise any objection to the search (Central News Agency, Taipei).

The original caption reads: "This picture shows Japanese recruits at bayonet drill in Nanking after the capture of the Chinese capital. They are using Chinese prisoners for their targets. In the center an unfortunate prisoner (or should we say fortunate) has just received the death thrust. In foreground, a bound Chinese is being 'lightly' pricked with the bayonet in order to get him into position for the coup de grace. As to the authenticity of the photo—it was sent to *Look* by W. A. Farmer of Hankow, who says the photograph was made by a Japanese soldier. The film was sent to Shanghai to be developed. Chinese employees in the Japanese-owned shop made extra prints and smuggled them out" (UPI/Bettmann).

Blindfolded and propped on two sticks, this poor man served as the living target for a Japanese officer's sword practice. Here an infantryman finishes the job with bayonet thrusts that continue even after the victim's death (Politburo of Military Committee, Taipei).

Five Chinese prisoners being buried alive by their Japanese captors outside Nanking after the fall of the Chinese capital. This is another picture that was sent to *Look* magazine by W. A. Farmer after it was taken by a Japanese soldier and smuggled out by Chinese film shop employees who "did the natural thing in exceeding the printing order" (UPI/Bettmann).

Beheadings by sword were popular in Nanking. Here the camera captures the moment of a victim's decapitation (New China News Agency).

The severed heads of Nanking victims (New China News Agency).

The head of a Chinese soldier placed on a barbed-wire barricade outside Nanking, with a cigarette butt inserted between his lips as a joke (Alliance for Preserving the Truth of Sino-Japanese War).

In Nanking the Japanese turned murder into sport. Note the smiles on the Japanese in the background (Revolutionary Documents, Taipei).

The Japanese media avidly covered the army's killing contests near Nanking. In one of the most notorious, two Japanese sublieutenants, Mukai Toshiaki and Noda Takeshi, went on separate beheading sprees near Nanking to see who could kill one hundred men first. The *Japan Advertiser* ran their picture under the bold headline, "Contest to Kill First 100 Chinese with Sword Extended When Both Fighters Exceed Mark—Mukai Scores 106 and Noda 105" (*Japan Advertiser*).

Japanese soldiers sometimes forced their victims to pose in pornographic pictures, which were kept as souvenirs of rape (courtesy of the Fitch family).

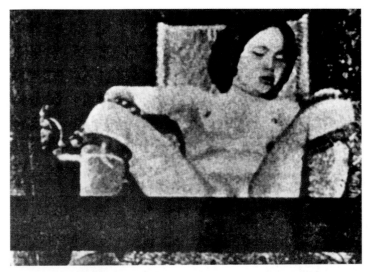

The Japanese bound this young woman to a chair for repeated attack (New China News Agency).

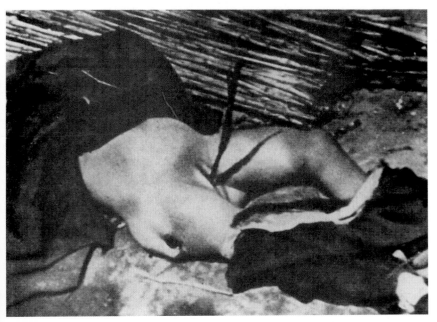

Nanking women were not only raped but tortured and mutilated (Modern China Publishing).

Arson destroyed one-third of Nanking during the massacre. Here Japanese troops set fire to a house in the suburbs (New China News Agency).

Japanese soldiers ride through a devastated neighborhood of Nanking (Yin and Young, *The Rape of Nanking*).

During the massacre thousands of Chinese refugees fled into the Nanking Safety Zone—war-free territory guarded by a handful of Westerners. The zone meant the difference between life and death for the remaining Chinese in the city and eventually housed more than three hundred thousand people (Nanking Municipal Archives).

The foreigners also established a rural safety zone outside Nanking (Ernest H. Forster, Yale Divinity School Library).

John Rabe, the Nazi hero of
Nanking (Ursula Reinhardt).

John Rabe, chairman of the International Committee for the Nanking Safety Zone, standing
with colleagues before zone headquarters at 5 Ninghai Road (Yale Divinity School Library).

A page from John Rabe's diaries of the Nanking massacre (John Rabe Collection, Yale Divinity School Library).

Feindliche Flieger
über Nanking.

Band VI.

Tagebuchblätter
von
John H. D. Rabe,
Nanking.

JOHN H. D. RABE
NANKING
—

z.Zt. Ueberseeheim, Dihlmannstr. 20.
Siemensstadt, den 8. Juni 1938.

Mein Führer !

Die Mehrzahl meiner Freunde in China ist der Meinung, dass Ihnen über die tatsächlichen Ereignisse in Nanking kein ausführlicher Bericht erstattet wurde.

Durch die Uebersendung der hier beiliegenden Niederschrift eines von mir gehaltenen Vortrages, der nicht für die breite Oeffentlichkeit bestimmt ist, erfülle ich ein meinen Freunden in China gegebenes Versprechen , Ihnen von den Leiden der chinesischen Bevölkerung in Nanking Kunde zu geben.

Meine Mission ist erfüllt, wenn Sie die Güte haben wollen mich wissen zu lassen, dass die anliegende Niederschrift Ihnen vorgelegt wurde.

Ich bin inzwischen verständigt worden, weitere Vorträge dieser Art zu unterlassen, sowie die dazugehörigen Aufnahmen nicht zu zeigen. Ich werde mich dieser Anordnung fügen, da ich nicht die Absicht habe der deutschen Politik und den deutschen Behörden entgegenzuarbeiten.

Ich versichere Sie meiner treuen Gefolgschaft und meiner aufrichtigen Ergebenheit

John Rabe

An
den Führer und Reichskanzler
Herrn Adolf Hitler ,
Berlin.

John Rabe's letter to Hitler, which he submitted along with a report and film of the atrocities. A few days later Rabe was arrested and interrogated by the Gestapo in Berlin (John Rabe Collection, Yale Divinity School Library).

Dr. Robert Wilson, the only surgeon in Nanking during the massacre (Yale Divinity School Library).

Dr. Wilson examines a gang-rape victim whose head was almost severed by the Japanese. In a deserted schoolhouse two soldiers struck this woman ten times with a bayonet—once on the wrist, once on the face, four times on the back, and four times on her neck, which slashed the muscles down to the vertebral column (John Magee).

Scenes from Nanking University Hospital, where Wilson worked. This teenage boy's head was charred black after the Japanese doused it with gasoline and set it on fire (John Magee).

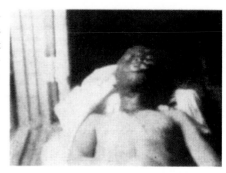

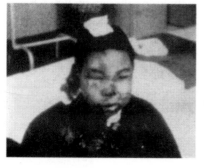

This fourteen-year-old boy was imprisoned by the Japanese, starved, and then severely beaten with an iron bar when he begged to go home (John Magee).

Li Xouyin, who barely eluded rape after fighting three Japanese soldiers and enduring thirty-seven bayonet wounds. Seven months pregnant during the fight, she suffered a miscarriage in the hospital. She did not recover from her wounds for another seven months (John Magee).

Minnie Vautrin, "The Living Goddess of Nanking" (Courtesy of Emma Lyon).

Miner Searle Bates, history professor at Nanking University and chairman of the International Committee after May 1939 (Yale Divinity School Library).

ORGANIZERS OF THE NANKING SAFETY ZONE

Christian Kröger *(above left)*, German engineer and Nazi member of the International Committee. He served as treasurer between December 1937 and February 1938 (Peter Kröger). John Gillespie Magee *(above right)*, Episcopalian minister who served as chairman of the International Red Cross Committee of Nanking during the massacre. An amateur filmmaker, Magee recorded many important images from Nanking University Hospital (Yale Divinity School Library).

Facing page: Lewis Strong Casey Smythe *(top left)*, a secretary of the International Committee and author of the study "War Damage in the Nanking Area, December 1937 to March 1938" (Yale Divinity School Library). Ernest Forster *(top right)*, Episcopalian missionary and one of the secretaries of the International Committee (Yale Divinity School Library). James Henry McCallum *(center)*, member of the United Christian Missionary Society and one of the treasurers of the Safety Zone. During the massacre McCallum drove an ambulance through the city to chauffeur patients home from the hospital (Disciples of Christ Historical Society). Wilson Plumer Mills *(bottom left)*, the Presbyterian missionary who first suggested that the Nanking Safety Zone be created (Angie Mills). George Ashmore Fitch *(bottom right)*, head of the YMCA in Nanking and an administrative director of the International Committee. He smuggled his and John Magee's films of Nanking atrocities out of the city (Edith Fitch Swapp).

During the war crimes trials in 1946, some of the dried bones from mass graves were unearthed for inspection by Chinese officials (Alliance for Preserving the Truth of the Sino-Japanese War).

tigious newspapers in the United States, but they also joined the International Safety Zone Committee in trying to save lives.

The Rape of Nanking forced the reporters out of their normal role as neutral observers and into the war drama as full-fledged participants. Sometimes they starred in their own stories by choosing to protect Chinese citizens from the Japanese invaders. For instance, C. Yates McDaniel assumed the responsibility of guarding the Chinese servants of the U.S. embassy. During the massacre most were so frightened they refused to leave the building even for water, and McDaniel spent hours filling buckets with well water and lugging them back to the embassy for the servants to drink. He tried to find their missing relatives (often retrieving only their bodily remains) and also chased away Japanese soldiers who tried to break into the embassy.

The reporters even tried to save people who were clearly beyond saving, if only to comfort those who were minutes away from death. During the massacre Durdin encountered a Chinese soldier lying on the sidewalk with his jaw shot away and his body bleeding. The soldier held out his hand, which Durdin picked up and held. "I didn't know where to take him or what to do," Durdin remembered years later. "So I just, stupidly, decided to do something. I just put a five-dollar bill in his hand. Which is utterly useless to him, of course, but anyway, somehow I felt the impulse to do something. He was just barely alive."

On December 15, most of the reporters left Nanking for Shanghai to file their stories. Their last day in the city was grisly. On the way to the waterfront, the reporters literally had to drive over several feet of bodies under the Water Gate, where dogs were already starting to gnaw on the corpses. Later, as they waited for their ship to arrive, they saw the Japanese military line up one thousand Chinese men, force them to kneel in small groups, and shoot each of them in the back of the head. During the execution some of the Japanese were laughing and smoking, as if they greatly enjoyed the entire spectacle.

The AP's McDaniel stayed in Nanking a day longer before boarding a destroyer for Shanghai. On December 16, his last day in the ruined Chinese capital, he saw more corpses and passed a long line of Chinese men with their hands tied. One of them broke away from the group, dropped on his knees, and begged McDaniel to save him from death. "I could do nothing," McDaniel wrote. "My last remembrance of Nanking—dead Chinese, dead Chinese, dead Chinese."

THE NEWSREEL MEN

There were also two American newsreel men near Nanking who risked their lives to film the bombing of the *Panay*. During the bombing Norman Alley of Universal and Eric Mayell of Fox Movietone happened to be on board and obtained superb footage of the action. Though they survived the attack unscathed (Alley emerged from the bombs and machine-gun fire with only a nicked finger and a bullet-perforated hat), another journalist was not so lucky. A splinter hit the Italian correspondent Sandro Sandri in the back of his eye when he followed Alley up a stairway on the *Panay*, and he died only hours later.

While hiding with the surviving *Panay* passengers under the riverbank reeds, Alley wrapped his film and Mayell's with canvas and buried it under the mud when he thought the Japanese were coming ashore to kill them. Later the film was safely unearthed and shipped to the United States, where parts of the newsreel footage of the event ran in movie houses across the country.

The sinking of the *Panay* caused more of an uproar in the United States than all the wholesale rape and slaughter in Nanking combined. On December 13, President Franklin D. Roosevelt announced that he was "shocked" at the bombing and demanded immediate compensation from Emperor Hirohito. A few days later, when the exhausted survivors finally reached civilization, the public response only grew worse. Filthy, cold, and wearing only blankets, Chinese quilts, and tatters of clothing, some of the survivors were still in shock or near death. Their stories, along with their photographs, soon appeared in every major newspaper in the country under headlines like "Panay Victims Under Japanese Fire for Full Hour," and "Butchery and Looting Reign in Nanking." When Alley's and Mayell's footage hit the theaters, it only aroused more outrage and anti-Japanese sentiment among American audiences.

JAPANESE DAMAGE CONTROL

The moment the foreign correspondents left Nanking, the Japanese sealed off the city to prevent other reporters from coming in. George Fitch witnessed the beginning of this on December 15, the day he drove some of the foreign correspondents out of the city to the riverfront so that they could board a gunboat for Shanghai. When Fitch tried to drive back into Nanking from Hsiakwan, a Japanese sentry stopped him at the gate and absolutely refused to let him reenter. Even Mr. Okamura, a member of the Japanese embassy from Shanghai who accompanied Fitch, was unable to persuade the man to let them through: "The embassy cuts no ice with the army in Japan." In the end Okamura had to take one of the cars to military headquarters to get a special pass for Fitch.

When the Japanese finally permitted a few foreigners to enter the city, they carefully controlled their movements. In February they allowed a few American naval officers to go ashore in Nanking, but only when accompanied by Japanese embassy representatives in a Japanese embassy car. As late as April the Japanese high command prevented most foreigners from freely leaving or entering the city.

To cover up the nauseating details of their military outrages, the Japanese even impeded the return of foreign diplomats to Nanking. But in the end they proved unsuccessful in hiding the truth—especially from the Germans and the Americans.

FOREIGN INTELLIGENCE ON THE RAPE OF NANKING

Hitler's government soon learned the Japanese motives for the delay. "The assumption I made in my previous report that the

Japanese delayed our return in order to have no official witnesses of the atrocities has been confirmed," a German diplomat reported to Berlin in January. "Once the intention of the foreign representatives to return to Nanking had been made known, according to Germans and Americans who were there, there were feverish cleanup efforts undertaken to remove the evidence of the senseless mass murders of civilians, women and children."

The American government also knew what the Japanese were trying to hide. A machine cipher had protected the Japanese Foreign Office's high-level diplomatic messages, but by 1936 cryptanalysts from the U.S. Army's Signal Intelligence Service had cracked the Japanese code, which the Americans dubbed "RED." American intelligence was thus able to intercept and read secret messages between the Japanese leadership in Tokyo and their representatives in Washington, D.C., during the Rape of Nanking. On December 26, 1937, Foreign Minister Hirota Koki sent one such message to Japanese Ambassador Saito Hirosi in Washington; it emphasized the need to stonewall the American embassy staff to prevent their immediate return to Nanking. "If they do return and receive unfavorable reports on the military's activities from their own nationals and if the diplomats, on receipt of such complaints, forward the reports to their home countries, we shall find ourselves in an exceedingly disadvantageous position," the message read. "We believe, therefore, that the best policy is to do our utmost to hold them here as long as possible. Even if this should cause some hard feeling, we believe that it would be better than running the risk of a clash on the scene."

But the U.S. government did not disclose to the public what it knew at the time and even contributed to Japanese censorship of the truth. For example, Norman Alley, the Universal newsreel man, had shot fifty-three hundred-foot rolls of movie film of the Japanese attack on the *Panay*, but before the film was released to the theaters, President Roosevelt asked him to excise some thirty feet of film that revealed several Japanese bombers shooting at the gunboat at nearly deck level. Alley agreed, even though those thirty feet were probably the best images in the entire film and certainly the most damning to the Japanese government. Hamilton Darby Perry, author of *The Panay Incident*, believes that Roosevelt wanted to give credence to the Japanese excuse that the attack was a case of mistaken identity, not deliberate design. No doubt the U.S. government was anxious to reach a financial and diplomatic settlement with the Japanese over the bombing and knew that those thirty feet of film would have made such a settlement impossible.

JAPANESE PROPAGANDA

Japanese attempts to influence public opinion were nothing new. Even before the Rape of Nanking, the American intelligence community had seen the Japanese plans, marked "utmost secrecy," to spread favorable propaganda of themselves in the United States. The Japanese government also had a large budget for wooing influential newspaper men, advertising in major newspapers and radio stations, and printing pamphlets and leaflets.

But during the Rape of Nanking the Japanese faced a public relations disaster so titanic it seems almost ridiculous today that they even tried to cover it up. Instead of bringing a measure of discipline to their forces in Nanking, the Japanese marshaled together their resources to launch a blitz of propaganda, which they hoped would somehow obscure the details of one of the greatest bloodbaths of world history.

The Japanese media first proclaimed that all was well and good in the city of Nanking. On December 20, Robert Wilson heard that Domei, the Japanese news agency, had reported that the Nanking population was returning home and everything was normal. "If that is all the news coming out of Nanking, it is due for a big shake up when the real news breaks," Wilson wrote.

Then the Japanese government authorized carefully prepared tours of the city for Japanese visitors. A week after the Domei report, a Japanese merchant ship arrived in Nanking from Shanghai, crowded with Japanese sightseers. "Carefully they were herded through the few streets now cleared of corpses," George Fitch wrote of the visit. "Graciously they passed sweets to Chinese children and patted their frightened heads." A number of ladies accompanied Japanese business representatives on a tour of the city, and Fitch observed that they seemed "tremendously pleased with themselves, also with Japan's wonderful victory, but of course they hear nothing of the real truth—nor does the rest of the world, I suppose."

In January Japanese newsmen came to Nanking to stage pictures of the city for distribution throughout Japan and the rest of the world. On New Year's Eve the Japanese embassy called together the Chinese managers of the refugee camps for a meeting and told them that "spontaneous" celebrations were to be held in the city the next day. The Chinese were ordered to make thousands of Japanese flags and carry them about in a parade for a motion picture that would illustrate crowds of joyful residents welcoming Japanese soldiers. Japanese photographers also came to Nanking to take pictures of Chinese children receiving medical care from a Japanese army doctor and candy from Japanese soldiers. "But," Lewis Smythe wrote in a letter to his friends, "these acts were not repeated when no camera was around!"

The rankest example of Japanese propaganda was an article that appeared on January 8, 1938, in the *Sin Shun Pao*, a Japanese-controlled newspaper in Shanghai. Under the headline "The Harmonious Atmosphere of Nanking City Develops Enjoyably," the article claimed that "the Imperial Army entered the city, put their bayonets into their sheaths, and stretched forth merciful hands in order to examine and heal," giving the starving and sick masses in Nanking medical aid and food.

> Men and women, old and young, bent down to kneel in salutation to the Imperial Army, expressing their respectful intention. . . . The vast hordes gathered around the soldiers beneath the sun flag and red cross flag shouting "Banzai" in order to express their gratitude. . . . Soldiers and the Chinese children are happy together, playing joyfully on the slides. Nanking is now the best place for all countries to watch, for here one breathes the atmosphere of peaceful residence and happy work.

Japanese attempts to gloss over the entire massacre with hokum provoked incredulous responses in the surviving missionary diaries. Here are a few samples:

From the diary of James McCallum, January 9, 1938:

> Now the Japanese are trying to discredit our efforts in the Safety Zone. They threaten and intimidate the poor Chinese into repudiating what we have said. . . . Some of the Chinese are even ready to prove that the looting, raping and burning was done by the Chinese and not the Japanese. I feel sometimes that we have been dealing with maniacs and idiots and I marvel that all of us foreigners have come through this ordeal alive.

From the diary of George Fitch, January 11, 1938:

> . . . we have seen a couple of issues of a Shanghai Japanese newspaper and two of the *Tokyo Nichi Nichi*. Those tell us that even as early as December 28th the stores were rapidly opening up and business returning to normal, that the Japanese were cooperating with us in feeding the poor refugees, that the city had been cleared of *Chinese* looters, and that peace and order now reigned! Well, we'd be tempted to laugh if it wasn't so tragic. It is typical of the lies Japan has been sending abroad ever since the war started.

From the diary of George Fitch, reprinted in *Reader's Digest*:

> In March, a government radio station in Tokyo flashed this message to the world: "Hoodlums responsible for so many deaths and such destruction of property in Nanking have been captured and executed. They were found to be discontented soldiers from Chiang Kai-shek's brigades. Now all is quiet and the Japanese army is feeding 300,000 refugees."

From a letter written by Lewis Smythe and his wife on March 8, 1938:

> Now the latest is from the Japanese paper that they have found eleven Chinese armed robbers who were to blame for it all!

> Well, if they each raped from 100 to 200 women per night and
> day for two weeks and got away with the reported $50,000 they
> were pretty powerful Chinese . . .

Leaflets were another form of Japanese propaganda. During
the mass executions Japanese army planes inundated the
Nanking population with messages dropped from the air; for
example: "All good Chinese who return to their homes will be
fed and clothed. Japan wants to be a good neighbor to those
Chinese not fooled by monsters who are Chiang Kai-shek's soldiers." The leaflets displayed colorful pictures of a handsome
Japanese soldier holding a Chinese child ("Christ-like," as one
observer put it) in his arms, with a Chinese mother at his feet
bowing her thanks for bags of rice. According to George Fitch,
thousands of Chinese actually left the refugee camps for their
ruined homes the day the leaflets were dropped.

The Japanese also pasted bright, colorful posters on or near
houses in which tragedies had occurred. One featured a Japanese soldier carrying a small child while giving a bucket of rice
to his mother and sugar and other food to the father. A German diplomatic report described the poster as depicting "a
charming, lovable soldier with cooking implements in hand
who carries on his shoulder a Chinese child whose poor but
honest Chinese farming parents gaze up at him (the soldier)
full of thankfulness and family happiness, up to the good uncle." The writing on the upper right corner said: "Return to
your homes! We will give you rice to eat! Trust and rely on the
Japanese army, you can get help!"

At the same time the Japanese hosted glamorous receptions
and media events in Nanking and Shanghai to divert attention
away from the atrocities. In early February a Japanese general
invited foreign diplomatic representatives to a tea at the Japanese embassy in Nanking. He boasted that the Japanese army
was world-renowned for its discipline, and that not a single violation against discipline had occurred during the Russo-Japanese War and Manchurian campaign. The general said that if
for some reason the Japanese had committed outrages in
Nanking, it was only because the Chinese people had resisted

them under the instigation of foreign nationals, meaning, of course, the International Safety Zone Committee. But oddly enough, in the same speech the general contradicted his previous statements by admitting that Japanese soldiers had vented their anger upon the population because they had found nothing edible or usable during their advance on Nanking.

The Japanese media circus, however, failed to fool the foreign diplomatic community about the arson, rape, and murder that raged through Nanking. In mid-February the Japanese held a military concert in Shanghai, complete with geishas and press photographers. A German diplomat observed, however, that while the gala affair was taking place, "a mother of an 11-year-old girl who did not want to release the young girl to rape by the soldiers was burnt down with her house."

THE SAFETY ZONE LEADERS FIGHT BACK

The International Safety Zone Committee did all it could to fight the barrage of propaganda. During the first few days of the massacre the zone leaders enlisted the aid of American foreign correspondents like Frank Tillman Durdin, Archibald Steele, and C. Yates McDaniel. But after their departure, the International Committee was left to its own devices. The Japanese government barred other reporters, like Max Coppening of the *Chicago Tribune*, from entering Nanking, and the behavior of the Japanese soldiers grew worse when they realized that their actions would not be observed by the world media.

But the Japanese government underestimated the ability of the International Committee to wage its own publicity campaign. One distinguishing trait that united the zone leaders was their superior training in the verbal arts. Almost without exception, they were eloquent writers and speakers. The missionaries, educated at the best universities in America and Europe, had devoted most of their adult years to delivering sermons, writing papers, and working the Christian lecture circuit; some of the professors on the committee had written books. Moreover, as a group they were sophisticated about working with the media; long before the fall of Nanking they had enjoyed broadcasting speeches over Nanking radio or penning articles about China for the popular press. Finally, the missionaries had an additional advantage the Japanese did not foresee: they had spent their entire lives contemplating the true meaning of hell. Having found one in Nanking, they wasted no time in describing it for the world public. Their hard, cogent prose recaptured the terror that they witnessed:

> Complete anarchy has reigned for ten days—it has been hell on earth . . . to have to stand by while even the very poor are having their last possession taken from them—their last coin, their last bit of bedding (and it is freezing weather), the poor ricksha man his ricksha; while thousands of disarmed soldiers who had sought sanctuary with you together with many hundreds of innocent civilians are taken out before your eyes to be shot or used for bayonet practice and you have to listen to the sounds of the guns that are killing them; while a thousand women kneel before you crying hysterically, begging you to save them from the beasts who are preying on them; to stand by and do nothing while your flag is taken down and insulted, not once but a dozen times, and your home is being looted, and then to watch the city you have come to love and the institution to which you have planned to devote your best deliberately and systematically burned by fire—this is a hell I had never before envisaged. (George Fitch, December 24, 1937)

> It is a horrible story to try to relate; I know not where to begin nor to end. Never have I heard or read of such brutality. Rape! Rape! We estimate that at least 1,000 cases at night and many by day. In case of resistance or anything that seems like disapproval there is a bayonet stab or bullet. We could write up hundreds of cases a day; people are hysterical; they get down on their knees and "kutow" any time we foreigners appear; they beg for aid. Those who are suspected of being soldiers, as well as others, have been led outside the city and shot down by the hundreds—yes, thousands. . . . Even the poor refugees in certain centers have been robbed again and again until the last cent, almost the last garment and last piece of bedding. . . . Women are being carried off every morning, afternoon and evening. (John McCallum, December 19, 1937)

I think I have said enough of these horrible cases—there are hundreds of thousands of them. Being so many of them finally makes the mind dulled so that you almost cease to be shocked anymore. I did not imagine that such cruel people existed in the modern world. . . . It would seem that only a rare insane person like Jack the Ripper would act so. (John Gillespie Magee, January 28, 1938)

The graphic details of Japanese excesses appeared not only in Safety Zone diaries but in letters and newsletters that were mimeographed or retyped over and over again so that friends, relatives, government officials, and the press could all receive copies. When mailing descriptions of the massacre, the zone leaders often begged the recipients not to disclose authorship of the documents if they were published, for fear that individual committee members would face retribution or expulsion from Nanking. "Please be very careful of this letter as we might all be kicked out if it were published, and that would be a disaster for the Chinese of Nanking," Magee wrote to his family. The Japanese, he explained, would allow the foreigners to leave, "with the greatest pleasure," but would not allow anyone to return.

In the end the persistence, hard work, and caution of the zone leaders paid off. George Fitch's diary was the first one to be leaked out of Nanking, and it created a "sensation" in Shanghai. His stories and others (often with key names deleted) swiftly found their way into mainstream print outlets like *Time, Reader's Digest,* and *Far Eastern* magazine, evoking widespread outrage among American readers. Some eventually reemerged in books, such as in the *Manchester Guardian* reporter Harold John Timperley's *Japanese Terror in China* (1938) and Hsu Shuhsi's *Documents of the Nanking Safety Zone* (1939).

To brace their readers, the zone leaders sometimes prefaced their documents with warnings. "What I am about to relate is anything but a pleasant story; in fact, it is so very unpleasant that I cannot recommend anyone without a strong stomach to read it," Fitch wrote in his diary before publication. "For it is a story of such crime and horror as to be almost unbelievable, the story of the depredations of a horde of degraded criminals of incredible bestiality, on a peaceful, kindly, law-abiding people. . . . I believe it has no parallel in modern history."

True to their predictions, the reports from the International Safety Zone Committee aroused skepticism from the American public. When the article "The Sack of Nanking" appeared in *Reader's Digest*, one subscriber wrote: "It is unbelievable that credence could be given a thing which is so obviously rank propaganda and so reminiscent of the stuff fed the public during the late war." Similar comments came from other subscribers. But the editors at *Reader's Digest* insisted that the stories were true. To defend their credibility, the editors took "considerable pains" to collect more letters from the Safety Zone leaders, which they reprinted in the October 1938 issue of the magazine. "The material we have seen," the editors hastened to add, "would fill an entire issue of this magazine, all of it corroborating the typical extracts which follow."

Fortunately, the crimes of Nanking were recorded not only on paper but on motion picture film, making them almost impossible to deny. John Magee, who possessed an amateur movie camera, filmed several bedridden victims at the University of Nanking Hospital. They were haunting images—the horribly disfigured, charred men the Japanese had tried to burn alive; the enamel-ware shop clerk whose head received a tremendous blow from a Japanese bayonet (six days after entering the hospital, the pulsation of his brain could still clearly be seen); the gang-rape victim whose head was almost cut off by Japanese soldiers.

George Fitch eventually smuggled the film out of China, though at great risk to his life. On January 19, he received a permit to leave Nanking and took a Japanese military train to Shanghai, where he shared the third-class coach with "as unsavory a crowd of soldiers as one could imagine." Sewn into the lining of his camel's hair coat were eight reels of 16-mm negative movie film of Nanking atrocities. There was no doubt in his mind, he told his family later, that if he had been searched and caught with the film, he would have been killed instantly. But luckily Fitch made it to Shanghai, where he took the negatives to the Kodak office and developed four sets of prints. One of them went to the Nazi Party leader John Rabe before he left Nanking for Germany. Some of the others ended up in the United States, where Fitch and other missionaries showed them during lectures before religious and political groups. Several frames from the films were reprinted in *Life* magazine; segments of actual footage later appeared in Frank Capra's newsreel documentary, *Why We Fight: Battle of China*. Decades later the film reappeared in two historical documentaries released during the 1990s: Magee's *Testament* and *In the Name of the Emperor*.

One can only imagine how the Japanese military leadership smoldered as these written reports, photographs, and even films of Japanese atrocities found their way into the world media. Many of the zone leaders lived in constant terror and believed that the Japanese would kill them all if they could get away with it. Some of the men barricaded themselves in their houses and after dark dared not venture outdoors except in twos or threes. At least one, George Fitch, suspected that there was a price on his head. But despite their fear, they continued to take turns guarding key areas of the zone at night and persisted in publicizing the Japanese atrocities. "The Japanese military hate us worse than the enemy for we have shown them up to the world," John Magee wrote on January 28, 1938. "We are all surprised that none of us have been killed and whether we all get out safely is yet a question."

7

THE OCCUPATION
OF NANKING

T HE RAPE of Nanking continued for
months, although the worst of it was
concentrated in the first six to eight
weeks. By the spring of 1938 the people of
Nanking knew that the massacre was over,
and that while they would be occupied they
would not necessarily all be killed. As
Nanking lay prostrate under Japanese rule,
the military began to implement measures to
subjugate the entire population.

At first there was not much to subjugate.
"You cannot imagine the disorganization of
the city," one foreigner wrote, "the dumping
of filth and every kind of waste everywhere."
Trash and human flesh putrefied in the streets
because the Japanese did not permit anything
to be done without their permission—not
even the disposal of garbage and corpses. Indeed, for days army trucks drove over several
feet of corpses under the Water Gate, grinding

over the remains in order to impress upon the populace the terrible results of resisting Japan.

Observers estimated that Japanese damage to public property totaled some $836 million, in 1939 U.S. dollars, and that the private property loss was at least $136 million. These figures do not include the cost of irreplaceable cultural artifacts taken by the Japanese army.

Under the direction of the sociologist Lewis Smythe, the International Safety Zone Committee conducted a systematic survey of damage to the Nanking area. Investigators visited every fiftieth inhabited house in the city and also went to every tenth family in every third village in the countryside. In a sixty-page report released in June 1938, Smythe concluded that the 120 air raids that Nanking experienced and the four-day siege of the city did only 1 percent of the damage inflicted by the Japanese army after it entered Nanking.

Arson caused most of the destruction. Fires in Nanking began with the fall of the city and lasted more than six weeks. Soldiers torched buildings under the guidance of officers and even used special chemical strips to set the fires. They burned down churches, embassies, department stores, shops, mansions, and huts—even areas within the Safety Zone. The zone leaders could not put out these fires because their pumps and fire equipment had been stolen by the Japanese. By the end of the first few weeks of the Rape of Nanking, the military had incinerated one-third of the entire city and three-fourths of all the stores.

They burned down the Russian legation embassy, defiled the American embassy, and ransacked almost every foreign house—even those marked clearly with flags or seals. The Japanese reserved American property for special insult: they tore down the American flag six times from the University of Nanking and trampled it in the dirt, threatening to kill anyone who dared to put it up again. But German property suffered almost as badly as American property, despite the alliance between the Nazi and Japanese governments. The Japanese tore down Nazi flags, burned German homes and businesses, and even stole pictures of Hitler and Hindenburg, a "remarkable" act, one German wrote, "considering the cult of the Japanese for their emperor pictures."

The consequences of the sack of Nanking extended far beyond the city walls. Japanese soldiers devastated the countryside around Nanking, torching entire villages by burning down straw huts and collecting furniture, tools, and farming implements into brick houses so that everything could be incinerated all at once. The region near the city was stripped clean of farm animals, both domestic and otherwise.

The Japanese also used acetylene torches, pistol shots, and hand grenades to blast open vaults in banks, including the personal safe deposit boxes of German officials and residents. Soldiers were permitted to mail back to Japan some of their booty, but most of the goods were confiscated and concentrated for official use. Warehouses filled rapidly with rare jade and porcelain artwork, rugs and paintings, gold and silver treasures. More than two hundred pianos were housed in a single storage hall. In late December the Japanese began to heap stolen goods— jewelry, art, furniture, metal, antiques—on the wharves for transport back to Japan.

Japanese looters usually sought big-ticket items. They coveted foreign cars, prompting committee members to believe that the army would have taken all of them in the city if foreigners were not sitting in them. (Trucks used to cart corpses away were also stolen.) But the Japanese also invaded Nanking University Hospital to steal trivial items—pens, flashlights, and wristwatches from the nurses—and broke into the Safety Zone repeatedly to steal bedding, cooking utensils, and food from the homeless. A German report noted that on December 15 the Japanese had forced five thousand refugees to line up so that they could steal a total of $180 from them. "Even handfuls of dirty rice were snatched from them by the soldiers," George Fitch wrote. "Death was the sure retort to any complaint."

In January 1938, not one shop was officially open in Nanking except for a military store and the International Committee's rice shop. The harbor was practically empty of ships. Most of the city lacked electricity, telephone, and water service because the Japanese had rounded up and executed some fifty employees from the local power plant. (The lack of running water made it difficult to bathe, but many women chose not to bathe anyway, in hopes that their unwashed flesh would repel Japanese soldiers intent on raping them.)

Slowly the city came back to life. People could be seen ransacking houses throughout Nanking—ripping out floorboards and wood paneling for firewood and carting away metal and brick to repair their own homes or to sell on the streets to others. On Shanghai Road in the Safety Zone, dense crowds of people clustered before hundreds of vendors who sold every kind of loot imaginable, including doors and windows. This activity jump-started the local economy, for next to the roadside merchants of booty mushroomed new teahouses and restaurants.

On January 1, 1938, the Japanese inaugurated a new city government: the Nanking Self-Government Committee (the *Nanjing zizhi weiyuanhui*)—or "Autonomous Government," as some of the Westerners in the city called it. The Self-Government Committee was staffed with Chinese puppet officials who controlled the city's administration, welfare, finance, police, commerce, and traffic. By spring Nanking was outwardly starting to function like a normal city again. Running water, electric lighting, and daily mail service resumed. A Japanese city bus service started, rickshas appeared in the streets, and people could take the train from Nanking to Shanghai. Nanking quickly became a busy shipping center for the Japanese as small locomotives, horses, field pieces, trucks, and other supplies were ferried daily from the city to nearby Pukow.

But signs of a brutal occupation were everywhere. Chinese merchants endured heavy taxes and rent extortion to finance the salaries of the new officials in power. The Japanese also opened up military shops for the Chinese populace that drained the city of Chinese gold and money and replaced it with worthless military currency. The Chinese puppet government compounded the poverty by confiscating valuables and stocks of inventory that remained in the city, even if the owner was still in town, leading some of the lower Chinese officials to joke cynically among themselves: "We are now doing an authorized plundering."

Far more alarming than the exploitation of the populace by taxes and confiscation was the reappearance of opium in the city. Before the Japanese occupation, opium was an underground narcotic, secretly smoked in the back rooms of Nanking by aristocrats and merchants. But it was not sold openly and brazenly in the streets, nor was it conspicuously paraded before young people. After the fall of the city, people could freely stroll into opium dens without interference from the police. These dens boldly advertised the drug with Chinese character shingles marked *Kuang To*, or "Official Earth"—a term used for opium.

To encourage addiction and further enslave the people, the Japanese routinely used narcotics as payment for labor and prostitution in Nanking. Heroin cigarettes were offered to children as young as ten. Based on his research, the University of Nanking history professor Miner Searle Bates concluded that some fifty thousand people in the Nanking area were using heroin—one-eighth of the population at the time.

Many of the downtrodden citizens of Nanking fell prey to drugs because it gave them the means to escape, if only temporarily, from the misery of their lives. Some even tried to use opium to commit suicide, swallowing large doses as poison. Others turned to crime to support their addiction, causing a wave of banditry to sweep through Nanking. After making conditions ripe for banditry in Nanking, the Japanese used the epidemic of crimes to justify their occupation, preaching the need for imperial law and order.

Japanese employers treated many of the local Chinese laborers worse than slaves, often killing them for the slightest infractions. Survivors later claimed that a harsh environment and capricious punishment were deliberately imposed upon the workplace to keep Chinese employees in a constant state of fear. One Chinese man who worked in a factory seized by the Japanese described the horrors that he witnessed there over the period of a few months. When a fellow employee was falsely accused by a Japanese overseer of stealing his sweater, he ended up being wrapped with rope, almost mummylike, from feet to throat and then stoned to death with a heap of bricks. By the end of the stoning, the body had lost all shape, and the flesh and bones, entwined with the rope, was thrown to the dogs as food. Another time, the Japanese found four small shoulder pads missing from the factory and discovered they had been used as toilet paper. A twenty-two-year-old woman who admitted that she had used the toilet that day was dragged behind the factory and beheaded with a knife. That very afternoon the same Japanese murderer also killed a teenage boy whom he accused of stealing a pair of slippers.

The Japanese even inflicted medical experiments on the Nanking people. In April 1939, they opened up a facility in the city to conduct research on human guinea pigs whom they called *zaimoku*, or "lumber." On East Chungshan (or Zhongsan) Street, only a short walk from the Yangtze River, the Japanese converted a six-story Chinese hospital into a laboratory for research in epidemics, which they named Unit Ei 1644. Though the laboratory was situated near a military airport, a geisha district, movie theaters, and conspicuous Japanese centers such as the Japanese consulate, the military police office, and the headquarters for the Chinese Expeditionary Force High Command, it remained a closely guarded secret. A high brick wall surrounded the compound, topped with barbed wire; the facility was patrolled by guards; the staff was ordered never to mention Ei 1644 in their letters back to Japan. Inside scientists injected or fed Chinese prisoners with a variety of poisons, germs, and lethal gases; the substances included doses of acetone, arsenate, cyanide, nitrite prussiate, and snake poisons such as cobra, habu, and amagasa venom. The Japanese scientists killed about ten or more people weekly in this manner and disposed of them in the Ei 1644 incinerator.

When the Japanese surrendered in August 1945, the staff of Ei 1644 destroyed their equipment and data, blew up the laboratory, and fled before Chinese troops could reach Nanking. We know about this secret laboratory only because some scientists of the unit confessed their activities to American interroga-tors after the war.

Those Chinese in the city fortunate enough to escape the physical brutality, the Japanese medical experiments, and the lure of drugs lived under a suffocating atmosphere of military intimidation. The Japanese authorities devised a method of mass control by organizing the population into a pyramidal hierarchy. Every ten households were ordered to appoint a head man, and every ten of those heads were ordered to ap-point another head, and so on. Under this system, every man in Nanking was required to carry a registration card signed by his heads of ten, one hundred, and one thousand men attest-ing to his loyalty to the new government. Every person was also required to report the presence in his household of any unknown or unregistered person to the immediate head of ten, who reported it to his direct head, and on up until the news reached the district officer of the city government. This was not a Japanese invention, but a traditional Chinese system called *baojia*, revived, no doubt, by the Japanese to legitimize their rule among the natives in Nanking.

The Japanese subjected this *baojia* system to frequent tests, sometimes releasing men without passes in the city to see if they could find a place to stay. If the men were not caught and reported within two hours, the heads of the groups in the neighborhoods where they stayed would be severely punished. "This," the committee member Albert Steward wrote in his di-ary in 1939, "is supposed to be the Japanese way of preserving loyalty to the new regime."

In spite of war, fire, and massacre, Nanking recovered. The dreaded famine never struck, not only because the Japanese eventually permitted shipments of food to enter the city, but because local farmers were able to harvest winter wheat crops after most of the Japanese troops left Nanking to pursue Chi-nese forces inland. Within the space of a year, much of the agri-culture in the fertile Yangtze delta area produced yields close to prewar levels. This is not to say that Nanking did not suffer food shortages under Japanese occupation. The gardens and farms inside the city walls failed to thrive because soldiers not only confiscated vegetables from them but forced the farmers to dig up and transport the produce for Japanese use. Also, as the war dragged on, Japanese authorities in Nanking tightened their hold on supplies and heavily rationed necessities such as coal and rice. But there is no evidence to suggest that Nanking endured worse hunger or malnutrition than other areas in China. Other cities, such as the new Nationalist capital of Chungking, had suffered far worse food shortages during the war.

Though the sale of opium and heroin thrived under Japanese rule, the population of Nanking remained relatively free of disease. After occupation, Japanese authorities in the city enacted rigorous policies to burn corpses that had perished from illness. They also began an aggressive inoculation program against cholera and typhoid, subjecting the people to shots several times a year. Chinese medical officers waited in the streets and in the train station to administer inoculations to pedestrians or visitors as they came into the city. This created great resentment among the civilians, many of whom feared the needles would kill them. Children of Western missionaries also remember that at the train station Chinese visitors to Nanking were ordered to step into pans of disinfectant—a requirement that many found deeply humiliating. (The Westerners themselves were often sprayed with Lysol upon entering the city.)

Within a few years Nanking pulled itself up from its ruins. In the spring of 1938, men started to venture back to the city—some to examine the damage, others to find work because they had run out of money, still others to see whether conditions were safe enough for their families to return. As reconstruction began, the demand for labor grew. Soon, more men were lured back, and before long their wives and children joined the influx of migration toward Nanking. Within a year and a half, the population had doubled, surging from an estimated 250,000–300,000 people in March 1938 to more than 576,000 people in December 1939. Though the population failed to reach the 1-million level that the city had enjoyed back in 1936, by 1942 the population peaked at about 700,000 people and stabilized for the duration of the war.

Life under the Japanese was far from pleasant, but a sense of resignation settled over the city as many came to believe that the conquerors were there to stay. Occasionally there was underground resistance—once in a while someone would run into a theater packed with Japanese officials and throw a bomb—but in general such rebellion was sporadic and rare. Most of the hostility against the Japanese was expressed nonviolently, such as in anti-Japanese posters, fliers, and graffiti.

The end of Nanking's ordeal came at last in the summer of 1945. On August 6, 1945, the United States dropped an untested uranium bomb on Hiroshima, Japan's eighth-largest city, killing 100,000 of its 245,000 people on the first day. When a Japanese surrender was not forthcoming, the Americans dropped, on August 9, a second, plutonium-type bomb on the Japanese city of Nagasaki. Less than a week later, on August 14, the Japanese made the final decision to surrender.

The Japanese remained in the former capital of China until the day of the surrender, then quickly left the city. Eyewitnesses reported that Japanese soldiers could be seen drinking heavily or weeping in the streets; some heard rumors of unarmed Japanese men being forced to kneel by the side of the road to be beaten by local residents. Retaliation against the Japanese garrison appears to have been limited, however, because many residents hid at home during this chaotic time, too fearful to even celebrate in case the news of a Japanese defeat turned out not to be true. The evacuation was swift, and there was no mass persecution or imprisonment of Japanese soldiers. One Nanking citizen recalls that she stayed in her house for weeks after the Japanese surrendered, and when she reemerged, they were gone.

8

JUDGMENT DAY

EVEN BEFORE World War II drew to a close, the Allies had organized war tribunals to bring Japanese military criminals to justice. Fully expecting a Japanese defeat, the American and Chinese Nationalist governments made preliminary arrangements for the trials. In March 1944, the United Nations created the Investigation of War Crimes Committee; a subcommittee for Far East and Pacific war crimes was established in Chungking, China's wartime capital, after the fall of Nanking. After the Japanese surrender, the planning of the tribunals began in earnest. The Supreme Command of the Allied Powers in Japan worked closely with the Chinese Nationalist government to gather information about Japanese atrocities in China. For the crimes committed during the Rape of Nanking, members of the Japanese establishment stood trial not only in Nanking but in Tokyo itself.

THE NANKING WAR CRIMES TRIAL

The Rape of Nanking had been a deep, festering wound in the city's psyche, a wound that hid years of repressed fear and hatred. When the trials for class B and C war criminals started in the city in August 1946, the wound ruptured, spilling forth all the poison that had accumulated during the war.

Only a handful of Japanese war criminals were tried in Nanking, but they gave the local Chinese citizens a chance to air their grievances and participate in mass catharsis. During the trials, which lasted until February 1947, more than 1,000 people testified about some 460 cases of murder, rape, arson, and looting. The Chinese government had posted notices in the streets of Nanking, urging witnesses to come forward with evidence, while twelve district offices collected statements from people all over the city. One after another, they appeared in the courtroom, listened to the Chinese judge warn them about the five-year sentence for perjury, and then swore an oath of truth by marking printed statements with signatures, seals, fingerprints, or crosses. The witnesses included not only Chinese survivors but some of the Safety Zone leaders, such as Miner Searles Bates and Lewis Smythe.

During the trials evidence that had been painstakingly hidden for years emerged. One of the most famous exhibits was a tiny album of sixteen photographs of atrocities taken by the Japanese themselves. When the negatives were brought to a film development shop during the massacre, the employees secretly duplicated a set of images, which were placed in an album, hidden in the wall of a bathroom, and later secreted under a statue of Buddha. The album passed from hand to hand; men risked their lives to hide it even when the Japanese issued threats and conducted searches for photographic evidence of their crimes. One man even fled from Nanking and wandered from city to city for years like a fugitive because of the sixteen photographs. (The long and complex journey that these pictures made from photo shop to war crimes trial to their final resting place in archives has inspired numerous articles and even a full-length documentary in China.)

But not all of the evidence had taken such a sensational, circuitous path to the courtroom. Some came straight from old newspaper clippings. A *Japan Advertiser* article was brought forth at the trial of two lieutenants, Noda Takeshi and Mukai Toshiaki, who had participated in the famous killing contest described in chapter 2. During the trial both soldiers, of course, denied killing more than 150 people each, one of them blaming the article on the imagination of the foreign correspondents and the other insisting that he lied about the contest to better attract a wife when he returned to Japan. When the verdict was read in the courtroom on December 18, 1947, the Chinese audience whooped, cheered, and wept for joy. Both lieutenants were executed by firing squad.

The focal point of the Nanking war crimes trials was Tani Hisao. In 1937 he had served as lieutenant general of the 6th Division of the Japanese army in Nanking, a division that perpetrated many of the atrocities in the city, especially around Chunghua Gate. In August 1946, Tani was brought back to China for his trial and hauled in a prison van to a detention camp in Nanking. To prepare for his prosecution, forensic experts in white overalls dug open five burial grounds near the Chunghua Gate and exposed thousands of skeletons and skulls, many cracked from gunshot wounds and still stained with dark blood.

It must have been frightening for Tani Hisao to face the concentrated fury of an entire city. As he stood in the docks, his yellow Japanese military uniform stripped of its stars and stripes, more than eighty witnesses came to court to recite an endless litany of horrors. The indictment had been long, listing hundreds of stabbings, burnings, drownings, strangulations, rapes, thefts, and destruction committed by Tani's division. As evidence mounted, all of it damning, Chinese prosecutors even paraded in experts who heightened the drama by displaying heaps of skulls on the courtroom table. On February 6, 1947, the day his verdict was announced, the courtroom was not large enough to accommodate everyone who wanted to attend. More than two thousand spectators packed the courtroom while a loudspeaker broadcast the proceedings to tens of thousands of residents gathered outside.

No one was surprised that the verdict was guilty. On March 10, 1947, the court sentenced Tani Hisao to death after concluding that his forces had violated the Hague Convention concerning "The Customs of War on Land and the Wartime Treatment of Prisoners of War" and helped perpetrate a slaughter that claimed an estimated three hundred thousand lives in Nanking. Most of the city turned out to watch his execution. On April 26, spectators lined the streets and sidewalks as guards led Tani Hisao, his arms bound behind his back, to the execution grounds at Yuhuatai, or Rain Flower Terrace, an area just south of Nanking. There he met his death by gunfire—a fate that many survivors believed to be infinitely more humane than what had befallen most of his victims.

THE INTERNATIONAL MILITARY TRIBUNAL FOR THE FAR EAST

The International Military Tribunal for the Far East (IMTFE), also known as the Tokyo War Crimes Trial, began in the capital of Japan on May 3, 1946. The scope of the trial was staggering. The IMTFE drew more than 200,000 spectators and 419 witnesses. The transcript of the trial spanned 49,000 pages, contained 10 million words, and included 779 affidavits and depositions and 4,336 exhibits. Dubbed "the trial of the century," it lasted for two and a half years—three times as long as the Nuremberg trials. Indeed, the IMTFE would become the longest war crimes trial in history.

The IMTFE commanded enormous media and legal attention, even though only twenty-eight Japanese military and political officials were prosecuted. On any given day more than one thousand people packed the courtroom, including judges, lawyers, foreign correspondents, newsreel camera men, legal staff, MPs, stenographers, and translators. To the left of the press section sat the justices from eleven Allied nations on an elevated platform, to the right the accused. Spectators sat perched in the balconies while lawyers, aides, and clerks stood below in the pit. Everyone wore earphones because the proceedings were conducted in both English and Japanese.

"At the IMTFE, a thousand My Lais emerged," wrote Arnold Brackman in his book *The Other Nuremberg: The Untold Story of the Tokyo War Crimes Trials*. During the trial thousands of horrific details of Japanese behavior across Asia came together in reams of news reports, surveys, statistics, and witness testimony. The IMTFE not only created an enduring oral history record of the Nanking massacre but proved that the massacre was just a tiny fraction of the totality of atrocities committed by the Japanese during the war. The prosecution learned, among other things, of Japanese medical experiments on their captives, of marches (such as the infamous Bataan Death March) in which gravely ill and starved prisoners dropped dead from exhaustion, of the savage conditions behind the construction of the Siam-Burma Death Railway, of the Japanese "water treatment" that pumped water or kerosene into the noses and mouths of victims until their bowels ruptured, of suspension of POWs by wrists, arms, or legs until their joints were literally ripped from their sockets, of victims being forced to kneel on sharp instruments, of excruciating extractions of nails from fingers, of electric shock torture, of naked women forced to sit on charcoal stoves, of every imaginable form of beating and flogging (a favored method of torture by military police officers involved tying prisoners to trees, surrounding them, and kicking them to death in a method they euphemistically called "triple attack," or "converging from three directions"), even of vivisection and cannibalism. It was later determined that Japanese treatment of their POWs surpassed in brutality even that of the Nazis. Only one in twenty-five American POWs died under Nazi captivity, in contrast to one in three under the Japanese.

The Rape of Nanking—perhaps the highlight of the IMTFE—served as a metaphor for Japanese behavior during the entire span of the war. Brackman, who had covered the IMTFE as a young United Press reporter, pointed out that "the Rape of Nanking was not the kind of isolated incident common to *all* wars. It was deliberate. It was policy. It was known in Tokyo.

For that matter, it was front-page news in the world's press. This was what the IMTFE was all about." The evidence presented at the trial overwhelmed the Japanese defense. Several members of the International Safety Zone Committee flew to Tokyo to read from their diaries, present their own research findings, and answer questions about the Rape of Nanking. The IMTFE verdict unequivocally denounced the Japanese for their crimes in Nanking, citing one observer's claim that the Japanese soldiers were "let loose like a barbarian horde to desecrate the city." The tribunal also concluded that the Japanese government had been well aware of the atrocities in Nanking. The crimes, after all, happened in plain view of the Japanese embassy. The International Committee had made daily visits to representatives at the Japanese Foreign Office and the Japanese embassy to report on the situation, even filing two protests a day for the first six weeks. Joseph Grew, the American ambassador in Tokyo, held personal meetings with top Japanese officials, including Hirota Koki, to inform them of the atrocities. Moreover, Ito Nobufumo, Japan's minister at large in China in 1937 and 1938, had also forwarded reports of Japanese outrages in China to Hirota.

The brunt of the blame for the Nanking atrocities fell on Matsui Iwane. As the commander of Japan's Central China Expeditionary Force at the time, Matsui served as the most obvious target: one month before the Nanking invasion, Matsui had boasted that his mission was to "chastise the Nanking government and the outrageous Chinese." On December 17, 1937, he had entered the city with great pomp and ceremony, perched on top of a chestnut horse, as soldiers cheered him on. But historians have suggested that Matsui may have served as the scapegoat for the Rape of Nanking. A sickly and frail man suffering from tuberculosis, Matsui was not even in Nanking when the city fell.

Because of the lack of literature on the subject, Matsui's responsibility for the crimes at Nanking remains a subject for further research and debate. The evidence suggests, however, that the tubercular general was guilt-stricken over the entire episode, no doubt because he was unable to maintain order in the Japanese army after Asaka took command. To atone for the sins of Nanking, Matsui erected a shrine of remorse on a hill in his hometown of Atami, a beach resort some fifty miles down the coast from Tokyo. Sacks of clay imported from the banks of the Yangtze River were mixed with native Japanese soil and then sculpted, baked, and glazed into the statue of Kanon, the Buddhist Goddess of Mercy. Before this statue a priestess was hired by the Matsui family to chant prayers and weep for the Chinese war dead.

But a public show of self-flagellation is one thing, and the willingness to seek justice for the wronged quite another. To this day Matsui's behavior at the IMTFE remains perplexing. During his testimony he failed to disclose the full story of what happened in Nanking, an account that would have implicated the imperial family. Instead, he waffled between lies and occasional self-denunciation. He tried to make excuses for the atrocities of Nanking, sometimes denied them completely, and irritated the prosecution with his circuitous, vaguely mystical discussions about Buddhism and the nature of Sino-Japanese friendship. But never once did he point accusatory fingers at the imperial throne. Rather, he blamed himself for failing to properly guide Prince Asaka and the emperor, and he told the prosecutors that it was his duty to die for them. "I am happy to end this way," he said. "I am really eager to die at any time."

He got his wish. The tribunal concluded that the Rape of Nanking was "either secretly ordered or willfully committed" and sentenced Matsui to death. He was not the only one; a total of seven Japanese class A war criminals, including Japanese Foreign Minister Hirota Koki, were judged guilty by the IMTFE and later hanged at the Sugamo Prison in Tokyo.

Unfortunately, many of the chief culprits of the Rape of Nanking—or those who might have exercised their royal authority to stop the Rape—never spent a day in court.

General Nakajima Kesago died shortly after Japan's surrender. The man whose troops had committed some of the worst Nanking outrages passed away on October 28, 1945, apparently of uremia and cirrhosis of the liver. There were rumors that Nakajima was an alcoholic and committed suicide, but his eldest son said that his illness was caused by inhalation of gases to which he was exposed when employed in chemical weapons research and education. By coincidence, an American MP who came to question Nakajima about war crimes arrived at his door just as a physician was informing the family that Nakajima had died. His biographer Kimura Kuninori—who believes Nakajima followed a "take no prisoners" policy in Nanking—quoted Nakajima's son as saying: "Had my father lived, he probably would not have escaped execution."

General Yanagawa Heisuke also died in 1945. Before his death by heart attack, however, he gave several interviews to his friend Sugawara Yutaka, who used seven volumes of notes from their conversations together to publish a book. Though the book is mostly laudatory of Yanagawa's military exploits ("He was a rare man and a great talent" Sugawara writes) it does address the subject of the Rape of Nanking. Yanagawa simply pooh-poohed the entire episode, assuring Sugawara that reports of his men's atrocities were "groundless rumors." Rather, he boasted that his soldiers had followed such strict military discipline in Nanking that even when quartered in Chinese homes they took care to wear slippers.

Hirohito lived long after Japan's surrender but never faced a full moral accounting for his activities during the war. In exchange for Japan's surrender, the American government granted him, the emperor of Japan, immunity from trial, so he was not called in as a defendant or even a witness. Because the terms of the surrender exonerated all members of the Japanese imperial family, Hirohito's uncle Prince Asaka (under whose command the "Kill All Captives" order was forged) also escaped justice, exempting him from having to appear at the IMTFE at all.

The decision to give Hirohito immunity from war responsibility and, still worse, the decision to keep him on the throne, later impeded the Japanese people's own historical awareness of their World War II crimes. According to Herbert Bix, a biographer of Hirohito and prominent Japan scholar: "Many would find it difficult to believe that they had been accomplices in aggression and murder on a near-genocidal scale when the emperor whom they had served so loyally never had to bear responsibility for his own speech and actions . . . MacArthur helped prepare the ground for future Japanese conservative interpretations of the postwar monarchy that denied the Showa emperor had ever held real power."

The details of Emperor Hirohito's role in the Rape of Nanking remain a controversial subject because of the dearth of primary source material available. Unlike the Nazi government records, which were confiscated and microfilmed by the Allies and later used as evidence in war crimes trials, the Japanese deliberately destroyed, hid or falsified most of their secret wartime documents before General MacArthur arrived. Even most of the Japanese high-level military records that the American occupation forces did manage to seize in 1945—documents which one professor called "a priceless historical treasure"—were inexplicably and irresponsibly returned to Japan by the American government little more than a decade later before they could be properly microfilmed. For these reasons it is practically impossible today to prove whether Emperor Hirohito planned, approved of, or even knew of the atrocities in Nanking.

Perhaps the only English-language book that has attempted to explain Hirohito's involvement in the Nanking massacre is *Japan's Imperial Conspiracy* by David Bergamini. In his book, Bergamini claims that the Japanese laid out an intricate blueprint for world conquest, and that the person who made the decision to invade Nanking was Hirohito himself. Bergamini offers a riveting narrative (complete, apparently, with quotes from Japanese top-secret messages) to explain the chain of events leading to the tragedy at Nanking. Unfortunately, Bergamini's book was seriously criticized by reputable historians who claimed that he cited sources that simply did not exist or quoted mysterious unnamed informants who said amazing but unverifiable things.

Adding to the confusion is the debate among scholars on whether a Japanese imperial conspiracy to conquer the world had ever existed. For years it was believed that Prime Minister Tanaka Gi-ichi had submitted a secret report to the throne during the Far Eastern Conference of 1927, a report known as the "Tanaka Memorial" that purportedly encapsulated Japanese ambitions at the time. "In order the conquer the world, we must first conquer China," the report allegedly dictated. "But in order to conquer China, we must first conquer Manchuria and Mongolia . . . If we succeed in conquering China the rest of the Asiatic countries and South Sea countries will fear us and surrender to us. Then the world will realize that Eastern Asia is ours and will not dare to violate our rights. This is the plan left to us by Emperor Meiji, the success of which is essential to our national existence."

Today, this report is generally considered by scholars to be a forgery, one with possible Russian origins. But when the Memorial first emerged in Peking in September 1929, it led many to believe that Japanese aggression against China was part of a well-coordinated Japanese plot to conquer the globe. The English text of the Tanaka Memorial later appeared in English in a Shanghai newspaper and even inspired the classic Hollywood movie *Blood on the Sun*, in which James Cagney attempts to steal Japan's master plan in order to save the world. Today the Tanaka Memorial still has a considerable grasp on the world imagination: many Chinese historians believe that the Tanaka Memorial is authentic, and Chinese encyclopedias and dictionaries as well as English-language newspaper and wire service articles continue to cite the Memorial as historical fact.

Currently, no reputable historian of Japan believes that there was a preplanned conspiracy by Japan to conquer the world. An examination of the chaos in the Japanese state administration in the 1920s and 1930s suggests that such a conspiracy was unlikely: the Japanese Army hated the Navy, the High Command in Tokyo didn't know what the Kwantung Army in Manchuria was doing until it was too late, and relations between the Foreign Ministry and the armed services were often chilly to the point of silence.

However, many scholars believe that Hirohito must have known about the Rape of Nanking. (Herbert Bix personally thinks it is "inconceivable" that Hirohito could not have known.) First, it was front-page news in the world press. Secondly, his own brother could have told him the gory details. Back in 1943, Prince Mikasa Takahito, the youngest brother of Emperor Hirohito, spent a year as a staff officer at the Nanking headquarters of the Japanese Imperial Army's expeditionary force in China, where he heard a young officer speak of using Chinese prisoners for live bayonet practice in order to train new recruits. "It helps them acquire guts," the officer told the prince. The appalled Mikasa described the practice as "truly a horrible scene that can only be termed a massacre." Out of a "desperate desire to bring the war to a close," the prince distributed a questionnaire to young staff officers to seek their opinions about the war, prepared a lecture that denounced Japanese aggression in China, and wrote the report "Reflections as a Japanese on the Sino-Japanese War." The paper was deemed controversial and dangerous, but Mikasa got away with writing it because of his royal blood. The Japanese military later confiscated and destroyed most of the copies, but a single copy survived, and it was later discovered in the microfilm collections of the national parliamentary archives.

If this story had come out during the Japanese war tribunals, it might have implicated the royal family and military command alike for their failure to crack down on war criminals when news of misdeeds reached them. (Mikasa admitted that he reported on the China situation in "bits and pieces" to his brother the emperor and even watched with him a newsreel about Japanese atrocities in China.) But Mikasa's confession did not emerge until 1994—almost half a century after the IMTFE.

We will probably never know exactly what news Hirohito received about Nanking as the massacre was happening, but the record suggests that he was exceptionally pleased by it. The day after the fall of the Chinese capital, the emperor expressed his "extreme satisfaction" to Prince Kanin, the grand-uncle of the empress and chief of the army general staff, and the prince, in turn, sent a telegram of congratulations to Matsui Iwane: "Not since history began has there been such an extraordinary military exploit." Hirohito even invited Matsui, Asaka, and Yanagawa to his summer villa to present them with silver vases embossed with the imperial chrysanthemum.

In the end, the royal family not only escaped scrutiny at the tribunal but went on to enjoy lives of leisure and national adoration. Prince Asaka, for one, retired to watch weekly newsreels with Hirohito, to sit with him on the Council of Princes of the Blood, and to play golf with him until the end of his days. (Asaka not only excelled at the sport but took an active interest in golf course development, becoming the architect of the Plateau Golf Course at the Dai-Hakone Country Club, in the resort town of Hakone on the east coast of Japan.) Hirohito himself lived peacefully and in dignity until his death in 1989.

9

THE FATE
OF THE SURVIVORS

MORE THAN one scholar of the Nanking massacre has commented upon the dismal manner in which justice was doled out after the IMFTE. While many of the Japanese who tormented the Nanking citizens received full military pensions and benefits from the Japanese government, thousands of their victims suffered (and continue to suffer) lives of silent poverty, shame, or chronic physical and mental pain.

The pivotal moment in this reversal of justice came with the advent of the cold war. The United States had originally sought to implement democracy in Japan by purging Japan's leadership of people involved in the war. But after the war the Soviet Union broke its promises at the Yalta Conference and seized Poland and part of Germany. As the "iron curtain" of communism descended on Eastern

Europe, so did a "bamboo curtain" in China; in 1949 the Communist forces of Mao Tse-tung defeated the armies of Chiang Kai-shek, forcing his government to retreat to the island of Taiwan. Then in 1950 the Korean War broke out, eventually killing 1 million Koreans, a quarter-million Chinese, and thirty-four thousand Americans. With China, the Soviet Union, and North Korea as its new postwar enemies, the United States suddenly viewed Japan as a country of strategic importance. Washington decided to maintain a stable government in Japan in order to better challenge communism in Asia. The United States left the prewar bureaucracy in Japan virtually intact, permitting many of its wartime perpetrators to go unpunished. Therefore, while the Nazi regime was overhauled and replaced and numerous Nazi war criminals were hunted down and brought to trial, many high-ranking wartime Japanese officials returned to power and prospered. In 1957 Japan even elected as prime minister a man who had been imprisoned as a class A war criminal.

At the same time, most if not all of the Nanking massacre survivors vanished from public view. During the cold war and the turbulent years of Mao's reign, Nanking—along with the rest of China—remained isolated from much of the international community. The Chinese Communist government not only severed communication with the West for several decades but expelled many of the remaining foreigners in Nanking, even those who had saved thousands of Chinese lives as administrators of the Nanking Safety Zone.

In the summer of 1995 I became one of the first people from the West to capture on videotape the oral testimonies of several survivors of the Rape of Nanking. Sad to say, if I had visited Nanking only a decade earlier, I would have found many sites of the massacre intact, for the city was then a model of historical preservation and much of its 1930s architecture was still standing. But in the late 1980s and 1990s the city underwent a frenzy of land speculation and construction, demolishing most of its ancient landscape and replacing it with new luxury hotels, factories, skyscrapers, and apartment buildings, under thick blankets of smog. Even much of the famous

Nanking Wall disappeared, with only a few gates remaining as tourist attractions.

If I did not know about the Rape of Nanking before my visit to this teeming, congested, and thriving city, I would have never suspected that it even took place, for the population of the city was at least ten times greater than it had been immediately after the massacre. Underneath the prosperity, however, hidden from view, were the last human links to the past—the elderly survivors of the Nanking massacre. Scholars in the city guided me to a few of them scattered throughout Nanking.

What I found shocked and depressed me. Most lived in dark, squalid apartments cluttered with the debris of poverty and heavy with mildew and humidity. I learned that during the massacre some had received physical injuries so severe they had been prevented from making a decent living for decades. Most lived in poverty so crushing that even a minimal amount of financial compensation from Japan could have greatly improved the conditions of their lives. Even $100 in reparations from the Japanese to buy an air conditioner could have made a world of difference for many of them.

After the war some of the survivors had clung to the hope that their government would vindicate them by pushing for Japanese reparations and an official apology. This hope, however, was swiftly shattered when the People's Republic of China (PRC), eager to forge an alliance with the Japanese to gain international legitimacy, announced at various times that it had forgiven the Japanese; in 1991 the PRC government even invited the Japanese prime minister to visit mainland China. Hearing such news was like being raped a second time, and some saw themselves as the victims of a double betrayal—first by the KMT soldiers who fled from Nanking before the city collapsed, then by the PRC government, which sold out their futures to the Japanese.

According to Karen Parker, an international human rights attorney, the PRC has never signed a treaty with the Japanese relinquishing its right to seek national reparations for wartime crimes, despite its conciliatory statements toward the Japanese. Moreover, Parker claims that even if such a treaty is made, it cannot, under the principle of *jus cogens,* infringe upon the right of individual Chinese people to seek reparations for wartime suffering.

But most of the survivors I spoke with in Nanking did not know the intricacies of international law and therefore believed that the PRC had already forfeited their right to seek reparations. Any news of friendly relations between the Chinese and Japanese governments is emotionally devastating to them. One man who was nearly roasted alive by the Japanese during the Rape of Nanking told me that he wept uncontrollably when he heard rumors that the PRC had forgiven the Japanese their past crimes. Another woman whose father was executed during the Nanking massacre said that her mother collapsed in a faint when the news of the prime minister's visit reached her over the radio.*

Equally sobering were the fates of many of the foreigners who organized the Nanking Safety Zone. Although they sacrificed their energy and health to help the Chinese in Nanking, many of these Westerners never quite got what they deserved from life or posterity. There are no famous books devoted to these forgotten heroes of World War II, and certainly there has been

---

*Not all of the survivors from the Rape of Nanking, however, suffered tragic fates. Sometimes I encountered numerous surprise endings, like the conclusion of the life of commander Tang Sheng-chih. Despite his fiasco at Nanking, Tang went on to enjoy a charmed existence in China. Things were rough for him at first, because the Nanking debacle left him in foul odor with the Nationalist party and forced him to return to his home province of Hunan without an official job. But after the Communists came to power, the new leadership embraced Tang—even though he had been a high-ranking military official in the enemy camp. Swiftly Tang rose to prominence, serving as lieutenant governor of Hunan and a member of the National People's Congress, the National Defense Committee, the Chinese National Party Revolutionary Committee and number of other organizations. Only after serving a long prestigious career in politics did he finally die on April 6, 1970—a revered official in his eighties.

no movie about them that has captured the imagination of the world public as intensely as *Schindler's List*. Their spirit lives mainly in a few archives and attics from Berlin to Sunnyvale—and in the minds of a handful of survivors in China who remember them simply as the living Buddhas who saved Nanking.

Most of the Nanking survivors know the deeds of the Safety Zone leaders, but few are aware of how their lives ultimately played out. The survivors I talked with in China were saddened to learn that some of their protectors eventually endured disgrace and expulsion from China, interrogation and ostracism in their home countries, and irreparable physical and mental wounds—even suicide. Several of these foreign heroes can be considered the belated victims of the Rape of Nanking.

The experiences of Miner Searle Bates and Lewis Smythe illustrate how the facts of their heroism during the Nanking massacre were twisted for political ends. During the Korean War the PRC distorted the history of the massacre in newspaper articles to depict the Americans as the villains of Nanking who assisted the Japanese in the carnage. In the local newspaper, Lewis Smythe saw articles that accused the Safety Zone foreigners of giving over the city to the Japanese and turning over thousands of women for raping. In a similar vein, an article in the national *Xinhua Yuebao* charged that the Americans who remained in Nanking in 1937 "not only responded well to the imperialist policies of the U.S. Government but also protected their companies, churches, schools and residences with the blood and bones of the Chinese people." The author insisted that the International Safety Zone Committee was an organization of imperialists who worked in "faithful collusion" with the Japanese invaders, and he quoted one Chinese survivor as saying "the American devils called out the names and the Japanese devils carried out the execution." Pictures of the atrocities were printed with the slogan, "Remember the Nanking massacre, stop American Remilitarization of Japan!"

Such propaganda shocked and frightened Smythe, though his Chinese teacher assured him of his safety. "Dr. Smythe, there are 100,000 people in this city [who] know what you people did," the teacher said. "There's nothing to worry about." Nevertheless, his days in Nanking were numbered. In 1951 he left his position at Nanking University to join the faculty of Lexington Theological Seminary in Kentucky the following year. Bates also left Nanking, but not before he had been placed under virtual house arrest by the Communists.

Smythe and Bates did not suffer as much as some of their colleagues. For several committee members, the massacre took years off their lives. David Magee, son of the Reverend John Magee, is certain that the stress of dealing with the Japanese caused the early death of his father. Other zone leaders endured years of mental agony. For example, Edith Fitch Swapp, the daughter of the YMCA secretary George Fitch, said her father had been so traumatized by the Japanese atrocities in Nanking that he often suffered complete amnesia when delivering lectures on the subject. This happened at least twice when Fitch spoke about the Sino-Japanese War in front of large organizations in the United States.

Robert Wilson, the Nanking University Hospital surgeon, paid the price of Nanking with his health. His widow recalled that while other doctors on the zone committee carefully paced themselves and went to Shanghai at least once a week to catch up on sleep, Wilson recklessly worked nonstop without taking breaks. Surgery consumed most of his energy during the day, while Japanese soldiers interrupted his sleep at night when he was called away from home time and again to stop a rape in progress. He operated, it seemed, on adrenaline alone. Finally, his body rebelled. In 1940 violent seizures and even a mental collapse forced Wilson to return to the United States, where he rested for a year in Santa Barbara, California. He never returned to China, nor did he fully recover from the strain. In the United States Wilson not only endured both seizures and nightmares but also experienced trouble focusing his eyes in the morning.

Minnie Vautrin paid the price with her life. The Nanking massacre took a deeper psychic toll on her than any of the other zone leaders or refugees had realized at the time. Few were aware that under a legend that had grown to mythic proportions was a vulnerable, exhausted woman who never recovered, either emotionally or physically, from daily exposure to Japanese violence. Her last diary entry, dated April 14, 1940, reveals her state of mind: "I'm about at the end of my energy. Can no longer forge ahead and make plans for the work, for on every hand there seem to be obstacles of some kind. I wish I could go on furlough at once but who will do the thinking for the Exp. course?"

Two weeks later she suffered a nervous breakdown. At the bottom of the last page of her diary is a sentence that was written, no doubt, by somebody else: "In May 1940 Miss Vautrin's health broke, necessitating her return to the United States." Her niece recalls that Vautrin's colleagues sent her back to the States for medical help, but during the voyage across the Pacific Ocean she tried repeatedly to kill herself. A friend who accompanied Vautrin could barely restrain her from jumping over the side of the ship. Once in the United States, Vautrin entered a psychiatric hospital in Iowa, where she endured electroshock treatment. Upon her release, Vautrin went to work for the United Christian Missionary Society in Indianapolis. Her family in Shepherd, Michigan, wanted to visit Vautrin, but she discouraged them by writing that she would be coming to see them soon. A fortnight later Vautrin was dead. On May 14, 1941, a year to the day she left Nanking, Vautrin sealed the windows and doors of her home with tape, turned on the gas, and committed suicide.

Then there was the fate of John Rabe, whose life remained a mystery to historians for years. Before he was summoned back to Germany, Rabe had promised the Chinese in Nanking that he would publicize the Japanese atrocities in his homeland and try to seek an audience with Hermann Göring and even Adolf Hitler. People in Nanking prayed that Rabe's presentation would compel Nazi leaders to exert pressure on the Japanese government to stop the carnage. Before Rabe's departure, a Chinese doctor had asked Rabe to tell the Germans that the Chinese were not Communists, but peace-loving people who wanted to live in harmony with other nations. After a round of tearful farewell parties in February 1938, Rabe departed for

Germany with a copy of John Magee's film of the Nanking atrocities. After that point in time, he vanished from all the records, and his whereabouts baffled scholars for decades.

I was determined to get to the bottom of the story for two reasons. First, the irony of a kind-hearted Nazi working with American missionaries to save Chinese refugees from Japanese soldiers was too intriguing for me to ignore. And second, I was convinced that something terrible must have happened to Rabe after he returned to Germany. Rabe, after all, did not appear at the International Military Tribunal of the Far East to testify with his colleagues about the horrors of Nanking. Also, an oral history interview with one of his friends indicated that Rabe had somehow run afoul of Hitler's government. But the friend failed to provide specific details, and by the time I came across the transcript he was no longer alive to give me the full story.

Questions nagged me at every turn. Did Rabe actually show the film and the report to Hitler? Or did he, God forbid, get sucked deeper into the Nazi machinery in Germany and contribute to the extermination of the Jews? (This I highly doubted, given his record of heroism at Nanking, but the possibility remained.) Perhaps he had been thrown in prison after the war. Or perhaps no one had ever heard from him again because he became a fugitive from the law, living out his remaining years in a Latin American country. I also wondered whether he had kept a personal diary of the Nanking massacre. But if he kept such papers, they must have been destroyed during the war, incinerated perhaps in an air raid; otherwise, any such diary should have ended up in archives by now, available to the rest of the world. Still, I figured that it would not hurt to write some letters to Germany to see what I could find.

I possessed one important clue about Rabe: he had been apprenticed in Hamburg around the turn of the century. Perhaps he had been born there and still had family in the city. Somehow I had to establish contact with a key source in Hamburg. I turned to an old friend for help. John Taylor, whom scholars called "a national treasure," had worked more than half a century at the National Archives in Washington, D.C., and knew just about every serious historian in the world. If there was an expert somewhere on the planet who had studied the history of the German community in China during World War II, Taylor would probably know who he was. Taylor suggested that I contact the historian Charles Burdick of Ferndale, California. Burdick in turn suggested that I write to the city historian of Hamburg; he also gave me the address of Martha Begemann, a friend of his and, he assured me, a "lovely lady" who was not only well connected in the city but generous with her help. Within a few days I wrote to Begemann about the Rabe mystery as well as to the editor of the largest newspaper in Hamburg, hoping that the latter would run a notice about my search. Then, expecting no immediate reply from either of them, I turned my attention to other things.

To my surprise, a letter came back from Begemann right away. Through a fortuitous chain of events, she had already located Rabe's family. "I am happy I could help you, and it was not so very difficult," she wrote on April 26, 1996. "First of all I wrote to Pastor Müller, in Bavaria, who collected the whereabouts of all former Germans in China. He promptly rang me up the other day telling me the names of Dr. Otto Rabe, son of John Rabe, and his sister Margarethe." She enclosed in her letter a message from Ursula Reinhardt, Rabe's granddaughter in Berlin.

From that moment on, things moved swiftly. Ursula Reinhardt, I learned, had been born in China; as a little girl, she even visited Nanking only months before the city fell. She was Rabe's favorite granddaughter. To my delight, Reinhardt proved endlessly helpful to my inquiries and sent me many long letters. With handwritten text, photographs, and news articles, Reinhardt filled in some of the missing details of Rabe's life.

Rabe kept his promise to the Chinese that he would inform the German authorities of the Japanese horrors in Nanking. On April 15, he and his wife returned to Germany, where he received numerous accolades for his achievements. In Berlin the German secretary of state officially commended Rabe for his work in China; Rabe was awarded the Service Cross of the Red Cross Order. In Stuttgart he was further decorated, receiving the Silver Poster for Service to Germany Award and the Diamond Order Award on a red, white, and blue necklace from the Chinese government. That May, Rabe publicized the Nanking massacre by lecturing and showing John Magee's film all over Berlin, speaking before packed audiences at the Siemens Company, the Ministry of Foreign Affairs, the Association for the Far East, and the War Ministry. Rabe failed to secure an audience with Adolf Hitler, however, and so on June 8 he sent a letter to the fuehrer, along with a copy of the film and a typewritten report on the Rape of Nanking.

But if Rabe had expected a sympathetic response from Hitler, he was gravely mistaken. A few days later two members of the Gestapo arrived on his doorstep to arrest him. Ursula Reinhardt was there when it happened. She was seven years old, trying on a pair of new roller skates near the door when she saw two official-looking men in black uniforms with white lapels take Rabe away to a waiting car. "My grandfather looked embarrassed and the two men very severe and stiff so that I didn't even dare hug him farewell."

Rabe was interrogated for several hours at Gestapo headquarters. The Gestapo released him only after his employer, Carl Friedrich von Siemen, vouched for his character and promised them that Rabe would refrain from talking of the Japanese so openly. Rabe was warned never to lecture, discuss, or write on the subject again and, most of all, never to show John Magee's film to anyone. After Rabe's release, the Siemens Company immediately sent him abroad, probably for his own protection. For the next few months Rabe worked in Afghanistan, helping German nationals leave the country by way of Turkey. In October the German government returned his report but kept the copy of John Magee's film. (Rabe never found out whether Hitler read the report or saw the film, although his family today is convinced that he did.) The German government informed Rabe that his report was sent to the Ministry of Economics, where it was read by the highest circles of government, but that he should not expect any change in German foreign policy toward Japan because of it.

The next few years proved nightmarish for Rabe. His apartment was bombed out, and the Russian invasion of Berlin reduced his family to poverty. Ursula Reinhardt is convinced that they survived only because they were living in the British, not the Soviet, section of Berlin. Rabe continued to work sporadically for the Siemens Company, translating economic correspondence into English. But the low wage was barely enough to keep his family alive.

The immediate postwar period for Rabe must have been one long string of angry accusations. First he was arrested by the Soviets, who interrogated him for three days and nights before the unrelenting glare of klieg lights. Then he was arrested by the British, who grilled him for an entire day but later gave him a work permit. (The permit, however, had little value for Rabe because the Siemens Company still did not have a permanent position for him.) The final humiliation came when a German acquaintance denounced Rabe and propelled him into a long, drawn-out "de-nazification" process; he had to pay for his own legal defense, in the process losing his work permit and depleting his savings and energy. Crowded into one tiny room with his family, fighting cold and hunger, Rabe was forced to sell, piece by piece, his beloved collection of Chinese artwork to the American army in order to buy beans, bread, and soap. Malnutrition caused him to succumb to skin disease, while sorrow and stress all but destroyed his health. In Nanking he was a legend, but in Germany he was a dying man.

Excerpts from Rabe's diary reveal his state of mind in 1945–46:

> *There is no job for me at Siemens—I am unemployed . . . According to the Military Government I must give my Standard Life Policies to be registered in Spandau* [a district in the northwest of Berlin] *at the Stadtkontorbank. The policies of over 1027.19 pounds (the rest of 5000) for which I worked and saved so many years are with Gretel* [Margarethe, his daughter] *in Bunde. As far as I can see this money is lost now!*

> *Last Sunday I was with Mommy* [Dora Rabe, John Rabe's wife] *in the Xantener Straße* [Rabe's bombed apartment]. *They*

broke the door in our cellar and stole my typewriter, our radio and more—Meo fatze!

Now Mommy weighs only 44 kg—we have grown very meager. The summer comes to an end—what will winter bring? Where will we get fuel, food and work? I am now translating Timperley's What War Means [a book of documents about the Nanking massacre]. *At the moment this brings no money, but perhaps I shall get a better food ration card . . . All Germans suffer as we do.*

We suffer hunger and hunger again—I had nothing to tell, so I didn't write down anything. In addition to our meager meal we ate acorn flour soup. Mommy collected the acorns secretly in autumn. Now as the provisions come to an end, day after day we ate stinging nettle, the young leaves taste like spinach.

Yesterday my petition to get de-nazified was rejected. Though I saved the lives of 250,000 Chinese people as the head of the International Committee of the Nanking Safety Zone, my request was refused because I was for a short time the leader of the Ortsgruppenleiter district of the NSDAP in Nanking and a man of my intelligence must not have sought membership of this party. I am going to appeal . . . If they don't give me any possibility to work at SSW [the Siemens Schuckert Werke, the name of Rabe's company] *I don't know what to live on. So I must go on to fight—and I am so tired. At the moment I am questioned every day by the police.*

If I had heard of any atrocities of the Nazis in China I wouldn't have entered the NSDAP and if any of my opinions as a German man had differed with the opinion of the foreigners in Nanking, the English, the Americans, Danes etc. etc. in Nanking wouldn't have chosen me Chairman of the International Security Committee in Nanking! In Nanking I was the living Buddha for hundreds of thousands of people and here I am a "pariah," an outcast. Oh, if I could only be cured of my homesickness!

On June the 3rd finally I was de-nazified by the de-nazifying commission of the British Sector in Charlottenburg.

The judgment runs: "Though you were deputy leader of the district of the NSDAP and though after your return to Germany you did not resign membership of the NSDAP [Ursula Reinhardt notes that doing so would have been suicide!] *the commission decided to sustain your objection because of your successful humanitarian work in China" etc.*

With this, the nerve torture finally came to an end. I was congratulated by many friends and directors of the SSW and given a holiday by the firm to recover from the strain.

Today Mommy is out with one of our Chinese wooden idols to go to Dr. Krebs, who now and then provided us with food and was in love with this idol. A Chinese carpet, a present from Kong, we gave to Mrs. Toepfer for three hundred weights of potatoes . . .

By 1948 news of Rabe's plight had reached China. When the Nanking city government announced to its people that Rabe needed help, the response was tremendous, almost reminiscent of the conclusion of Frank Capra's classic film *It's a Wonderful Life.* Within a matter of days the survivors of the massacre raised for Rabe's support $100 million in Chinese dollars, roughly equivalent at the time to $2,000 in U.S. dollars—no small amount in 1948. In March that year the mayor of Nanking traveled to Switzerland, where he bought large quantities of milk powder, sausages, tea, coffee, beef, butter, and jam to be delivered to Rabe in four huge packages. From June 1948 until the fall of the capital to the Communists, the people of Nanking also mailed Rabe a bundle of food each month to express their heartfelt thanks for his leadership of the International Safety Zone. The Kuomintang government even offered Rabe free housing in China and a lifelong pension if he ever chose to return.

The packages were a godsend for Rabe and his family. In June 1948 the city of Nanking learned just how badly Rabe had needed them when they received from him several letters of profuse thanks, letters that remain to this day in Chinese archives. Before the packages arrived, the family had been collecting wild weeds, which the children would eat with soup. The adults subsisted on barely more than dry bread. But at the time when Rabe wrote his letters to Nanking, even bread had disappeared from the Berlin market, making the packages all the more precious to them. The entire family was grateful for the support of the Nanking people, and Rabe himself wrote that the gesture had restored his faith in life.

Rabe died from an artery stroke in 1950. Before his death, he left behind a written legacy of his work in China: more than two thousand pages of documents on the Rape of Nanking that he had meticulously typed, numbered, bound, and even illustrated; these documents included his and other foreigners' eyewitness reports, newspaper articles, radio broadcasts, telegrams, and photographs of the atrocities. No doubt Rabe recognized the historical value of this record; perhaps he even predicted its future publication. A decade after his death, Ursula Reinhardt's mother found the diaries among his papers and offered to give them to her, but the offer came at a bad time: Reinhardt was pregnant and immersed in school examinations; more significantly, she was afraid to read the gruesome contents of the diaries. When she politely declined the offer, John Rabe's son, Dr. Otto Rabe, inherited the papers instead. With him they remained unknown to the world public and even to German historians for half a century.

There are a number of possible reasons for this secrecy. According to the Reinhardts, John Rabe himself had warned his son not to disclose the existence of the diaries. The treatment he had endured under the Gestapo may very well have had something to do with his caution. But there was a more fundamental reason for the family's reluctance to advertise the diaries' existence. Rabe's previous status as a Nazi raised understandable concerns among some members of his family, and in the immediate postwar years it was simply not politically correct to publish the documents of a Nazi or boast about his accomplishments, however worthy they might have been.

The other Nazis on the Nanking International Safety Zone Committee kept quiet about their records as well. Shortly after the discovery of the Rabe papers, I learned of the existence of another Nazi diary of the Rape of Nanking, entitled "Days of Fate in Nanking" by Christian Kröger. His son, Peter Kröger, had found a copy of the diary in his father's desk after his death at the age of ninety. It was fortunate, he wrote, that my letter reached him when it did; if it had arrived only a month earlier, he would have told me that his father had possessed only a few newspaper articles on the subject. To this day he wonders why his father never told him about the Rape of Nanking or the diary. I suspect the reason is linked to Rabe's downfall and persecution in Germany after he sent the report on the great Rape to Hitler. In fact, at the bottom of the diary is a handwritten scrawl, no doubt Kröger's, that warns: "Contrary to the current opinions of the Hitler government. Consequently I had to be very careful with this."

It was Ursula Reinhardt who finally told the world about Rabe's heroic efforts. When my letter reached her, she decided that the diaries merited closer examination. She borrowed the documents from her uncle and steeled herself to read them. The contents were violent beyond her wildest expectations, causing her to reel from descriptions of women gang-raped by Japanese soldiers in the public streets, of Chinese victims burned alive in Nanking. Months later Reinhardt remained so horrified by her grandfather's report that she did not hesitate to tell a reporter from the *Renming Ribao* (People's Daily) her honest opinion of the Nanking massacre, an opinion certain to provoke controversy: that the Japanese torture of their victims in Nanking surpassed even the Nazis in cruelty, and that the Japanese were far worse than Adolf Hitler himself.

Reinhardt worried about the implications of releasing the diaries to the world. She saw the diaries as political dynamite with the potential to wreck Sino-Japanese relations. But at my urging, and also at the urging of Shao Tzuping, a past president of the Alliance in the Memory of Victims of the Nanking Massacre who worked for the United Nations, she decided to make the diaries public. She spent fifteen hours photocopying them. Shao, who was fearful that right-wing Japanese might break into her house and destroy the diaries or offer the family large sums of money to buy up the originals, hastily flew Ursula

Reinhardt and her husband to New York City, where copies of the diaries were donated to the Yale Divinity School library at a press conference that was first announced by a prominent story in the *New York Times* and then covered by Peter Jennings of ABC-TV, CNN, and other world media organizations on December 12, 1996—the fifty-ninth anniversary of the fall of Nanking.

Historians were unanimous in their proclamation of the diaries' value. Many saw the diaries as more conclusive proof that the Rape of Nanking really did occur, and as an account told from the perspective of a Nazi, they found it fascinating. Rabe's account added authenticity to the American reports of the massacre, not only because a Nazi would have lacked the motive to fabricate stories of the atrocities, but also because Rabe's records included translations of the American diaries from English to German that matched the originals word for word. In the PRC, scholars announced to the *Renming Ribao* that the documents verified and corroborated much of the existing Chinese source material on the massacre. In the United States, William Kirby, a professor of Chinese history at Harvard University, told the *New York Times:* "It's an incredibly gripping and depressing narrative, done very carefully with an enormous amount of detail and drama. It will reopen this case in a very important way in that people can go through the day-by-day account and add 100 to 200 stories to what is popularly known."

Even Japanese historians pronounced the Rabe finding important. Kasahara Tokushi, a professor of modern Chinese history at Utsunomiya University, testified to the *Asahi Shimbun:* "What makes this report significant is the fact that, not only was it compiled by a German, an ally of Japan, Rabe submitted the report to Hitler to make him aware of the atrocities occurring in Nanking. The fact that Rabe, who was a vice-president of the Nazi Party, entreated Hitler, the top leader of a Japanese ally, to intervene testifies to the tremendous scale of the massacre." Hata Ikuhiko, a professor of modern Japanese history at the University of Chiba, added: "The meaning of this report is significant in the sense that a German, whose country was allied with Japan, depicts the atrocity of Nanking objectively. In that sense, it has more value as a historical document than the testimony of the American pastor. At the time, Germany was not sure which side to take, either Japan's or China's. However, Ribbentrop's inauguration as foreign minister fostered Germany's alliance with Japan. It is amazing how brave he was by trying to let Hitler know of the atrocity in Nanking at such a critical time."

10

THE FORGOTTEN HOLOCAUST: A SECOND RAPE

S THERE a child today in any part of the United States, and perhaps in many other parts of the world, who has not seen the gruesome pictures of the gas chambers at Auschwitz or read at least part of the haunting tale of the young Anne Frank? Indeed, at least in the United States, most schoolchildren are also taught about the devastating effects of the atomic bombs the United States dropped over the Japanese cities of Hiroshima and Nagasaki. But ask most Americans—children and adults alike, including highly educated adults—about the Rape of Nanking, and you will learn that most have never been told what happened in Nanking sixty years ago. A prominent government historian admitted to me that the subject had never once come up in all her years of graduate school. A Princeton-educated lawyer told me sheepishly that she was not even aware that China and Japan had been at war; her knowledge of the Pacific conflict of World War II had been limited to Pearl Harbor and Hiroshima. The ignorance extends even to Asian Americans in this country. One of them revealed her woeful grasp of geography and history when she asked me, "Nanking? What was that, a dynasty?"

An event that sixty years ago made front-page news in American newspapers appears to have vanished, almost without a trace. Hollywood has not produced a mainstream movie about the massacre—even though the story contains dramatic elements similar to those of *Schindler's List*. And until recently most American novelists and historians have also chosen not to write about it.

After hearing such remarks, I became terrified that the history of three hundred thousand murdered Chinese might disappear just as they themselves had disappeared under Japanese occupation and that the world might actually one day believe the Japanese politicians who have insisted that the Rape of Nanking was a hoax and a fabrication—that the massacre never happened at all. By writing this book, I forced myself to delve into not only history but historiography—to examine the forces of history and the process by which history is made. What keeps certain events in history and assigns the rest to oblivion? Exactly how does an event like the Rape of Nanking vanish from Japan's (and even the world's) collective memory?

One reason information about the Rape of Nanking has not been widely disseminated clearly lies in the postwar differences in how Germany and Japan handled their wartime crimes. Perhaps more than any other nation in history, the Germans have incorporated into their postwar political identity the concession that the wartime government itself, not just individual Nazis, was guilty of war crimes. The Japanese government, however, has never forced itself or Japanese society to do the same. As a result, although some bravely fight to force Japanese society to face the painful truth, many in Japan continue to treat the war crimes as the isolated acts of individual soldiers or even as events that simply did not occur.

In Japan competing stories of what happened during World War II continue to appear. According to a currently popular revisionist view, the country bears no responsibility for the wholesale murder of civilians anywhere during the war. The Japanese fought the war to ensure its own survival and to free Asia from the grip of Western imperialism. Indeed, in return for its noble efforts, Japan itself ended up as the ultimate victim at Hiroshima and Nagasaki.

This soothing perception of history still finds its way into Japanese history textbooks, which have either ignored the massacre at Nanking altogether or put a decidedly Japanese spin on the actions of the military. At the far end of the political spectrum, Japanese ultranationalists have threatened everything from lawsuits to death, even assassination, to silence opponents who suggest that these textbooks are not telling the next generation the real story.

But it is not just fanatical fringe groups that are trying to rewrite history. In 1990 Ishihara Shintaro, a leading member of Japan's conservative Liberal Democratic Party and the author of best-selling books such as *The Japan That Can Say No*, told a *Playboy* interviewer: "People say that the Japanese made a holocaust there [in Nanking], but that is not true. It is a story made up by the Chinese. It has tarnished the image of Japan, but it is a lie."

Naturally, this statement enraged scholars and journalists around the world. One proclaimed that "Japan's denial of the rape of Nanjing would be politically the same as German denial of the Holocaust." But the denunciations failed to silence Ishihara, who responded with a furious stream of counterattacks. In his rebuttals, Ishihara, in the face of overwhelming evidence to the contrary, asserted that the world never learned about the Nanking massacre until the International Military Tribunal of the Far East put people on trial for their role in it; that neither Japanese war correspondents nor Western reporters wrote about the massacre as it was occurring; that the *New York Times* correspondent Frank Tillman Durdin failed to witness any massacre; and that the Episcopalian minister John Magee saw only one person killed.

By the 1990s John Magee was, of course, no longer alive to defend himself, but his son, David Magee, made an effort to disprove Ishihara's statements. He gave interviews to the media and attended conferences on the Nanking massacre at which he read from his father's papers and displayed the actual camera his father used to film Japanese atrocities. Frank Tillman Durdin was alive, and he took direct action. Stepping out of retirement in San Diego to hold a press conference to refute Ishihara's remarks, Durdin explained to reporters that he had indeed written an article in 1937 that described the countryside from Shanghai to Nanking as peaceful, but that this article was written two months before the Japanese started their advance on Nanking.

Ishihara's other statements are readily refutable. Contemporaneous reports of the Rape appeared in dozens of Western newspapers, and even Japanese newspapers ran detailed stories about the massacre. As for Durdin, his articles were not only contemporaneous but published on the front pages of the *New York Times*. John Magee's letters contained descriptions like, "The raping of the women has been beyond description or imagination," and, "There were dead bodies in every street and alley in the city, so far as I could tell, and I went around quite extensively including Hsiakwan."

Not to be stopped, however, Ishihara went on to suggest that the Chinese claims of a massacre at Nanking helped influence the U.S. decision to bomb Hiroshima and Nagasaki. As each refutation of his earlier claims made it impossible for Ishihara to repeat them, he shifted his position slightly, but on one point he remained inflexible: even if the Germans had apologized for killing the Jews, that did not mean that the Japanese should do the same; under no circumstances should the Japanese ever admit they were guilty of any wrongdoing.

Ishihara's career remained intact despite the *Playboy* interview, but eventually others were not so lucky.

—One man who was sucked into the vortex of controversy was General Nagano Shigeto. In the spring of 1994, within days of his appointment to the cabinet-level position of justice minister, he gave an interview to the *Mainichi Shimbun* newspaper that turned out to be political suicide. "I think the Nanking Massacre and the rest was a fabrication," he told the newspaper. "I was in Nanking immediately afterwards." He went on to call the Korean comfort women "licensed prostitutes," not sex slaves, and to argue that Japan had no choice but to go to war because it was "in danger of being crushed." The violent reaction to his statements across Asia forced Nagano to resign in disgrace.

—In September 1986, Fujio Masayuki, the Japanese minister of education, sabotaged his career when he declared that the Rape of Nanking was "just a part of war." In an interview with *Bungei Shunju* magazine, Fujio defended the actions of the Japanese during the Nanking massacre and claimed that the number of dead had been exaggerated. He also said that Korea was partly to blame for its annexation by Japan in 1910, that Korea willingly accepted colonization, and that the Tokyo War Crimes Trial was "racial revenge" meant to "rob Japan of her power." Though Fujio made these comments only "to restore the Japanese spirit through history and tradition," they cost him his job. That month Japanese Prime Minister Nakasone Yasuhiro dismissed him from his post.

—Okuno Seisuki, who had been the prefectural director of the notorious *Kempeitai* (the secret Japanese military police) during the war, rose after the war to become the Japanese minister of justice and even the minister of education. By 1988 Okuno had become the Japanese land agency chief and the third most senior member of the cabinet. But Okuno's undoing came that spring when he visited the Yasukuni Shrine in Tokyo (where Japanese class A war criminals are enshrined and worshipped) and revealed his true attitudes about World War II. "There was no intention of aggression," Okuno told reporters. "The white race made Asia into a colony, but only Japan has been blamed. Who was the aggressor country? It was the white race. I don't see why Japanese are called militarists and aggressors." His statements provoked an uproar across Asia, prompting Okuno to adjust his wording: "I didn't say Japan wasn't an aggressor. I said it wasn't the only aggressor." By May, Okuno had been forced to resign, but he remained unrepentant to the end. He had stepped down, Okuno said, only under pressure from the government, not because he wished to retract his statements.

—In August 1994, Sakurai Shin, the director general of the Japanese environmental agency, remarked that Japan did not go to war with the intent to commit aggression. In response to China's angry protests (a PRC Foreign Ministry spokesman announced that "the Chinese government regrets that, once again, a Japanese cabinet minister has brazenly made remarks which distort historical facts"), Murayama Tomiichi ended up apologizing for Sakurai's remarks. He also rebuked Sakurai by calling the remarks "inappropriate" and forced the director general to hold a midnight press conference to retract his statement.

—In 1995 Hashimoto Ryutaro, the minister for international trade and industry and a powerful man in the Liberal Democratic Party (he would later become the prime minister of Japan), announced that it was Japan's intention only to fight the United States, Britain, and "others" during World War II. While Japan was aggressive toward China, he said, it really had no intention of invading other Asian countries.

The official denials continued even as this book was going to press. Kajiyama Seiroku, the Japanese chief cabinet secretary, outraged several Asian countries when he stated that the sex slaves and rape victims of the Japanese imperial army during World War II were not slaves at all but willingly engaged in prostitution. In January 1997, he proclaimed that the comfort women of the Japanese army "went for the money" and were no different from the Japanese prostitutes who were working legally in Japan at the time. Amazingly, these comments came on the eve of weekend summit talks between Japanese Prime Minister Hashimoto Ryutaro and South Korean President Kim Young-sam, both of whom expressed deep anger over Kajiyama's remarks.

Kajiyama later made a gesture to apologize, though he infuriated critics because the apology seemed insulting and insincere. The cabinet secretary regretted that his comments "caused some unpleasantness at the Japan–South Korean summit, and misunderstanding among the South Korean people," but he refused to retract his original comments. This was not the first time Kajiyama's mouth had landed him in trouble. In 1990 he was forced to resign from his position as Japanese justice minister after comparing African Americans to prostitutes who come in and ruin a neighborhood.

THE TEXTBOOK CONTROVERSY

Perhaps one of the most sinister aspects of the malaise in Japanese education is the deliberate obstruction of important historical information about World War II through textbook censorship.

Almost from birth, Japanese children fight for footholds in the slippery pyramid of education, striving to reach the tip, which is admission to Todai, or Tokyo University. There are cram elementary schools to get into the right high school, where kids study from 9:00 P.M. to 6:00 A.M.; cram preparatory kindergartens to ensure admission into the right elementary school; even exclusive maternity wards that guarantee babies a ticket into the right nursery school.

But despite the "examination hell" for which the Japanese are famous, what do their schoolchildren learn about World War II?

Very little, as it turns out. The entire Japanese education system suffers from selective amnesia, for not until 1994 were Japanese schoolchildren taught that Hirohito's army was responsible for the deaths of at least 20 million Allied soldiers and Asian civilians during World War II. In the early 1990s a newspaper article quoted a Japanese high school teacher who claimed that his students were surprised to learn that Japan had been at war with the United States. The first thing they wanted to know was who won.

How does this happen? All textbooks used in Japan's elementary and secondary schools must first be approved by the Japanese Ministry of Education. Critics in Japan note that social studies textbooks come under the heaviest scrutiny. For example, in 1977 the Ministry of Education reduced a section on World War II within a standard history book of several hundred pages to only six pages, which consisted mainly of pictures of the American firebombing of Tokyo, a picture of the ruins of Hiroshima, and a tally of Japan's war dead. The text neglected to mention the casualties on the other side, Japanese war atrocities, or the forced evacuations of Chinese and Korean prisoners to labor camps in Japan.

Much of this censorship might have gone unchallenged had it not been for the efforts of one brave crusader. In 1965 the Japanese historian Ienaga Saburo sued the Japanese government. This lawsuit was the beginning of a legal battle that would span three decades and gain the backing of thousands of sympathetic Japanese followers.

Those who have met Ienaga are struck by his frailty. The bald octogenarian historian trembles when he walks and his voice is hardly louder than a whisper. But underneath a powerful will is at work.

The Ministry interfered with Ienaga's attempts to document the Nanking massacre for schoolchildren. For example, in his textbook manuscript Ienaga wrote: "Immediately after the occupation of Nanking, the Japanese Army killed numerous Chinese soldiers and citizens. This incident came to be known as the Nanking Massacre." The examiner commented: "Readers might interpret this description as meaning that the Japanese Army unilaterally massacred Chinese immediately after the occupation. This passage should be revised so that it is not interpreted in such a way."

Finally, over Ienaga's protests, the passage was changed to: "While battling the fierce resistance of the Chinese armed forces, the Japanese Army occupied Nanking and killed numerous Chinese soldiers and civilians. This incident came to be known as the Nanking Massacre." That statement may have satisfied textbook censors as a compromise between Ienaga's argument and the ministry's position on the massacre. Unfortunately, the statement is simply not true, because it implies that the massacre occurred in the heat of battle.

The examiner demanded that Ienaga delete his description

of the Rape itself, claiming that "the violation of women is something that has happened on every battlefield in every era of human history. This is not an issue that needs to be taken up with respect to the Japanese Army in particular."

Even the word *aggression* was deemed taboo. *"Aggression,"* the censors wrote, "is a term that contains negative ethical connotations." The Ministry of Education also bristled at Ienaga's efforts to condemn Japanese wartime behavior. It took offense at the following passage: "The war was glorified as a 'holy war' and the Japanese Army's defeat and their brutal acts on the battlefield were completely concealed. As a result, the majority of the Japanese people were not able to learn the truth and they were placed in a position where they had no choice but to cooperate enthusiastically in this reckless war." The Ministry of Education deleted this passage on the grounds that the expressions "the Japanese Army's brutal acts" and "this reckless war" were "unilateral criticism of Japan's position and actions" during World War II.

In 1970, when he actually won his case (Sugimoto Ryokichi, the judge for the Tokyo district court, ruled that the screening of textbooks should not go beyond correction of factual and typographical errors), extremists fired off death threats to the plaintiff attorneys, the judge, and Ienaga himself, while thugs kept the scholar awake by banging pots and pans outside his home and screaming slogans. The police had to escort Ienaga and his counsel in and out of court through a secret door.

With the exception of an award that Ienaga received in 1948 (when, he admits, he was "politically tone deaf"), he has been consistently ignored by the official committees that dole out national prizes in history. The historian has won, nevertheless, a place in history itself. The tremendous publicity that Ienaga receives for his efforts arouses foreign protests that force change upon the highly conservative Ministry of Education. By the 1980s years of lawsuits and political activism were beginning to pay off. In 1982 the distortion of the history of the Rape of Nanking in Japanese high school history textbooks had become such a hot issue in Japan that it created an international diplomatic crisis. All four of Japan's major national newspapers carried headlines on the subject. Chinese and Korean officials also filed formal protests, accusing the Japanese of trying to obliterate from memory the history of their aggression to lay the basis for reviving militarism in the younger generation. The Japanese textbook examination council, however, tried to defend itself by telling reporters: "It was not fair to describe the Nanking atrocity in three to five lines while mentioning Soviet or American atrocities against the Japanese in only one line or two."

In the end, the publicity from the textbook controversy accomplished two things. One was the dismissal of Japan's education minister, Fujio Masayuki, who had rigorously defended the ministry's policy of whitewashing World War II history. The second was a heightened awareness inside the ministry that the Nanking massacre was something they could no longer ignore. Before Fujio's dismissal, the National Conference for the Defense of Japan had prepared a right-wing history textbook that summed up the Nanking massacre in this manner: "The battle of Nanking was extremely severe. China has asked Japan to reflect regarding casualties on the part of the Chinese army and civilians." But after Fujio's dismissal, the Ministry of Education rewrote the passage to read: "The battle in Nanking was extremely severe. After Nanking fell, it was reported that the Japanese army killed and wounded many Chinese soldiers and civilians, thus drawing international criticism."

Of course, the issue of textbook censorship is far from over. Rather than denying the massacre outright, some officials in Japan now focus on minimizing its scale. In 1991 screeners at the ministry ordered textbook authors to eliminate all reference to the numbers of Chinese killed during the Rape of Nanking because authorities believed there was insufficient evidence to verify those numbers. Three years later the ministry even forced a textbook author to reduce the number of killings by Japanese soldiers during one day of the Nanking massacre from twenty-five thousand to fifteen thousand people. The original version of the textbook cited a diary account that twenty-five thousand captives were "put away" in a single day. But under pressure from the ministry, the textbook publisher backed down and shortened a quotation from the diary so that it read: "The Sasaki unit disposed of 15,000 people."

THE ACADEMIC COVER-UP

With few exceptions, the academic community in Japan has shied away from studying the Rape of Nanking. Some have argued that not enough time has gone by to render the subject worthy of historical study, or for historians to judge Japanese wrongdoing. Some even react indignantly to criticism of Japanese wartime misdeeds. ("How long must we apologize for the mistakes we have made?" one said heatedly.)

Others act as apologists for Japan and have even allied themselves with conservative Japanese ultranationalists to minimize the significance of the massacre and its death toll. One prominent revisionist who has launched his own crusade to distort the history of the Rape of Nanking and other aspects of World War II history is Fujioka Nobukatsu, a professor of education at Tokyo University. Among his incendiary statements are the assertions that far fewer people were killed in the Rape of Nanking than the Chinese claim; that most of the victims of Nanking were guerrilla soldiers, not civilians; and that the Asian sex slaves, or "comfort women," of the Japanese military were ordinary prostitutes. Fujioka equated the women's receipt of financial compensation with "hitting the lottery" and demanded that the Japanese government not only retract the apologies it has offered to these women but strike information about them from Japanese history textbooks.

In Japan serious research on the Rape of Nanking has largely been left up to the efforts of those operating outside of traditional academic communities, such as freelance authors and journalists. Ono Kenji, a factory worker, is a prime example. In 1988 he started to interview farmers in his area who had served in the Aizu Wakamatsu Battalion during the Rape of Nanking. The bachelor Ono had time to devote himself to the subject because he enjoyed thirty-six-hour breaks between long factory shifts and had no family responsibilities. Six years later it was reported that Ono Kenji had visited some six hundred homes, interviewed two hundred people, photocopied twenty out of some thirty diaries, and videotaped interviews with seven people. Some of his findings appeared in the weekly magazine *Shukan Kinyobi* and were hailed as the first work on the Nanking massacre to be based solely on Japanese sources. In 1996, he coedited an important book on the subject of the Nanking massacre, but he continues to live under the constant shadow of possible Japanese retaliation, refusing even to be photographed for fear of falling prey to right-wing fanatics.

SELF-IMPOSED CENSORSHIP

In Japan censorship is practiced not only by the government when it tampers with textbooks but by the media, which police themselves. In many ways private-sector self-censorship can be more insidious than government censorship because it is subtler and harder to pinpoint.

What distributors did to a scene of the Rape of Nanking in the film *The Last Emperor* is a revealing illustration of Japanese self-censorship at work. In 1988 the Shochiku Fuji Distribution Company removed from Bernardo Bertolucci's film biography of Pu Yi a thirty-second scene depicting the Rape of Nanking. Bertolucci was furious, of course, when he found out. "Not only did the Japanese distributor cut the whole sequence of the 'Rape of Nanking' without my authorization and against my will, without even informing me, but they also declared to the press that myself and the producer, Jeremy Thomas, had made the original proposition to mutilate the movie," he announced. "This is absolutely false and revolting."

Bertolucci's outcry forced the distributors to restore the excised scene immediately. They offered a variety of excuses for their behavior. Kubotani Motoyuki, director of Shochiku Fuji, apologized for the "confusion and misunderstanding," explaining that his company thought the Nanking scene was simply "too sensational" to be shown in Japan. "Cutting the film was our voluntary decision. We had no idea that it would become such a big issue," he said. Saito Mitsuhiro, another spokesman for Shochiku Fuji, told reporters that the scene was removed "out of respect for Japanese audiences." Nakane Takehiko, a Japanese film critic, speculated that the decision to cut the scene arose from both the distributors' pusillanimity and the threat of ultranationalist violence. "I believe the film's distributors and many theatre owners were afraid these right-wing groups might cause trouble outside the theaters," the critic told reporters. "Some of these people still believe that Japan's actions in China and during the war were part of some sacred crusade."

DEBATES ON THE NANKING MASSACRE

Japanese who find the courage to write books about the Rape of Nanking often face unrelenting attacks. Take the example of Hora Tomio and Honda Katsuichi. Hora, a professor of Japanese history at Waseda University, visited China in 1966 to investigate Japanese atrocities in China; he later published his research on the Nanking massacre in several books. Honda Katsuichi was a prize-winning journalist at the *Asahi Shimbun* who broke the taboo against discussing the Nanking massacre in the Japanese press by going to mainland China in the 1970s and 1980s to interview survivors. His findings, serialized first in the *Asahi Shimbun* and other journals, were later expanded into full-length books. Both Hora and Honda reached the conclusion that Japanese soldiers had killed some three hundred thousand people in Nanking between 1937 and 1938.

Both also faced a vicious backlash in Japan. One vociferous critic of Hora and Honda was the ultraconservative author Suzuki Akira, who challenged their findings in an article entitled "The Illusion of the Nanjing Massacre." Suzuki charged that some of Honda's and Hora's stories were fabricated, that insufficient primary source material existed to substantiate the massacre, and that the Rape of Nanking was an "illusion." The book that resulted from his articles won the *Bungei Shunju* Prize in nonfiction and received eulogies from literary critics as "admirable" and "courageous." When Hora published a series

of rebuttals to Suzuki, several famous Japanese writers immediately sprang to Suzuki's defense.

Another critic was Tanaka Masaaki, a man who claimed to
be Matsui Iwane's protégé. In 1984 he published an
anti-Honda book called *The Fabrication of the "Nanking Massacre,"* using material from Matsui's wartime diary. Accusing
Honda of spreading "enemy propaganda," Tanaka argued that,
unlike in Europe or China, "you won't find one instance of
planned, systematic murder in the entire history of Japan."
This is because, he wrote, the Japanese have "a different sense
of values" from Westerners and the Chinese. Revisionists ral-
lied behind Tanaka and joined his attacks on Honda and Hora.
The right-wing author Watanabe Shoichi, who wrote a foreword to Tanaka's book, also blasted Honda for heaping guilt
"not only on the Japanese officers and men of the time, but on
all Japanese, indeed on our children yet to be born."

A debate soon raged between the two camps. There was the
liberal "massacre faction," which consisted of Hora, Honda,
and their supporters, and the conservative "illusion faction"
led by Suzuki and Tanaka. The liberal camp published its findings in the *Asahi Shimbun* and other journals, while the conservatives contributed to right-wing publications like *Bungei
Shunju, Shokun!,* and *Seiron.* The liberals demanded that the
Japanese government apologize for its crimes in China, while
the conservatives considered such an apology an insult to veterans and a foreign interference in Japanese internal affairs.

Ironically, attempts to disprove the Nanking massacre back-
fired when the revisionists themselves began to probe into the
subject for ammunition against the "massacre faction." For instance, in the 1980s *Kaikosha*, a fraternity of army cadet school
graduates, asked its eighteen thousand members to come forward with eyewitness accounts to discredit the Nanking massacre. To the dismay of the "illusion faction," many *Kaikosha*
members confirmed the details of the Rape of Nanking and described atrocities that horrified even hard-core Japanese conservatives. A former officer under Matsui estimated that some
120,000 captives were killed under the orders of a staff officer,
although later, no doubt under pressure, he changed the figure

to "no less than tens of thousands." But his testimony scuttled the entire purpose of the survey, and moved even an editor of *Kaikosha*'s journal to write in the concluding part of the series that "there was no excuse for such massive illegal executions. As someone related to the old Japanese Army, I have to apologize deeply to the Chinese people."

But the most embarrassing incident was yet to come. In 1985 a popular history journal, *Rekishi to jinbutsu*, discovered as many as nine hundred errors in the newly published Matsui wartime diary. Most of them were intentional attempts to falsify primary documents, a revelation that scandalized historians across Japan. Still more disturbing, the author of these alterations was none other than Tanaka Masaaki, who had proclaimed himself a staunch critic of historical distortion.

INTIMIDATION

What happened to Azuma Shiro, the first Japanese veteran to admit openly his crimes in Nanking, is a spectacular example of the system of Japanese intimidation at its worst. In 1987 he created a sensation when he became the first former Japanese soldier to apologize in public for his role in the Nanking massacre. On the eve of his departure to Nanking to participate in a fifty-year memorial ceremony of the great Rape, he gave interviews to newspaper and television reporters at a press conference in Kyoto. The result was an avalanche of criticism and death threats. To protect himself, Azuma retired from his company and moved with his wife into a house in a tiny village outside Kyoto, where he kept an arsenal of weapons, such as truncheons, clubs, pepper sprays, chains, and knuckle dusters.

The troubles for Motoshima Hitoshi, the mayor of Nagasaki, began when he was asked by a Communist Party member in the city assembly what he thought of the emperor's wartime guilt. It was December 7, 1988, the forty-seventh anniversary of the attack on Pearl Harbor. Emperor Hirohito was slowly dying of cancer, and the nation was mourning the passing of the Showa era by muting the holiday festivities.

Motoshima responded that, having read accounts of the war from abroad and served as a soldier himself, he believed that the emperor bore responsibility for the war. The response to his statement was immediate. The next day enraged city legislators and the local branch of the Liberal Democratic Party demanded that the mayor retract his words. But Motoshima refused, announcing that he could not "betray his own heart."

His opponents then embarked on a violent campaign of harassment and intimidation calculated to bring the mayor to his knees. The Liberal Democrats not only dismissed him as the counsel to their organization but succeeded in convincing the prefectural governor to refuse to cooperate politically with the mayor. Right-wing groups even called for Motoshima's death. On December 19, 1988, twenty-four ultranationalist groups drove through Nagasaki on thirty loudspeaker trucks, blasting their demands for "divine retribution" through Motoshima's death. Two days later the number of groups demonstrating in Nagasaki had grown to sixty-two, and the number of loudspeaker trucks to eighty-two. Representatives from numerous conservative organizations, including the office for Shinto shrines, called for his impeachment. Less than two weeks after Hirohito's death on January 7, 1989, a right-wing fanatic shot Motoshima in the back. The bullet punctured his lungs, but miraculously, the mayor survived. The assassination attempt thrilled extremists across the nation, many of whom proclaimed the deed as nothing less than "divine punishment."

EPILOGUE

THE RAPE OF NANKING was only one incident in a long saga of Japanese barbarism during nine years of war. Before the great massacre, Japan had already earned notoriety as the first country in Asia to break the taboo and use airpower not only as a battlefield weapon but as a means of terrorizing civilian populations. Then it launched its armed forces on a campaign of slaughter that started in Shanghai, moved through Nanking, and proceeded inland.

While there was no Japanese equivalent of a "final solution" for the Chinese people, the imperial government endorsed policies that would wipe out everyone in certain regions in China. One of the deadliest was the "Three-all" policy ("Loot all, kill all, burn all") in northern China, where Communist Chinese guerrillas had fought the Japanese furiously and effectively. In his diary, a frustrated Japanese colonel reveals the cruel simplicity of this policy: "I have received orders from my superior officer that every person in this place must be killed."

The result was a massive terrorist campaign in 1941 designed to exterminate everyone in the northern Chinese countryside. It reduced the population there from 44 million to 25 million people. At least one author on China, Jules Archer, believes that the Japanese killed most of the 19 million people who disappeared from the region, though other scholars speculate that millions must have fled to safer ground. R. J. Rummel, author of *China's Bloody Century*, points out that even if only 5 percent of the population loss consisted of murder victims, that would still amount to nearly 1 million Chinese.

The Japanese also waged ruthless experiments in biological warfare against the Chinese. Some of it was retaliatory and directed against Chinese villages suspected of helping American fliers during the April 1942 Doolittle raid of Tokyo. In areas that may have served as landing zones for the bombers, the Japanese massacred a quarter-million civilians and plowed up every Chinese airfield within an area of twenty thousand square miles. Here as well as elsewhere during the war, entire cities and regions were targeted for disease. We now know that Japanese aviators sprayed fleas carrying plague germs over metropolitan areas like Shanghai, Ningpo, and Changteh, and that flasks of disease-causing microbes—cholera, dysentery, typhoid, plague, anthrax, paratyphoid—were tossed into rivers, wells, reservoirs, and houses. The Japanese also mixed food with deadly germs to infect the Chinese civilian and military population. Cakes laced with typhoid were scattered around bivouac sites to entice hungry peasants; rolls syringed with typhoid and paratyphoid were given to thousands of Chinese prisoners of war before they were freed.

The final death count was almost incredible, between 1,578,000 and 6,325,000 people. R. J. Rummel gives a prudent estimate of 3,949,000 killed, of which all but 400,000 were civilians. But he points out that millions more perished from starvation and disease caused in large part by Japanese looting, bombing, and medical experimentation. If those deaths are added to the final count, then one can say that the Japanese killed more than 19 million Chinese people in its war against China.

It is impossible for most people to imagine exactly what went through the minds of Japanese soldiers and officers as they committed the atrocities. But many historians, eyewitnesses, survivors, and the perpetrators themselves have theorized about what drove the naked brutality of the Japanese imperial army.

Some Japanese scholars believe that the horrors of the Rape of Nanking and other outrages of the Sino-Japanese War were caused by a phenomenon called "the transfer of oppression." According to Tanaka Yuki, author of *Hidden Horrors: Japanese War Crimes in World War II*, the modern Japanese army had great potential for brutality from the moment of its creation for two reasons: the arbitrary and cruel treatment that the military inflicted on its own officers and soldiers, and the hierarchical nature of Japanese society, in which status was dictated by proximity to the emperor. Before the invasion of Nanking, the Japanese military had subjected its own soldiers to endless humiliation. Japanese soldiers were forced to wash the underwear of officers or stand meekly while superiors slapped them until they streamed with blood. Using Orwellian language, the routine striking of Japanese soldiers, or *bentatsu*, was termed an "act of love" by the officers, and the violent discipline of the Japanese navy through *tekken seisai*, or "the iron fist," was often called *ai-no-muchi*, or "whip of love."

It has often been suggested that those with the least power are often the most sadistic if given the power of life and death over people even lower on the pecking order, and the rage engendered by this rigid pecking order was suddenly given an outlet when Japanese soldiers went abroad. In foreign lands or colonized territories, the Japanese soldiers—representatives of the emperor—enjoyed tremendous power among the subjects. In China even the lowliest Japanese private was considered superior to the most powerful and distinguished native, and it is easy to see how years of suppressed anger, hatred, and fear of authority could have erupted in uncontrollable violence at Nanking. The Japanese soldier had endured in silence whatever his superiors had chosen to deal out to him, and now the Chinese had to take whatever he chose to deal out to them.

A second factor in the atrocities, scholars believe, is the virulent contempt that many in the Japanese military reserved for Chinese people—a contempt cultivated by decades of propaganda, education, and social indoctrination. Though the Japanese and the Chinese share similar if not identical racial features (which in a distorted way may have threatened the Japanese vision of themselves as unique), there were those in the imperial army who saw the Chinese as subhuman beings whose murder would carry no greater moral weight than squashing a bug or butchering a hog. In fact, both before and during the war members of the Japanese military at all levels frequently compared the Chinese to pigs. For example, a Japanese general told a correspondent: "To be frank, your view of Chinese is totally different from mine. You regard the Chinese as human beings while I regard the Chinese as pigs." A Japanese officer in Nanking who bound Chinese captives together in groups of ten, pushed each group into a pit, and burned them excused his actions by explaining that his feelings when committing these murders were identical to those he had when he slaughtered pigs. In 1938 the Japanese soldier Azuma Shiro confided in his diary at Nanking that "a pig is more valuable now than the life of a [Chinese] human being. That's because a pig is edible."

A third factor was religion. Imbuing violence with holy meaning, the Japanese imperial army made violence a cultural imperative every bit as powerful as that which propelled Europeans during the Crusades and the Spanish Inquisition. "Every single bullet must be charged with the Imperial Way, and the end of every bayonet must have the National Virtue burnt into it," one Japanese general declared in a speech in 1933.

Few Japanese doubted the righteousness of their mission in China. Nagatomi Hakudo, a former Japanese soldier who participated in the Rape of Nanking, said he had been reared to believe that the emperor was the natural ruler of the world, that the Japanese were racially superior to the rest of the world, and that it was the destiny of Japan to control Asia. When a local Christian priest asked him, "Who is greater, God or the emperor of Japan?," he had no doubt that "the emperor" was the correct answer.

With an entity higher than God on its side, it was not difficult for the Japanese military to take the next step—adopting the belief that the war, even the violence that came with it, would ultimately benefit not only Japan but its victims as well. Some perceived atrocity as a necessary tool to achieve a Japanese victory that would serve all and help create a better China under Japan's "Greater East Asian Co-Prosperity Sphere." This attitude echoes that of the Japanese teachers and officers who beat their students and soldiers senseless while insisting, between blows, that it was all done for their own good.

Perhaps it was General Matsui Iwane who summed up the prevailing mentality of self-delusion best when he attempted to justify Japanese oppression of China. Before he left for Shanghai in 1937, he told his supporters: "I am going to the front not to fight an enemy but in the state of mind of one who sets out to pacify his brother." Later he would say of the invasion of China:

> The struggle between Japan and China was always a fight between brothers within the "Asian Family." . . . It had been my belief during all these days that we must regard this struggle as a method of making the Chinese undergo self reflection. We do not do this because we hate them, but on the contrary *we love them too much*. It is just the same as in a family when an elder brother has taken all that he can stand from his ill-behaved younger brother and has to chastise him in order to make him behave properly.

Whatever the course of postwar history, the Rape of Nanking will stand as a blemish upon the honor of human beings. But what makes the blemish particularly repugnant is that history has never written a proper end for the story. Even in 1997, the

Japanese as a nation are still trying to bury the victims of Nanking—not under the soil, as in 1937, but into historical oblivion. In a disgraceful compounding of the offense, the story of the Nanking massacre is barely known in the West because so few people have tried to document and narrate it systematically to the public.

This book started out as an attempt to rescue those victims from more degradation by Japanese revisionists and to provide my own epitaph for the hundreds upon thousands of unmarked graves in Nanking. It ended as a personal exploration into the shadow side of human nature. There are several important lessons to be learned from Nanking, and one is that civilization itself is tissue-thin. There are those who believe that the Japanese are uniquely sinister—a dangerous race of people who will never change. But after reading several file cabinets' worth of documents on Japanese war crimes as well as accounts of ancient atrocities from the pantheon of world history, I would have to conclude that Japan's behavior during World War II was less a product of dangerous people than of a dangerous government, in a vulnerable culture, in dangerous times, able to sell dangerous rationalizations to those whose human instincts told them otherwise. The Rape of Nanking should be perceived as a cautionary tale—an illustration of how easily human beings can be encouraged to allow their teenagers to be molded into efficient killing machines able to suppress their better natures.

Another lesson to be gleaned from Nanking is the role of power in genocide. Those who have studied the patterns of large-scale killings throughout history have noted that the sheer concentration of power in government is lethal—that only a sense of absolute unchecked power can make atrocities like the Rape of Nanking possible. In the 1990s R. J. Rummel, perhaps the world's greatest authority on *democide* (a term he coined to include both genocide and government mass murder), completed a systematic and quantitative study of atrocities in both the twentieth century and ancient times, an impressive body of research that he summed up with a play on the famous Lord Acton line: "Power kills, and absolute power kills absolutely." The less restraint on power within a government, Rummel found, the more likely that government will act on the whims or psychologically generated darker impulses of its leaders to wage war on foreign governments. Japan was no exception, and atrocities such as the Rape of Nanking can be seen as a predictable if not inevitable outgrowth of ceding to an authoritarian regime, dominated by a military and imperial elite, the unchallenged power to commit an entire people to realizing the sick goals of the few with the unbridled power to set them.

And there is yet a third lesson to be learned, one that is perhaps the most distressing of all. It lies in the frightening ease with which the mind can accept genocide, turning us all into passive spectators to the unthinkable. The Rape of Nanking was front-page news across the world, and yet most of the world stood by and did nothing while an entire city was butchered. The international response to the Nanking atrocities was eerily akin to the more recent response to the atrocities in Bosnia-Herzegovina and Rwanda: while thousands have died almost unbelievably cruel deaths, the entire world has watched CNN and wrung its hands. One could argue that the United States and other countries failed to intervene earlier to prevent the Nazis from carrying out their "final solution" because the genocide was carried out in wartime secrecy and with such cold efficiency that until Allied soldiers liberated the camps and saw with their own eyes the extent of the horror, most people could not accept the reports they had been getting as literally true. But for the Rape of Nanking, or for the murders in the former Yugoslavia, there can be no such excuse. The Nanking atrocities were splashed prominently across the pages of newspapers like the *New York Times*, while the Bosnia outrages were played out daily on television in virtually every living room. Apparently some quirk in human nature allows even the most unspeakable acts of evil to become banal within minutes, provided only that they occur far enough away to pose no personal threat.

Sad to say, the world is still acting as a passive spectator to the second Japanese rape—the refusal of the Japanese to apologize for or even acknowledge their crimes at Nanking, and the attempts by Japanese extremists to erase the event from world history. To get a better handle on the magnitude of the injustice, one only has to compare the postwar restitution that the governments of Japan and Germany have made to their wartime victims. While it is certainly true that money alone cannot give back to murder victims their lost lives or erase from memory the tortures the survivors endured, it can at least convey that what was done to the victims represented the evil of others.

As of 1997 the German government has paid at least DM 88 billion in compensation and reparations and will pay another DM 20 billion by the year 2005. If one factors in all the money the Germans have paid in compensation to individual victims, restitution for lost property, compensatory pensions, payments based on state regulations, final restitution in special cases, and money for global agreements with Israel and sixteen other nations for war damages, the total comes to almost DM 124 billion, or almost $60 billion. The Japanese have paid close to nothing for their wartime crimes. In an era when even the Swiss have pledged billions of dollars to create a fund to replace what was stolen from Jewish bank accounts, many leading officials in Japan continue to believe (or pretend to believe) that their country did nothing that requires compensation, or even apologies, and contend that many of the worst misdeeds their government has been accused of perpetrating never happened and that evidence that they did happen was fabricated by the Chinese and other Japan bashers.

The Japanese government has taken the position that all wartime reparation issues were resolved by the 1952 San Francisco Peace Treaty. A close reading of the treaty, however, reveals that the issue was merely postponed until Japan was in a better financial situation. "It is recognized that Japan should pay reparations to the Allied Powers," the treaty states in chapter 5, article 14. "Nevertheless it is also recognized that the resources of Japan are not presently sufficient, if it is to maintain a viable economy, to make complete reparations for all such damage and suffering and at the same time meet its other obligations."

One of the greatest ironies of the cold war is that Japan not only eluded its responsibility to pay reparations but received billions of dollars in aid from the United States, which helped build its former enemy into an economic powerhouse and competitor. Now there is considerable concern in Asia about the prospect of renewed militarism among the Japanese people. During the Reagan administration the United States pushed Japan to beef up its military power—something that alarmed many who had suffered years of Japanese wartime agression. "Those who ignore history tend to become its victims," warned Carlos Romulo, the Philippine foreign minister and Pulitzer Prize winner who served as General Douglas MacArthur's aide-de-camp during World War II and understood the competitive national spirit engendered by the Japanese culture. "The Japanese are a very determined people; they have brains. At the end of World War II, no one thought that Japan would become the foremost economic power in the world—but they are. If you give them the chance to become a military power—they will become a military power."

But the cold war has ended, China is fast emerging from the chrysalis of communism, and other Asian nations that were bullied by Japan during the war may challenge it as they grow ascendant in the international economic arena. The next few years may well witness giant strides in activism regarding Japanese wartime crimes. The American public is growing demographically more Asian. And unlike their parents, whose careers were heavily concentrated in scientific fields, the younger generations of Chinese Americans and Chinese Canadians are fast gaining influence in law, politics, and journalism—professions historically underrepresented by Asians in North America.

Public awareness of the Nanking massacre increased substantially between the time I first started to research this book and the time I finished it. The 1990s saw a proliferation of novels, historical books, and newspaper articles about the Rape of Nanking, the comfort women, Japanese medical experimentation on wartime victims, and other Japanese World War II atrocities. As of 1997 the San Francisco school district plans to include the history of the Rape of Nanking in its curriculum, and blueprints have even been drawn up among Chinese real estate developers to build a Chinese holocaust museum.

As this book neared completion, the U.S. government was starting to respond to activist demands to pressure the Japanese to confront their wartime past. On December 3, 1996, the Department of Justice established a watch list of Japanese war criminals in order to bar them from entering the country. In April 1997, former U.S. Ambassador Walter Mondale told the press that Japan needs to face history honestly and directly and expressed his wish that Japan make a full apology for its war crimes. The Rape of Nanking even made its way into a bill that will soon be introduced into the U.S. House of Representatives. Through the spring of 1997, legislators worked with human rights activists to draft a bill that will condemn Japan for the maltreatment of U.S. and other prisoners during World War II and demand an official apology and compensation for its wartime victims.

The movement to force the Japanese government to face the full truth about the legacy of its wartime government is gaining support even in Japan, where official denials of wartime atrocities have aroused considerable shame and embarrassment among those citizens who see themselves as more than simply and solely Japanese. A vocal minority is convinced that their government must acknowledge its past if it expects to command trust from its neighbors in the future. In 1997 the Japanese Fellowship of Reconciliation released the following statement:

> In the past war, Japan was arrogant and pompous, behaved as aggressors in other Asian countries and brought misery to a great number of people, especially in China. For fifteen years around the 1930s, Japan continued to make war against the Chinese. War actions continued and victimized tens of millions of people. Here, we sincerely would like to apologize for Japan's past mistakes and beg your forgiveness.

The present generation in Japan faces a critical choice. They can continue to delude themselves that the war of Japanese aggression was a holy and just war that Japan happened to lose solely because of American economic power, or they can make a clean break from their nation's legacy of horror by acknowledging the truth: that the world is a better place because Japan lost the war and was not able to impose its harsh "love" on more people than it did. If modern Japanese do nothing to protect the truth, they run the risk that history will leave them as tarnished as their wartime ancestors.

Japan carries not only the legal burden but the moral obligation to acknowledge the evil it perpetrated at Nanking. At a minimum, the Japanese government needs to issue an official apology to the victims, pay reparations to the people whose lives were destroyed in the rampage, and, most important, educate future generations of Japanese citizens about the true facts of the massacre. These long-overdue steps are crucial for Japan if it expects to deserve respect from the international community—and to achieve closure on a dark chapter that stained its history.

EPILOGUE FOR
THE 2011 EDITION

by Brett Douglas,
September 23, 2011

W HEN I FIRST MET my wife, Iris Chang, in October of 1988, she was a beautiful, brilliant, charming girl who was full of life. I wouldn't have been surprised if someone had told me she would someday write a best-selling book that would be translated into 15 languages. What does surprise me is that I am now writing an epilogue to *The Rape of Nanking* seven years after her death. With the energy, passion, and drive that Iris showed at age thirty, I thought it was likely she would be writing great books well in her eighties and nineties.

When we met, neither of us had dated more than a few times, but we soon both knew we were a perfect match. We were blessed to have sixteen very happy years together. At the time of this writing, two books have been published about Iris's life: *Finding Iris Chang* by Paula Kamen and *The Woman Who Could Not Forget* by her mother, Ying-Ying Chang. These are both good works, and I encourage those who want to learn more about Iris to read them. Iris's life ended far too soon, and because she was a private person, much of her life and death has been shrouded in some mystery. I'm grateful to Basic Books for giving me the opportunity to fill in some of the holes and to remove some of the mystery associated with Iris's life so her legacy and the legacy of her book can endure.

Ying-Ying Chang's *The Woman Who Could Not Forget* provides a detailed description of Iris's entire life, and I have no desire to try to improve upon that work. Instead, I'll focus on a few key factors I believe led to her success. Both of her parents were Harvard PhDs who spent their careers doing scientific research. Thus, Iris learned to value intellectual achievement at a very early age. She spent thousands of hours as a youth at the University of Illinois library and other local libraries learning to read and process information quickly. Iris compiled an exhaustive list of all Nobel Prize- and Pulitzer Prize–winning books and Academy Award–winning films, and she proceeded to read and watch each and every one. Her days off consisted of methodically working her way through these books and films.

Iris attended the University of Illinois's University High School, a tiny academic pressure cooker populated primarily by academically driven professors' children who had all passed a rigorous entrance exam. The high school has produced several Nobel Prize winners and many other graduates who went on to achieve extraordinary success. In 1985, Iris was one of the few women who entered the University of Illinois Urbana-Champaign's competitive Math and Computer Science program. She was on track to graduate in just over three years, but she changed her major to journalism when she was a few hours short of a degree. At the time, it was relatively rare for a girl to study Math and Computer Science, it was rare for someone to complete the program that quickly, and it was extremely rare for someone who had completed the program so easily to change majors at the very end.

Most would expect someone who changed majors after almost three years to be significantly behind her peers, but Iris soon made up the difference and won internships at *Newsweek,* the *Associated Press,* and the *Chicago Tribune.* While at the *Tribune,* she discovered her real passion was writing lengthy feature stories, so she applied and was admitted to the prestigious Writing Seminars program at Johns Hopkins University. While she was there, at the age of only twenty-two, she met her editor and later her agent, Susan Rabiner. Susan gave her a topic, and Iris started research on her first book, *The Thread of the Silkworm.*

When Iris completed her degree from Johns Hopkins, she moved to Santa Barbara, California, to live with me. Iris was always interested in film, so she took a portfolio of photos to a talent agency and was soon selected to be a dancer in an MC Hammer video. However, Iris had a MacArthur Foundation grant proposal due the very next day, so she declined their offer. We thought it was probably the first time anyone had ever turned down MC Hammer and his production company for that reason. Iris made the right decision. She won the MacArthur Foundation grant.

Iris later went on to win a National Science Foundation grant to continue her research on *The Thread of the Silkworm.* What was truly amazing was that Iris never completed a science degree, and she had no formal affiliation with any university or research institution.

Along with her beauty, her intelligence, and her education, two other factors contributed greatly to Iris's success. She was never shy about asking someone, no matter how famous, for help or advice, and she was always trying to improve herself. For instance, in 1991 Iris was very nervous about the prospect of giving a short toast in front of two hundred people at our wedding reception. Yet she consciously worked at public speaking so that by the time *The Rape of Nanking* was published in 1997, she could hold the attention of a thousand people for an hour or longer while she talked about her research and her books.

During the first ten years of our relationship, it was a true pleasure to watch Iris build herself from a sometimes shy and introverted person into "Super Iris," the famous author and historian who could write best-selling books, keep audiences enthralled with her speeches, and win debates on national television. It was much sadder to see "Super Iris" rapidly succumb to mental illness during the summer of 2004.

There remain a number of myths and misunderstandings about the life and career of Iris Chang. Even I still have a few questions of my own. I can, however, offer information that I think will offer clarity to readers of this book. The first misunderstanding has to do with whether there was a "Eureka! Moment." Iris attended a conference in Cupertino, California, late in 1994 where she saw photos from the Rape of Nanking. There is a common myth that Iris saw the photos and decided then and there that she had to write a book on the atrocity. This is a nice story, but it is entirely contrary to the way Iris did her work. Iris maintained a meticulous file of book ideas, which grew to 400 potential projects by 2004. Iris had heard stories about the Rape of Nanking as a child from her parents and grandparents. She told me shortly after we started dating in October 1988 of her desire to write a book about the Nanking massacre. As soon as she completed the final draft of her first book *The Thread of the Silkworm*, she determined that Japan's assault on Nanking was the most promising topic for her second book, and so she started research. A month later, in the fall of 1994, she attended the conference in Cupertino where she met with the group of activists who sponsored it. She saw many photographs of victims, and she became acquainted with many people who were to become extremely helpful to her in her research. Yet, somehow the idea got started that looking at the photographs at the conference gave her the inspiration to write the book, and that myth has continued to grow. Iris never made an impulsive career decision like that. Writing *The Rape of Nanking* was something she had planned for years, and she was researching the book already when she attended the conference.

Another myth is that the subject matter of *The Rape of Nanking* and the Bataan Death March led to her breakdown and her death. Iris completed *The Rape of Nanking* in early

1997 but never showed any real signs of mental illness until 2004. While she was researching *The Rape of Nanking* and the Bataan Death March, she read through an enormous amount of information. She provided almost daily updates of her progress to me, and she also discussed the material with her parents and several close friends. My impression was that rather than upsetting her, seeing the photos and reading the material energized her and drove her to do the best job she could to tell the stories. She expressed sadness that the people of Nanking who suffered so much in 1937 and 1938 were still living in severe poverty sixty years later. She developed a close attachment to many Bataan Death March veterans who suffered at the hands of the Japanese from 1942 through 1945. Many of those Bataan veterans were small-town Midwestern boys like me and many of her childhood friends, so she identified closely with them. Most were in their mid-eighties by that time, and by 2004, many had passed away or were diagnosed with terminal illnesses. The only time I saw Iris break down and cry on a work-related issue was when she heard that one of the Bataan veterans she befriended had passed away.

There is another myth that the demands of being a working mother contributed to her mental illness. During the two years between our son's birth and her breakdown, a full-time nanny cared for Christopher and did all the household cooking, cleaning, laundry, and grocery shopping. I spent a great deal of time caring for Christopher, and both my parents and Iris's parents helped care for him. It's difficult to conceive anyone having a better support system for childcare and domestic work than Iris had.

Another myth is that the CIA and the US government were responsible for her breakdown and her death. Iris herself believed this because she was forcefully apprehended and confined against her will in a psychiatric ward in Louisville. It was a terrifying experience for her, and after going several days with very little food, water, or sleep, she believed that the US government was behind it. She related this belief to several people during the last three months of her life, but I never saw any evidence to support her belief.

The final myth is that the Japanese government was somehow responsible for Iris's eventual suicide. Iris's life experiences gave her plenty of reason to be fearful of the Japanese. Iris's parents and their families all experienced the Japanese invasion and occupation of China from 1937 to 1945, so Iris heard terrifying stories about Japanese atrocities growing up. While she researched *The Rape of Nanking*, many of the people she worked with had lived through the Japanese invasion of China. When she was on tour promoting her books many former US servicemen, as well as people from Korea, China, Taiwan, Vietnam, Thailand, Malaysia, and the Philippines would seek her out to tell her their horror stories of the Japanese occupation and their fears about the Japanese government. The Japanese press and Japanese activists attacked her in every verbal way they could. She received a good deal of hate mail during 1998 and 1999 while she was actively promoting *The Rape of Nanking*. During that time, almost everything in Iris's life was giving her reason to fear the Japanese and providing positive feedback for that fear. However, the hate mail decreased and then stopped almost entirely after she focused her attention on her next book *The Chinese in America*. During the entire thirteen years I lived with Iris, I never saw any evidence of someone from Japan threatening her physical safety or doing anything to contribute to Iris's breakdown or her suicide.

Many have speculated that Iris was mentally ill prior to 2004. Part of this perception may be due to her background, and part of it may come from her career and lifestyle choices. Iris's parents lived through the Japanese invasion of China and the civil war between Mao's Communist forces and Chiang's Nationalist forces. They told Iris many of the horrific stories that they had seen and heard. During her writing career, she researched the Armenian Genocide, the rise of the Nazis and their persecution of the Jews, multiple World War II atrocities, the Chinese Civil War, the Great Leap Forward, and the Cultural Revolution. During the last few years of her life, the US government took several actions that disturbed Iris, most notably the Bush Administration's attack on Iraq in 2003. She was also disturbed by the attack and killing of the Branch

Davidians, the Clinton Administration's bombing of multiple Middle Eastern nations during the Monica Lewinsky scandal, the "Humanitarian Bombing" in Kosovo, the Bush Administration's hostility towards China in 2001, the loss of privacy and personal liberties from the Patriot Act, and the indefinite detention of suspected terrorists without charging them with a crime. Iris saw these as a progression of changes leading the United States towards becoming a society capable of atrocities similar to those she had studied. She would often engage people in lengthy discussions on these and similar subjects and on the potentially disastrous consequences should the current trends continue. In public, Iris always kept a tight hold on emotions, but in private conversations she would often get emotional discussing a topic that was important to her. Someone who engaged in occasional private conversations with Iris might have concluded that this was manic behavior. I think it was due to the fact that she had a great deal of passion on a variety of topics, and she had the energy and intellect to aggressively discuss her point of view. I didn't see a change in that aspect of her behavior from 1988 through 2004.

Iris was a goal-oriented person rather than a relationship-oriented person, so many times she was more focused on achieving her goals than on how she would be perceived by others. This created some problems early in her career when she was expected to ingratiate herself to employers, co-workers, editors, and publishers. After *The Rape of Nanking* was published, however, she knew she would never have to work for anyone else because her writing and speaking skills would be in demand. Very few people experience that kind of freedom at the age of thirty. Working for a company or organization does a great deal to make people conform. While workers get almost constant feedback from their supervisors and co-workers, Iris got none for the last thirteen years of her life. I think what some may have perceived to be unusual behavior was not a result of any mental illness but a reflection of the fact that she had the good fortune to behave as she wished.

Book tours took a heavy toll on her. The closest analogy I can make to Iris's book tours is a rock star on tour. Most mornings, Iris would wake up, head to the airport, fly to a new city, do the event, attend parties afterward, and then get to her hotel room late at night. At the events, people often told her their horror stories about what had happened to the Japanese's Prisoners of War and the civilians who lived in areas occupied by the Japanese during World War II. She would often repeat that same routine many days in a row. Iris lived that life for most of 1998, the first half of 1999, six weeks in 2003, and five weeks in 2004. Most of the people who met with her during the last seven years of her life did so when she was living this chaotic lifestyle.

Many have speculated about what caused Iris's breakdown. I don't know myself. Several different factors could have contributed to it. She *may* have had a genetic predisposition towards mental illness. Like Iris, one of her relatives had had a successful career until her mid-thirties when it abruptly fell apart, and she never worked again. During the first minute I met her, I thought she was a very charming lady, but she soon shifted the conversation to the people who hated her and wanted to kill her. She was tormented by the same thoughts that would plague Iris during the last three months of her life.

Iris finally stopped her one and a half years of promoting *The Rape of Nanking* in the summer of 1999. She intended to spend time at home resting and recuperating, and we tried to start a family. During the next months, Iris went through several miscarriages, causing wild hormonal swings that we later learned could hasten the onset of bipolar disorder. She was more volatile and excitable than at any other time prior to 2004. Someone meeting her then—who didn't understand her exhaustion from the travel and the hormonal swings—might have concluded she was mentally ill.

Iris also had unusual work habits. She went directly from being a college student to being a self-employed writer, so she never fell into the nine-to-five routine of most Americans. Throughout her career, she pulled frequent all-nighters to meet mostly self-imposed deadlines. Iris used a Franklin Planner to help squeeze in as much productivity as she possibly could each day. When she would receive a request to write a blurb for a soon to be published book, she always read the book cover to cover, then produced a carefully written endorsement for the book. As a result, she would work late into the night to avoid falling behind on her own projects. These work habits undoubtedly put her under more physical and mental stress as she entered her thirties and may have contributed to her breakdown.

Iris had other medical issues such as thrombophilia and a thyroid condition that accelerated her metabolism. She once told me the thyroid condition could cause mental illness if not treated properly with medication. When Iris had her breakdown, one doctor asked me to write down all the vitamins and supplements she was taking because the overuse of unregulated herbal supplements is a frequent cause of mental illness. When I opened up the cabinet where she kept them, I couldn't believe my eyes. Along with her multivitamins, I found many different bottles full of the following ingredients:

Hymenaea Courbaril Bark, Tabebuia Impiginosa barb, Schinus Molle bark, Peiveria Alliacea whole herb, and Cassia Occidentalis leaf, Cat's Claw vine bark, Physalis Angulata whole herb, Boerhaavia Diffusa whole herb, Petiveria Alliacea whole herb, Cassia Occidentalis leaf, Smilaxsp. root, Physalis Angulata leaf and stem, Schinus Molle bark, Petiveria Alliacea leaf and stem, Mirabilis Jalapa leaf, Achyrocline Satureoides leaf, Urva Usi leaf, Jatoba bark, Hymeneaea Courbaril, Chlorella, Garlic, Carageenan, L-Methioninie,L-Cysteine, L-Lysene Hcl, Activated Attapulgite (clay), Sodium Alginae, EDTA Calcium Disodium, Alpha Lipic Acid, Betaine Vanadyl, Sulfate Choline, Inositol, Para-Amino-Benzoic Acid, Rutin, Lemon Bioflavonoid Complex, Hesperidin Complex, Quercetin, Milk Thistle Extract, Coenzyme Q-10, L-Glutathione, Grape Seed Extract, L-Camitine, Artichoke Powder, Beet Juice Powder, Ginko Bilboa Extract, Lycopene, Chondroitin Sulfate A, Cilantro, Methyl Sulfonyl Methane, Taurine, L-Prline Hawthorne Berry Extract, Green Tea Extract, Aphanizomenon, Fresh Water Algae, Acacia Amylase, Glucomylase, Lipase, Protease, Invertase, Malt Diastese, Celulase, Bromelain, Lactase, Papain, Green Papaya, Apple Pectin, Ginger, Turmeric, Fennel, Bladderwrack, Nori, Wakeme, Peppermint,

Beets, Habanero Peppers, Jalapeno Peppers, African Peppers, Chinese Peppers, Thai Peppers, Korean Peppers, Japanese Peppers, Pumpkin Seed Oil, Burdock, PeachTree Leaves, Chamomile, Jaborandi, Sage Leaves, SD Alcohol and Methyl Salicylate Iodine from Kelp, Alfalfa, Dicalcium Phosphate, Stearic Acid, Magnesium Stearate, and Bilbery Extract.

Iris started promoting *The Rape of Nanking* at age twenty-nine, and she finished at age thirty-one. During her tour, she visited at least sixty-five cities, many of them multiple times. At that age, she seemed to be able to bounce back from the stresses of travel. However, she was thirty-five and thirty-six when she was promoting *The Chinese in America*. Her travel schedule was shorter but even more intense, and she wasn't able to recover like she had six years earlier. The Iris Chang who went on book tour in March 2004 was a very different person than the Iris Chang who returned five weeks later.

I believe Iris's prolonged fear and apprehension about Japanese right-wing extremists, her genetics, her multiple miscarriages, her countless all-nighters, her strenuous book tours, and her herbal supplements all may have contributed to her breakdown in Louisville in August of 2004. Paula Kamen wrote that one form of mental illness is the inability to control one's fears. This is how Iris's fears escalated:

When our son Christopher started showing signs of autism, she discovered that many believed vaccines were the cause. She dug deeper and found that vaccines and drugs given to Gulf War veterans caused various illnesses. Around the same time, we went to see the 2004 version of *The Manchurian Candidate*, in which the government used mind control on Gulf War soldiers. The movie heightened her anxiety. She spent the next few days preparing for an upcoming business trip to Louisville to meet with Colonel Arthur Kelly and interview survivors of the Bataan Death March. Instead of sleeping, she spent the next few nights visiting web sites on autism, Gulf War Syndrome, and many conspiracy theories. We were all quite concerned about her at the time she left for Louisville, but we thought if she went on the research trip she would focus on her work and not on all the conspiracies. However, her mind began to play tricks on her due to the lack of sleep. She believed that the government was trying to poison her, so she refused to eat or drink anything after she left our home. Her condition deteriorated rapidly due to the deprivation of food, water, and sleep. She called her mother in terrible condition, and her mother contacted Colonel Kelly. When Colonel Kelly and his wife, a retired nurse, saw her condition, they called for an ambulance. Iris had never met Colonel Kelly in person; she became convinced they were part of a conspiracy to do harm to her, so she tried to flee. Police and paramedics forced her to go to the Louisville Hospital for extensive tests. She was placed in the psychiatric ward, where, according to Iris, she was repeatedly threatened by the orderlies. By this time she was firmly convinced that they were trying to drug her or poison her, so she once again refused to eat, drink anything, or sleep while she was there. If Iris had her breakdown at home surrounded by people she loved and trusted, it would not have been nearly as traumatic for her. Instead, she concluded that the people who had tried to help her in Louisville were all part of a Bush Administration conspiracy to harm her. During the last three months of her life, we could never get her to let go of that belief.

After her parents brought her home from the Louisville hospital, we had trouble finding a good psychiatrist to treat her. To compound the problem, Iris was not a cooperative mental health patient. Iris's experience solving our fertility problems caused her to lose respect for most medical doctors. Iris would so thoroughly research the topic that she would overwhelm the doctors she met. After that experience, she had very little faith in most medical doctors. This was a time when we desperately needed to find a good psychiatrist. We even more desperately needed Iris to follow the treatment plan, but she fought it every step of the way.

Iris's parents and I thought it would be a good idea to bring her to a bipolar personality support group, so they brought her to a meeting at Stanford University. The people she saw there were not winning the battle with bipolar disorder. Almost none of them were working, and many were on five or six medications. Iris described them as zombies, and she said she would never allow herself to be medicated like that. Shortly afterwards, her psychiatrist formally diagnosed her with bipolar personality disorder, meaning she should be treated with mood-stabilizing drugs rather than antidepressant and antipsychotic drugs. The suicide risk for mental health patients goes up during changes in medication.

After Iris's death, her mother did a lot of research on the drugs prescribed to Iris, and she discovered that Asians may be more sensitive to many of the commonly prescribed drugs. These drugs have been tested on very few Asians because they make up such a small portion of the US population, so the medications pose more risk of side effects to Asian patients. This was likely the case with Iris. The powerful antipsychotic and mood-altering drugs she took seemed to cause many side effects on her.

Two days after the diagnosis and change in medication her mother found a gun safety course brochure from Reed's Gun Shop in Iris's purse. This was the first indication we had that she had any plans to buy a gun. When we questioned her, she told us she believed the US government was out to get her, and she needed a gun to protect herself. The combination of meeting the heavily medicated bipolar personality disorder patients, Iris's formal diagnosis of bipolar personality disorder, her change of medications, and the resulting side effects all put Iris in a very unstable state. Iris's parents, her psychiatrist, and I tried to find people who were successfully coping with bipolar personality disorder to talk to Iris and to give her encouragement, but we ran out of time.

After her experience in Louisville, Iris firmly believed the Bush Administration meant to do harm to her. She was hopeful that John Kerry would defeat George Bush in the November 2004 election, but Bush's victory was announced on November 3. Her thoughts of four more years of persecution were too much for her. The police investigation after her death concluded that she purchased the first handgun on the very next day.

The last factor that I believe led to Iris's suicide was something that no one else has mentioned: Pride. In her suicide note, she wrote:

"It is far better that you remember me as I was—in my heyday as a best-selling author—than the wild-eyed wreck who returned from Louisville."

On a personal level, Iris was completely unpretentious. She drove a Geo Metro for five years. If someone had stopped by our home unannounced, they would likely find Iris wearing glasses, no makeup, a t-shirt, and a baggy pair of sweats. However if Iris made a public appearance, her hair and makeup were always perfect, she wore her contacts and a conservative business suit, and she always had a speech prepared and rehearsed. She invested a tremendous amount of time and effort into building up and maintaining her public persona. I don't believe she felt like she could maintain that after her breakdown.

Iris wrote three books in her short life. Her first book, *The Thread of the Silkworm*, was a topic chosen by her editor at Basic Books, Susan Rabiner. Her last book, *The Chinese in America*, was a topic chosen by her publisher at Viking Penguin. *The Rape of Nanking* was the only book chosen by Iris. The one book she intended to write from a very young age spent several weeks on the best-seller list and was translated into 15 languages She was in a position where she had the financial resources and the influence in the publishing industry to write whatever she wanted for the rest of her life. It is difficult to say what she would have been able to accomplish if she had continued writing for another fifty years.

Since Iris has passed away, many people have said that she has inspired them to carry on her work. I've guided people to visit the Iris Chang collections in the Hoover Archives at Stanford University, at the University of California Santa Barbara, and at the University of Illinois. That's the only way to fully appreciate the tremendous amount of original research that went into all three of her books. The Hoover Archives contains a list of other books she had planned to write. I encourage anyone who wants to carry on her legacy to complete one of these projects.

Iris's dream was to have her books made into documentaries and feature films. Many claim to have done films based on *The Rape of Nanking*; however as of this writing, no producer has done a documentary film or a feature film on any one of her three books. Iris was not a religious person, but if she is looking down on us, nothing would make her happier than to see this happen.

There are many unsung heroes who are truly carrying on the work of Iris Chang. When our son Christopher started to show the first signs of autism in the summer of 2004, he could have had no better mother than the Iris Chang who researched and wrote three books from 1991 through 2002. That Iris Chang would have done the research necessary to put the best possible program in place to help Christopher achieve his potential. However, the Iris Chang of 2004 was already well on her way towards a mental breakdown. When Iris committed suicide, she left Christopher as a motherless two-year-old autistic child. Several women stepped in and partially filled the void left by Iris's mental illness and death. Our neighbor, Sun-Mi Cabral, and her sister, Sunny Park, cared for Christopher like he was their own child for most of the next year. Iris's mother, Ying-Ying Chang, cooked nutritious dinners for him for the next two years. After Christopher was diagnosed with autism, my girlfriend, Jiebing Shui, quit her job, moved in with us, became his step-mother, and focused full-time on getting him to his therapy sessions. His first adaptive behavioral analysis therapist, Hanna Almeda, made tremendous progress getting Christopher to communicate verbally with other people. However after Jiebing Shui became busy with our newborn son and Hanna Almeda accepted a position with the Palo Alto public schools, Christopher started to regress.

It was then that my parents, Ken and Luann Douglas, sold their retirement home and moved to Normal, Illinois, to be near Illinois State University because it had one of the best special education programs in the United States. I moved my family from San Jose, California, to the same community. My parents have spent their retirement years devoted to giving Christopher a chance to develop to his full potential. Melissa Watson has been Christopher's adaptive behavioral analysis therapist since 2007. Melissa has done more to help Christopher develop than any other person. Many other therapists have also worked with Christopher: Hannah Gomez, Monica Bozek, Tricia Ferguson, Susan Konkal, Sarah Conklen, Megan Watson, Grace Watson, Angela Watson, Rachael Wrage, Kristin Hunsburger, Bethany Ingrum, Gavin Meador, many therapists at Easter Seals in Bloomington, Illinois, and many therapists at The Autism Place in Normal, Illinois.

Iris was a hero for telling the story of the people who had suffered so much in Nanking during the winter of 1937 and 1938. She may have been a tragic hero because the same extraordinary motivation and drive that led her to achieve so much by age twenty-nine probably contributed to her breakdown and early death at age thirty-six. Iris influenced hundreds of thousands of people through her writing and on her books tours. I've met only a small fraction of the people she knew, and I'm still learning more about her seven years after her death.

ACKNOWLEDGMENTS

IN WRITING *The Rape of Nanking* I have incurred many debts. Many organizations and individuals were endlessly supportive of the book from its inception. While it is impossible to acknowledge all the people who shared their time and expertise with me over the years, many deserve special mention here.

My parents, Drs. Shau-Jin Chang and Ying-Ying Chang, were the first ones to tell me about the Rape of Nanking and to emphasize its importance in history. I am deeply moved by the countless hours they have spent reading the manuscript in draft form, translating key documents for me, and offering invaluable advice during lengthy discussions over the phone. They are the kind of parents most authors can only dream of having—wise, passionate, and inspirational. No one but me can truly understand what they have meant to me during the writing of this book.

My editor, Susan Rabiner, also recognized the historical significance of this book and encouraged me to write it. Over a period of weeks and months she not only gave this manuscript line-by-line scrutiny but greatly improved it with her brilliant perceptions. This she did for me despite her intense administrative responsibilities as editorial director and the personal pressures she endured shortly before her departure from Basic Books. There are few editors in the publishing world today who possess Susan Rabiner's combination of literary talent, knowledge of the craft of serious nonfiction, and genuine concern for the author. To have worked with her as extensively as I did was not only a joy but a privilege.

The Global Alliance for Preserving the History of World War II in Asia was tremendously supportive as I researched the Rape of Nanking and provided me with photographs, articles, and important contacts throughout the world. Within the Alliance, I am especially indebted to Ignatius and Josephine Ding, David and Cathy Tsang, Gilbert Chang, Eugene Wei, J. J. Cao, and Kuo-hou Chang.

Flesh was given to the text by those who helped translate important documents. To finish a book that exploited primary source material in four different languages (English, Chinese, Japanese, and German) I had to rely heavily on the kindness of friends, colleagues, and even strangers. My friend Barbara Masin, a brilliant high-tech executive fluent in five languages, gave freely of her valuable time to translate numerous German diplomatic reports and diaries into English. Satoko Sugiyama in San Diego volunteered to translate not only Japanese wartime diaries for me but also my correspondence with Shiro Azuma, a former Japanese soldier at Nanking.

The historian Charles Burdick and Martha Begemann of Hamburg helped me find the descendants of John Rabe, the former leader of the International Committee for the Nanking Safety Zone. I am beholden to Ursula Reinhardt, the granddaughter of John Rabe, for giving me detailed descriptions of Rabe's life and copies of his reports and diaries. Many thanks go also to Jeff Heynen of the *Asahi Shimbun* for giving me, out of the kindness of his heart, his excellent translations of Rabe's papers.

Several friends helped make my research trip to the East Coast a success. Nancy Tong in New York loaned me materials related to her excellent documentary, *In the Name of the Emperor.* Shao Tzuping and his family graciously gave me room, board, and hospitality in Rye, New York—even loaning me their car to make the commute to the Yale Divinity School Library in New Haven. Shen-Yen Lee (the former publisher of the *Chinese American Forum*), his wife, Winnie C. Lee, and historian Marian Smith selflessly provided me with transportation, housing, and emotional support during my stay in Washington, D.C. At the National Archives, John Taylor steered me to an incredible store of information on the Nanking massacre, helping me locate military and diplomatic reports, intercepts of Japanese Foreign Office communications, OSS records and transcripts, and exhibits of the International Military Tribunal for the Far East (IMTFE). At the Yale Divinity School Library, the archivists Joan Duffy and Martha Smalley were unfailingly kind as they introduced me to missionary diaries and photographs of the massacre.

The Pacific Cultural Foundation paid for my travel to Asia. In Nanking, Sun Zhaiwei, a professor and vice director of the Institute of History at the Jiangsu Academy of Social Sciences, and Duan Yueping, the assistant director of the Memorial Hall of the Victims of the Nanking Massacre by Japanese Invaders, shared with me invaluable Chinese documentation about the Rape of Nanking and gave me a thorough tour of the execution sites in the city. The interpreters Yang Xiaming and Wang Weixing worked long hours to help me translate the documents and the transcripts of videotaped interviews with survivors.

In the Republic of China, Lee En-han at the Institute of Modern History arranged for me to stay at the Academia Sinica as I continued my research on the massacre. Caroline Lin, a reporter at the *China Times*, graciously provided me with her contacts and files on the subject. The veterans Lin Baoding, Lin Rongkun, Cheng Junqing, Wang Wanyong, and Liu Yongzhong also gave me unprecedented access to their files.

Several survivors of the Nanking massacre relived the horror of the past to narrate their stories to me. They include Niu Xianming in Los Angeles; Chen Deguai, Hou Zhanqing, Li Xouyin, Liu Fonghua, Niu Yongxing, Pang Kaiming, Tang

Shunsan, and Xia Shuqing in Nanking; and Shang Zhaofu (Jeffrey Shang) and Zhu Chuanyu in the Republic of China.

Most of the surviving American and European eyewitnesses of the massacre and their families were unstintingly generous with their time and information, giving me telephone interviews, photographs, documents, and even films of the massacre. They include Robert and Morton Bates, Tanya Condon, Frank Tillman Durdin, Marion Fitch Exter, Robert Fitch, Marge Garrett, Peter Kröger, Emma Lyon, David Magee, Angie and Harriet Mills, Fred Riggs, Charles Sone, Leland Steward, Edith Fitch Swapp, Marjorie Wilson, and Robert Wilson Jr.

Drs. Rana Mitter and Christian Jessen-Klingenberg of the University of Oxford, Carol Gluck of Columbia University, and William Kirby of Harvard University, took the time to review my book before publication and to enrich it with their important scholarly suggestions.

In San Francisco, several Japanese and Asians met with me to discuss their viewpoints on the Rape of Nanking and Japanese denial of World War II responsibilities. I am grateful for Haru Murakawa's help in organizing this March 30, 1997, workshop, and for Citania Tam's generosity in providing office space for the meeting. Many thanks go to the workshop participants, who include Akira Donuma, Keiko Ito, Kenji Oka, Ching Jeng, Sueko Kawamshi, Connie Yee, Hirokiu Yamaji, Noriko Yamaji, and Yasuhiro Yamaji.

Other people who assisted me in various important ways while I was completing the book include Simon Avenell, Marilyn Bolles, Frank Boring, Mark Cajigao, Julius Chang, Barbara Culliton, Jim Culp, Edward Dodds, Mark Eykholt, David Farnsworth, Robert Friedly, Richard Fumosa, Chris Goff, Paul Golob, Gilbert Hair, Hiro Inokuchi, Ron King, Petrus Liu, David McWhirter, Dale Maharidge, Karen Parker, Axel Schneider, John Sweeney, Shigehisa Terao, Marjorie Traverso, Ao Wang, Gail Winston, Wu Tien-wei, James Yin, and Shi Young.

Finally, I must thank my husband, Dr. Bretton Lee Douglas, who endured, without complaint, story after gruesome story of Japanese atrocities in China. His love, wisdom, and encouragement gave me the strength to finish this book.

NOTES

A Chinese-language edition of this book is available to those interested in obtaining the Chinese character names of people and places mentioned in the text. Write to Commonwealth Publishing Company Ltd., 87 Sung-Chiang Road, 4F, Taipei, Taiwan, Republic of China, or E-mail the publisher, Charles Kao, at ckao@cw.com.tw.

INTRODUCTION

page 4. *Years later experts at the . . . IMTFE:* "Table: Estimated Number of Victims of Japanese Massacre in Nanking," document no. 1702, Records of the International Military Tribunal for the Far East, court exhibits, 1948, World War II War Crimes Records Collection, box 134, entry 14, record group 238, National Archives.

5. *One historian has estimated:* estimates by Wu Zhikeng, cited in *San Jose Mercury News,* January 3, 1988.

5. *Romans at Carthage:* Frank Chalk and Kurt Jonassohn, *The History and Sociology of Genocide: Analyses and Case Studies* (New Haven, Conn.: Yale University Press, 1990), p. 76.

5. *The monstrosities of Timur Lenk:* Arnold Toynbee, 1947, p. 347, cited in Leo Kuper, *Genocide: Its Political Use in the Twentieth Century* (New Haven, Conn.: Yale University Press, 1981), p. 12.

5. *Indeed, even by the standards of history's most destructive war:* For European numbers, see R. J. Rummel, *China's Bloody Century: Genocide and Mass Murder Since 1900* (New Brunswick, N.J.: Transaction, 1991), p. 138.

6. *It is likely that more people died in Nanking:* Statistics from the Bombing of Dresden come from Louis L. Snyder, *Louis Snyder's Historical Guide to World War II* (Westport, Conn.: Greenwood Press, 1982), pp. 198–99.

6. *Indeed, whether we use the most conservative number:* Brigadier Peter Young, ed., *The World Almanac Book of World War II* (Englewood Cliffs, N.J.: World Almanac Publications/Prentice-Hall, 1981), p. 330. For numbers on the blasts at Hiroshima and Nagasaki, see Richard Rhodes, *The Making of the Atomic Bomb* (New York: Simon & Schuster, 1996), pp. 734, 740. Rhodes claims that by the end of 1945 some 140,000 people had died in Hiroshima and 70,000 in Nagasaki from the nuclear explosions. The dying continued, and after five years a total of some 200,000 in Hiroshima and 140,000 in Nagasaki had perished from causes related to the bombing. But it is significant to note that even after five years the combined death toll in both cities is still less than the highest casualty estimates for the Rape of Nanking.

6. *An estimated 20,000–80,000 Chinese women were raped:* Catherine Rosair, "For One Veteran, Emperor Visit Should Be Atonement," Reuters, October 15, 1992; George Fitch, "Nanking Outrages," January 10, 1938, George Fitch Collection, Yale Divinity School Library; Li En-han, a historian in the Republic of China, estimates that 80,000 women were raped or mutilated. ("'The Great Nanking Massacre' Committed by the Japanese Army as Related to International Law on War Crimes," *Journal of Studies of Japanese Aggression Against China* [May 1991]: 74).

6. *Many soldiers went beyond rape:* Author's interviews with survivors.

6. *"bestial machinery":* Christian Kröger, "Days of Fate in Nanking," unpublished diary in the collection of Peter Kröger; also in the IMTFE judgment, National Archives.

7. *"Nothing the Nazis under Hitler would do":* Robert Leckie, *Delivered from Evil: The Saga of World War II* (New York: Harper & Row, 1987), p. 303.

10. *During the conference I learned of two novels:* R. C. Binstock, *Tree of Heaven* (New York: Soho Press, 1995); Paul West, *Tent of Orange Mist* (New York: Scribners, 1995); James Yin and Shi

Young, *The Rape of Nanking: An Undeniable History in Photographs* (Chicago: Innovative Publishing Group, 1996).

12. *"erecting a cathedral for Hitler in the middle of Berlin"*: Gilbert Hair, telephone interview with the author.

CHAPTER 1: THE PATH TO NANKING

19. *For as far back as anyone could remember*: Tanaka Yuki, *Hidden Horrors: Japanese War Crimes in World War II* (Boulder, Co.: Westview, 1996), pp. 206–8. (Although Tanaka is the author's surname, he uses an American-style of presenting his name as Yuki Tanaka for this English-language book.) According to Tanaka, the modern Japanese corrupted the ancient code of *bushido* for their own purposes. The original code dictated that warriors die for just causes, not trivial ones. But during World War II, officers were committing ritual suicide for the most absurd of reasons, such as for stumbling over their words when reciting the code. The concept of loyalty in *bushido* was also replaced by blind obedience, and courage by reckless violence.

20. *It is striking to note*: Meirion Harries and Susie Harries, *Soldiers of the Sun: The Rise and Fall of the Imperial Japanese Army* (New York: Random House, 1991), p. vii.

21. *"A parallel situation"*: Samuel Eliot Morison, *"Old Bruin": Commodore Matthew C. Perry 1794–1858* (Boston: Atlantic–Little, Brown, 1967), p. 319.

22. "As we are not the equals of foreigners,": Delmer M. Brown, *Nationalism in Japan: An Introductory Historical Analysis* (Berkeley and Los Angeles: University of California Press, 1955), p. 75. (Italics mine.) (Brown's citation: Satow, trans., *Japan 1853–1864*, or Genji Yume Monogatari, p. 4).

24. *"destined to expand and govern other nations"*: Taiyo, July 1905, quoted in ibid., p. 144.

24. *Modernization had earned for the country*: Ibid., p. 152.

26. *The population had swollen*: Paul Johnson, *Modern Times: The World from the Twenties to the Nineties* (New York: HarperCollins, 1991), p. 189.

26. *"There are only three ways left to Japan"*: W. T. deBary, ed., *Sources of the Japanese Tradition* (New York, 1958), pp. 796–97, quoted in ibid., p. 189.

27. *Why, the military propagandist Sadao Araki:* Quoted in ibid., p. 189.

27. *Nor were Japan's covetous intentions:* Ibid., p. 393. For more information about the ambitions of some Japanese ultranationalists regarding the United States during that era, see Records of the Deputy Chief of Naval Operations, 1882–1954, Office of Naval Intelligence, Intelligence Division—Naval Attaché Reports, 1886–1939, box 525, entry 98, record group 38, National Archives. As early as December 1932, a U.S. naval intelligence report noted that best-sellers in Japan tended to be books on war—particularly on the possibility of American-Japanese war. This report and others analyzed the content of Japanese books, articles, pamphlets, and lectures that dwelled on the topic of a Japanese invasion of the United States. Some of these publications bore titles such as "The Alaska Air Attack," "The Assault on Hawaii," and "The California Attack." Here are a few examples of Japanese propaganda from the early 1930s that made their way into American naval intelligence files (the following names come directly from an English-language report and may be misspelled):

—A lecture by Captain K. Midzuno revealed that the Japanese military not only developed strategies for attacking Pearl Harbor from the air but also foresaw the possibility of American raids on Tokyo.

—In *Japan in Danger: A Great Naval War in the Pacific Ocean*, Nakadzima Takesi described scenarios of a victorious war waged by the Japanese against the United States through naval battles and air bombardment.

—In *Increasing Japanese-American Danger*, Vice Admiral Sesa Tanetsugu wrote that he was convinced of the inevitability of Japanese-American conflict.

—Ikedzaki Talakta presented in *The Predestined Japanese-American War* a compilation of articles on the subject of the inevitability of a Japanese-American war. A newspaper review lauded this book as "a work of passionate love for the native land" and assured readers that "if Japan draws its sword, the false, haughty America will be powerless" (February 3, 1933, report, p. 260).

27. *"Before a new world appears":* Delmer Brown, *Nationalism in Japan*, p. 187; see also Okawa Shumei, "Ajia, Yoroppa, Nihon (Asia, Europe, and Japan)," p. 82, translated in "Analyses,"

IPS document no. 64, pp. 3–4 (italics added).

29. *To prepare for the inevitable war with China:* Tessa Morris-Suzuki, *Showa: An Inside History of Hirohito's Japan* (New York: Schocken, 1985), pp. 21–29.

30. *"We appear to be standing in the vanguard of Asia":* Quoted in Ian Buruma, *The Wages of Guilt* (New York: Farrar, Straus & Giroux, 1994), pp. 191–92.

30. *"Why are you crying about one lousy frog?":* Ibid., p. 172.

30. *"deep ambivalence in Japanese society":* Letter from Rana Mitter to author, July 17, 1997.

31. *It was reputed that more than one teacher:* Harries and Harries, *Soldiers of the Sun,* p. 41.

31. *A visitor to one of its elementary schools:* Iritani Toshio, *Group Psychology of the Japanese in Wartime* (London and New York: Kegan Paul International, 1991), pp. 177, 191.

31. *abuse:* Ibid.

32. *"I do not beat you because I hate you":* Ibid., p. 189.

32. *The intensity of the training in Japan:* 106/5485, February 1928 report, p. 136, Papers of the British War Office in the Public Record Office, Kew, London. An OSS report on Japanese army training summarizes the process of indoctrination: "The smallest infraction or error in regulations brings instant and severe punishment. Act tough—shout, don't talk—scowl, don't look pleasant—be tough—have no desires—forget your family at home—never show emotionalism—do everything the hard way—don't let yourself be comfortable—train and discipline your desires for comfort, food and water—suffer pain and hardship in silence—you are a son of Heaven"; report no. 8974-B, dissemination no. A-17403, distributed December 28, 1943, Research and Analysis Branch Divisions, Intelligence Reports "Regular" Series, 1941–45, box 621, entry 16, record group 226, National Archives.

32. *"During these impressionable years":* 106/5485, February 1928 report, p. 84, Papers of the British War Office.

33. *That August, while attempting to land thirty-five thousand fresh troops:* David Bergamini, *Japan's Imperial Conspiracy* (New York: Morrow, 1971), p. 11.

33. *In the 1930s Japanese military leaders:* John Toland, *The Rising Sun: The Decline and Fall of the Japanese Empire* (New York: Random House), p. 47. "Crush the Chinese in three months and they will sue for peace," Minister Sugiyama predicted.

CHAPTER 2: SIX WEEKS OF TERROR

37. *"specialist in thought control, intimidation and torture"*: David Bergamini, *Japan's Imperial Conspiracy* (New York: William Morrow and Company, 1971), p. 16.

37. *"a beast"*: Kimura Kuninori, *Koseiha Shogun Nakajima Kesago [Nakajima Kesago, General of the Individualist Faction].* (Tokyo: Kôjinsha, 1987), p. 212.

37. *"masked shogun"*: Sugawara Yutaka, *Yamatogokoro: Fukumen Shogun Yanagawa Heisuke Seidan [Spirit of Japan: Elevated Conversation from the Masked Shogun Yanagawa Heisuke].* (Tokyo: Keizai Oraisha, 1971), p. 9.

37. *Consider the example of Suchow:* Wu Tien-wei, "Re-study of the Nanking Massacre," *Journal of Studies of China's Resistance War against Japan* (China Social Science Academy), no. 4 (1994): 43; Central Archive Bureau, China No. 2 Historical Archive Bureau; Jilin Province Social Science Academy, ed., *Pictorial Evidence of the Nanjing Massacre* (Changchun, PRC: Jilin People's Publishing House, 1995), p. 31; Dick Wilson, *When Tigers Fight: The Story of the Sino-Japanese War, 1937–1945* (New York: Viking, 1982), p. 69.

38. *The invasion, according to the* China Weekly Review: *China Weekly Review* (March 1938).

38. *"There is hardly a building standing"*: Manchester Guardian reporter Timperley wrote this account, which was telegraphed to London by another correspondent on January 14, 1938.

38. *On December 7, as the Japanese troops:* For this section on Asaka's replacement of Matsui, see Bergamini, *Japan's Imperial Conspiracy,* ch. 1, p. 22.

39. *"not good"*: Kido, Nikki, 468, quoted in ibid., p. 23.

39. *"sparkle before the eyes"*: Nakayama Yasuto, testimony before IMTFE, "Proceedings," p. 21893 (see also pp. 33081ff., 37238ff., and 32686 [Canberra]), quoted in ibid., p. 23.

39. *"The entry of the Imperial Army"*: Quoted in ibid.; see also IMTFE judgment, pp. 47171–73, National Archives.

40. *After Asaka heard this report:* Bergamini, *Japan's Imperial Conspiracy,* p. 24; Information on footnote on Tanaka Ryukichi comes from *Pictorial Evidence of the Nanjing Masacre,* p. 35. (Bergamini's book is poorly footnoted so it must be used with caution. However, the citation suggests that he interviewed Tanaka.)

41. *"BATTALION BATTLE REPORTER"*: Quoted in Jilin Province Social Science Academy, ed., *Pictorial Proof of the Nanking Mas-*

sacre, p. 62. The English translation of this command appears in Yin and Young, *The Rape of Nanking*, p. 115.

42. *"To deal with crowds of a thousand"*: Kimura, "The Battle of Nanking: Diary of 16th Division Commander Nakajima," *Chuo Kouron Sha* [Tokyo] (November 24, 1984). Nakajima's diary appeared in a December 1984 supplement to the Japanese periodical *Historical Figures*. The English translation of parts of his diary appears in Yin and Young, *The Rape of Nanking*, p. 106.

43. *"It was a magnificent view"*: Azuma Shiro, *Waga Nankin Puratoon [My Nanjing Platoon]* (Tokyo: Aoki Haruo, 1987).

44. *fifty-seven thousand:* IMTFE verdict.

45. *"The [Japanese] army encountered great difficulties"*: Quoted in Honda Katsuichi, *Studies of the Nanking Massacre* (Tokyo: Bansei Sha Publishing, 1992), p. 129.

45. *"After three or four hours"*: Kurihara Riichi, *Mainichi Shimbun*, August 7, 1984.

46. *"The result was a mountain of charred corpses"*: Honda Katsuichi, *The Road to Nanking* (*Asahi Shimbun*, 1987), quoted in Yin and Young, p. 86.

46. *After the soldiers surrendered en masse:* For this section, "The Murder of Civilians," see Gao Xingzu, Wu Shimin, Hu Yungong, and Zha Ruizhen (History Department, Nanjing University), "Japanese Imperialism and the Massacre in Nanjing— An English Translation of a Classified Chinese Document on the Nanjing Massacre," translated from Chinese into English by Robert P. Gray (pgray@pro.net). See also *China News Digest*, special issue on the Nanjing massacre, part 1 (March 21, 1996).

46. *Corpses piled up outside the city walls:* Gao Xingzu, "On the Great Nanking Tragedy," *Journal of Studies of Japanese Aggression Against China* (November 1990): 70.

47. *These atrocities shocked many of the Japanese correspondents:* The English translations of the Japanese journalists' accounts of the Nanking massacre appear in Yin and Young, *The Rape of Nanking*, pp. 52–56.

47. *"One by one the prisoners fell down"*: Ibid.

47. *"On Hsiakwan wharves"*: Imai Masatake, "Japanese Aggression Troops' Atrocities in China," *China Military Science Institute*, 1986, pp. 143–44.

48. *"Those in the first row were beheaded"*: Omata Yukio, *Reports and Recollections of Japanese Military Correspondents* (Tokyo: Tokuma Shoten, 1985).

48. *"Before the 'Ceremony of Entering the City'"*: Quoted in Moriyama Kohe, *The Nanking Massacre and Three-All Policy: Lessons Learned from History* (Chinese-language edition, People's Republic of China: Sichuan Educational Publishing, 1984), p. 8.

48. *"I've seen piled-up bodies"*: Quoted in Yang Qiqiao, "Refutation of the Nine-Point Query by Tanaka Masaaki," *Baixing* (Hong Kong), no. 86 (1985).

49. *"Women suffered most"*: Quoted in Hu Hua-ling, "Chinese Women Under the Rape of Nanking," *Journal of Studies of Japanese Aggression Against China* (November 1991): 70.

49. *Surviving Japanese veterans claim*: Azuma Shiro, undated letter to the author, 1996.

49. *Soldiers were even known to wear amulets*: George Hicks, *The Comfort Women: Japan's Brutal Regime of Enforced Prostitution in the Second World War* (New York: Norton, 1994), p. 32.

49. *"At first we used some kinky words"*: Interview with Azuma Shiro in *In the Name of the Emperor* (film), produced by Nancy Tong and co-directed by Tony and Christine Choy, 1995.

49. *"After raping, we would also kill them"*: Quoted in Hu Hua-ling, "Chinese Women Under the Rape of Nanking," p. 70.

50. *"Perhaps when we were raping her"*: Shiro Azuma, undated letter to the author, 1996.

50. *raping some twenty women*: "The Public Prosecution of Tani Hisao, One of the Leading Participants in the Nanking Massacre," *Heping Daily*, December 31, 1946.

50. *"Either pay them money or kill them"*: Quoted in Bergamini, *Japan's Imperial Conspiracy*, p. 45.

50. *"Great Field Marshal on the Steps of Heaven"*: Quoted in Bergamini, *Japan's Imperial Conspiracy*, p. 39.

50. *The next day the Western news media*: Hallett Abend, "Japanese Curbing Nanking Excesses," *New York Times*, December 18, 1937.

51. *"I now realize that we have unknowingly wrought"*: Okada Takashi, testimony before IMTFE, p. 32738.

51. *"I personally feel sorry"*: Ibid., pp. 3510–11.

51. *"Never before"*: Dick Wilson, *When Tigers Fight*, p. 83.

51. *"the Japanese army is probably the most undisciplined army"*: Ibid., p. 83.

51. *"It is rumored that unlawful acts continue"*: Bergamini, *Japan's Imperial Conspiracy*, p. 43; IMTFE exhibit no. 2577; "Proceedings" (Canberra), p. 47187.

52. *"My men have done something very wrong"*: Hidaka Shun-rokuro's testimony, IMTFE, p. 21448.

52. *"Immediately after the memorial services"*: Hanayama, p. 186, quoted in Bergamini, p. 41.

52. *"The Japanese Expeditionary Force in Central China"*: Yoshimi Yoshiaki, "Historical Understandings on the 'Military Comfort Women' Issue," in *War Victimization and Japan: International Public Hearing Report* (Osaka-shi, Japan: Toho Shuppan, 1993), p. 85.

53. *But in 1991 Yoshimi Yoshiaki unearthed:* For English-language information on Yoshimi's discovery in the Defense Agency's archives, see *Journal of Studies of Japanese Aggression Against China* (February 1992): 62. The discovery made the front page of the *Asahi Shimbun* just as Prime Minister Miyazawa Kiichi was visiting Seoul, South Korea, in January 1992.

54. *"a black hole"*: Theodore Cook, telephone interview with the author.

54. *"To this day"*: "Some Notes, Comparisons, and Observations by Captain E. H. Watson, USN (Ret) (Former Naval Attaché) After an Absence of Fifteen Years from Japan," Office of the Chief of Naval Operations, Division of Naval Intelligence, general correspondence, 1929–42, folder P9–2/EF16#23, box 284, record group 38, National Archives.

54. *In her book* The Chrysanthemum and the Sword: Ruth Benedict, *The Chrysanthemum and the Sword: Patterns of Japanese Culture* (Boston: Houghton Mifflin, 1946).

56. *"Sub-Lieutenants in Race"*: Bergamini, *Japan's Imperial Conspiracy*, p. 21. The Osaka newspaper *Mainichi Shinbun* as well as the Tokyo newspapers *Nichi Nichi Shinbun* and the *Japan Advertiser* (English edition) all reported this killing competition.

56. *"One day Second Lieutenant Ono said to us"*: Quoted in Wilson, *When Tigers Fight*, p. 80.

57. *"All new recruits are like this"*: Ibid.

57. *"They had evil eyes"*: Oral history interview with Tominaga Shozo, in Haruko Taya Cook and Theodore F. Cook, *Japan at War: An Oral History* (New York: New Press, 1992), p. 40.

58. *"loyalty is heavier than a mountain"*: Azuma Shiro, undated letter to the author, 1996.

59. *"I remember being driven in a truck"*: Quoted in Joanna Pitman, "Repentance," *New Republic*, February 10, 1992, p. 14.

59. *"Few know that soldiers impaled babies"*: Ibid.

CHAPTER 3: THE FALL OF NANKING

61. *A city long celebrated:* For Nanking's literary and artistic legacy, ancient history, and the treaty to end the Opium Wars, see *Encyclopedia Britannica,* vol. 24 (1993).

61. *And it was in Nanking in 1911:* Encyclopedia Americana, vol. 29 (1992).

62. *The picture would include the intricately carved stone statues:* for Drum Tower history, see Julius Eigner, "The Rise and Fall of Nanking," *National Geographic* (February 1938). Eigner's article, which includes color photographs, provides an excellent description of life in Nanking immediately before the massacre.

62. *"like a coiling dragon and a crouching tiger":* Encyclopedia of Asian History, vol. 3 (1988).

62. *The first invasion occurred:* On the invasions of Nanking, see Julius Eigner, "The Rise and Fall of Nanking," *National Geographic* (February 1938): 189; Jonathan Spence, *The Search for Modern China* (New York: Norton, 1990), pp. 805, 171–74.

63. *Vestiges of the old China remained in the streets:* Julius Eigner, "The Rise and Fall of Nanking"; Anna Moffet Jarvis, "Letters from China, 1920–1949," box 103, record group 8, Jarvis Collection, Yale Divinity School Library; interview with Pang Kaiming, a survivor of the Nanking massacre and former ricksha puller, July 29, 1995.

63. *Surely, he proclaimed:* Rev. John Gillespie Magee, "Nanking Yesterday and Today," lecture given over the Nanking Broadcasting Station, May 28, 1937, archives of David Magee.

64. *In the summer of 1937:* Author's interviews with survivors.

64. *"Are they giving us an air-raid practice?":* Chang Siao-sung, letter to friends, October 25, 1937, Ginling correspondence, folder 2738, box 136, series IV, record group 11, UBCHEA, Yale Divinity School Library. The facts in her letter were confirmed by the author in her 1997 telephone interview with Chang Siao-sung, now residing in Waltham, Massachusetts.

65. *Frank Xing, now a practitioner of Oriental medicine:* Frank Xing, interview with the author, San Francisco, January 28,1997.

65. *My own grandparents nearly separated forever:* Interviews with my maternal grandmother, Yi-Pei Chang, my mother, Ying-Ying Chang, and my aunt, Ling-Ling Chang, May 25, 1996, in New York City.

67. *Long files of Chinese soldiers:* For descriptions of Nanking as the fighting continued in Shanghai in November, see Commanding Officer J. J. Hughes to Commander in Chief, U.S. Asiatic Fleet (letterhead marked "Yangtze Patrol, U.S.S. *Panay*"), November 8, 1937, intelligence summary for week ending November 7, 1937, Office of the Chief of Naval Operations, Division of Naval Intelligence, general correspondence, 1929–42, folder A8-2/FS#2, box 194, entry 81, record group 38, National Archives.

67. *More than two hundred thousand Japanese troops:* 793.94/11378A, general records of the Department of State, record group 59, National Archives; Yin and Young, *The Rape of Nanking,* p. 9.

67. *Neither really trusted the other:* Sun Zhaiwei, *1937 Nanjing Beige* (1937: The Tragic Ballad of Nanking) (Taipei: Shenzi Chubanshe, 1995), pp. 31–32.

68. *"Either I stay or you stay":* Ibid., pp. 27–31.

68. *Before reporters he delivered a rousing speech:* 106/5353, January 2, 1938, Papers of the British War Office in the Public Record Office, Kew, London; Sun Zhaiwei, *1937 Nanjing Beige,* p. 33.

68. *"dazed if not doped":* Harries and Harries, *Soldiers of the Sun,* p. 219.

68. *He sweated so profusely:* Sun Zhaiwei, *1937 Nanjing Beige,* p. 33.

69. *First Chiang ordered most government officials to move:* Commander E. J. Marquart to Commander in Chief, U.S. Asiatic Fleet (letterhead marked "Yangtze Patrol, U.S.S. *Luzon* [Flagship]"), November 22, 1937, intelligence summary for week ending November 21, 1937, Office of the Chief of Naval Operations, Division of Naval Intelligence, general correspondence, 1929–42, folder A8-2/FS#2, box 194, entry 81, record group 38, National Archives.

69. *Within days official-looking cars packed with luggage:* Minnie Vautrin, diary 1937–40, November 16 and 19, December 4, 1937, pp. 71–72, 94–95, Yale Divinity School Library.

69. *And then, in mid-November, fifty thousand Chinese troops:* Ibid., November 17, 1937, p. 72.

69. *Arriving from upriver ports:* Commanding Officer J. J. Hughes to Commander in Chief, U.S. Asiatic Fleet (letterhead marked "Yangtze Patrol, U.S.S. *Panay*"), November 29, 1937, intelligence summary for week ending November 28, 1937, Office of the Chief of Naval Operations, Division of Naval Intelli-

gence, general correspondence, 1929–42, folder A8–2/FS, box 194, entry 81, record group 38, National Archives.

69. *By December an estimated ninety thousand Chinese troops:* Sun Zhaiwei, "Nanjing datusha yu nanjing renkou (The Nanking Massacre and the Nanking Population)," *Nanjing shehuai kexue* (*Nanking Social Science Journal*) 37, no. 3 (1990): 79.

69. *The troops transformed the face of Nanking:* F. Tillman Durdin, "Japanese Atrocities Marked Fall of Nanking After Chinese Command Fled," *New York Times,* December 22, 1937; "21 U.S. Citizens Now in Nanking: Only Eight Heed Warning to Evacuate Besieged City," *Chicago Daily News,* December 7, 1937; 793.94/11466, General Records of the Department of State, microfilm, record group 59, National Archives; Harries and Harries, *Soldiers of the Sun,* p. 219.

69. *In early December the military also resolved:* A. T. Steele, "Nanking Ready for Last Stand; Defenders Fight Only for Honor: Suburban Areas Aflame; Chinese May Destroy City in Defeat," *Chicago Daily News,* December 9, 1937, p. 2; Durdin, "Japanese Atrocities Marked Fall of Nanking," p. 38; Minnie Vautrin, diary 1937–40, December 7, 1937, p. 99, Yale Divinity School Library.

70. *"an outlet for rage and frustration":* Durdin, "Japanese Atrocities Marked Fall of Nanking," *New York Times,* p. 38.

70. *On December 2, hundreds of boxes of Palace Museum treasures:* Minnie Vautrin, diary 1937–40, December 2, 1937, p. 93, Yale Divinity School Library.

70. *Six days later, on December 8, Chiang Kai-shek:* For information on the departure of Chiang, see Reginald Sweetland, "Chiang Flees to Escape Pressure of 'Red' Aides," *Chicago Daily News,* December 8, 1937; Frank Tillman Durdin, "Japanese Atrocities Marked Fall of City after Chinese Command Fled," *New York Times,* December 22, 1937, p. 38; 793.94/12060, report no. 9114, December 11, 1937 (day-by-day description of Japanese military maneuvers), restricted report, General Records of the Department of State, record group 59, National Archives.

70. *During the battle of Shanghai:* For statistics on the Chinese and Japanese air forces, see Sun Zhaiwei, *1937 Nanjing Beige,* p. 18. See also Julian Bloom, "Weapons of War, Catalyst for Change: The Development of Military Aviation in China, 1908–1941" (Ph.D. dissertation, University of Maryland,

n.d.), San Diego Aerospace Museum, document no. 28–246; Rene Francillon, *Japanese Aircraft of the Pacific War* (London: Putnam, 1970); Eiichiro Sekigawa, *Pictorial History of Japanese Military Aviation*, ed. David Mondey (London: Ian Allan, 1974); Robert Mikesh and Shorzoe Abe, *Japanese Aircraft, 1910–1941* (Annapolis: Naval Institute Press, 1990).

71. *During the battle of Shanghai, Italian-trained Chinese pilots:* Bergamini, *Japan's Imperial Conspiracy*, p. 11.

71. *On December 8, the day Chiang and his advisers left the city:* A. T. Steele, "China's Air Force, Disrupted by Superior Planes of Foes, Leaves Nanking to Its Fate," *Chicago Daily News*, December 8, 1937.

71. *Second, the government officials who moved to Chungking:* Nanking Massacre Historical Editorial Committee, ed., (Zhongguo dier lishe dang an gan guan, Nanjing shi dang an guan) *Archival Documents Relating to the Horrible Massacre Committed by the Japanese Troops in Nanking in December 1937*, No. 2, National Archives, Nanking Municipal Archives (Nanking: Jiangsu Guji chubanshe [Jiangsu Ancient Books Publisher], November 1987), p. 46.

71. *Third, the troops did not come from the same regions:* Wei Hu, former paramedic for the Chinese military in Nanking, interview with the author, January 17, 1997, in Sunnyvale, California.

71. *Fourth, many of the "soldiers" in this army:* Ibid.

71. *Tired, hungry, and sick: Archival Documents Relating to the Horrible Massacre* (1987), p. 46.

71. *Worst of all, Chinese soldiers:* Ibid.

72. *"protect innocent civilians":* Quoted in Yin and Young, *The Rape of Nanking*, p. 32; Xu Zhigeng, *Lest We Forget: Nanjing Massacre, 1937* (Beijing: Chinese Literature Press, 1995), p. 43.

72. *"Our army must fight to defend":* Sun Zhaiwei, *1937 Nanjing Beige*, pp. 98–99; Xu Zhigeng, *Lest We Forget*, p. 44.

72. *Privately, however, Tang negotiated for a truce:* General Records of the Department of State, 793.94/11549, record group 59, National Archives; "Deutsche Botschaft China," document no. 203 in the German diplomatic reports, National History Archives, Xingdian, Taipei County, Republic of China. Chiang's rejection of the proposal came as a shock to Tang and the International Committee for the Nanking Safety Zone. In a letter of January 24, 1938, W. Plumer Mills wrote, "General

Tang had assured us that he was confident that Gen. Chiang would accept the truce proposal, so we were surprised to receive a wire from Hankow the next day to the effect that he would not"; from the family archives of W. Plumer Mills's daughter, Angie Mills.

73. *On December 10, the Japanese waited for the city to surrender:* Xu Zhigeng, *Lest We Forget,* p. 44; Bergamini, *Japan's Imperial Conspiracy,* p. 29.

73. *"From the 9th to the 11th of December":* Tang Sheng-chih to Chiang Kai-shek, telegram, reprinted in *Archival Documents Relating to the Horrible Massacre* (1987), p. 35.

73. *At noon on December 11, General Gu Zhutong placed a telephone call:* Sun Zhaiwei, *1397 Nanjing Beige,* pp. 122–23.

74. *Tang received a telegram:* Ibid, p. 123.

74. *At 3:00 A.M. on December 12:* Ibid., p. 124.

75. *But then electrifying reports reached Tang:* Yin and Young, *The Rape of Nanking,* p. 38.

75. *Sperling agreed to take a flag:* Commanding Officer C. F. Jeffs to the Commander in Chief, U.S. Asiatic Fleet (letterhead marked the U.S.S. *Oahu*), February 14, 1938, intelligence summary for the week ending February 13, 1938. The report included an excerpt from a missionary letter (from George Fitch's diary, name not given), which was not given to the press for fear of reprisals from the Japanese; Office of the Chief of Naval Operations, Division of Naval Intelligence, General Correspondence, 1929–42, folder A8–21/FS#3, box 195, entry 81, record group 38, National Archives; see also George Fitch, *My Eighty Years in China* (Taipei: Mei Ya Publications, 1974), p. 102.

75. *That afternoon, just minutes before his commanders:* Sun Zhaiwei, *1937 Nanjing Beige,* pp. 124–26.

76. *Not surprisingly, the order to retreat:* Ibid.

76. *Their soldiers continued to fight the Japanese:* Wilson, *When Tigers Fight,* p. 70.

76. *Even in the larger, tragic scheme of things:* Durdin, "Japanese Atrocities Marked Fall of Nanking"; A. T. Steele, "Reporters Liken Slaughter of Panicky Nanking Chinese to Jackrabbit Drive in US," *Chicago Daily News,* February 4, 1938; F. Tillman Durdin, "U.S. Naval Display Reported Likely Unless Japan Guarantees Our Rights; Butchery Marked Capture of Nanking," *New York Times,* December 18, 1937; author's interviews with survivors.

77. *But before the gate lay a scene:* For details of the congestion, fire and deaths before the gate and the desperate attempts to cross the river, see A. T. Steele, "Panic of Chinese in Capture of Nanking, Scenes of Horror and Brutality Are Revealed," *Chicago Daily News,* February, 3, 1938, p. 2; Arthur Menken, "Witness Tells Nanking Horror as Chinese Flee," *Chicago Tribune,* December 17, 1937, p. 4; Durdin, "Japanese Atrocities Marked Fall of Nanking," p. 38; Fitch, *My Eighty Years in China,* p. 102; Wilson, *When Tigers Fight;* Gao Xingzu, Wu Shimin, Hu Yungong, and Zha Ruizhen, "Japanese Imperialism and the Massacre in Nanjing"; author's interviews with survivors.

77. *Tang witnessed much of this chaos:* For information on Tang's journey to the docks, see Sun Zhaiwei, *1937 Nanjing Beige,* pp. 133–35.

78. *Terrified crews tried to ward off the surging mob:* Author interview with survivor Niu Xianming in Montery Park, California, and interviews with other survivors in Nanking, People's Republic of China.

78. *That evening a fire broke out on Chungshan Road:* How the fire started near the Water Gate is a matter of dispute. A. T. Steele wrote that Chinese soldiers torched the Ministry of Communications—a beautiful $1 million office building and ceremonial hall—to destroy all the ammunition that had been stored inside ["Power of Chinese in Capture of Nanking, Scenes of Horror and Brutality Are Revealed," *Chicago Daily News,* February 3, 1938]. Another speculates that stray Japanese shells might have ignited nearby to ignite the ammunition; still another believes that two military vehicles had collided and burst into flames in the tunnel under the Water Gate [Dick Wilson, *When Tigers Fight,* pp. 66–85].

79. *Never experienced a day as dark:* Sun Zhaiwei, pp. 133–35.

CHAPTER 4: SIX WEEKS OF HORROR

81. *Approximately half the original population:* Sun Zhaiwei, "The Nanking Massacre and the Nanking Population," pp. 75–80.

82. *Weary of fire, weary of bombardment:* Frank Tillman Durdin, "Japanese Atrocities Marked Fall of Nanking after Chinese Command Fled," *New York Times,* December 22, 1937, p. 38; Minnie Vautrin, diary 1937–40, December 14, 1937, p. 110.

82. *Eyewitnesses later claimed:* Hsu Chuang-ying, testimony before IMTFE, Records from the Allied Operational/Occupation Headquarters, IMTFE transcript, entry 319, record group 331, p. 2562, National Archives. Hsu testifies: "The Japanese soldiers, when they entered the city—they were very very rough, and they were very barbarous; they shoot at everyone in sight. Anybody who runs away, or on the street, or hanging around somewhere, or peeking through the door, they shoot them—instant death." Several newspaper articles, diary entries, and letters echo Hsu's words. "Any person who, through excitement or fear, ran at the approach of the Japanese soldiers was in danger of being shot down," F. Tillman Durdin wrote (*New York Times,* December 22, 1937). "Often old men were to be seen face downward on the pavement, apparently shot in the back at the whim of some Japanese soldier." See also George Fitch's diary entries reprinted in *Reader's Digest* (July 1938): "To run was to be plugged instantly," he wrote. "Many were shot in seemingly sporting mood by the Japs, who laughed at the terror plainly visible on faces of coolies, merchants, and students alike. It reminded me of a picnic of devils."

83. *Unlike thousands of hapless civilians:* Tang Shunsan, interview with the author, Nanking, July 25, 1995.

87. *Live burials:* Committee for the Historical Materials of the Nanking Massacre and the Nanjing Tushuguan (Nanking Library), ed., *Nanjing datusha shiliao bianji weiyuanhei* (Source Materials Relating to the Horrible Massacre Committed by the Japanese Troops in Nanking in December 1937) (Nanking: Jiangsu guji chubanshe [Jiangsu Ancient Books Publisher], July 1985), p. 142.

87. *Mutilation:* On nailing prisoners to wooden boards, see Ling Da, "Xuelui hua jingling (Using Blood and Tears to Describe Nanjing)," *Yuzhou Feng (The Wind of the Universe)* 71 (July 1938), reprinted in ibid., pp. 142–44. Ling Da was not a witness but someone who interviewed a survivor called Tan.

On the crucifixion of prisoners on trees and electrical posts and bayonet practice, see Zhu Chengshan, *Qinghua rijun Nanjing datusha xingcunzhe zhengyanji (The Testimony of the Survivors of the Nanking Massacre Committed by the Invading Japanese)* (Nanking: Nanjing daxue chubanshe [University of Nanking Press], December 1994), p. 53; *Source Materials Relating to the Horrible Massacre* (1985), pp. 142–44.

On the Japanese carving strips of flesh from victims, see *Archival Documents Relating to the Horrible Massacre* (1987), pp. 68–77.

On eye-gouging, see Gao Xingzu, Wu Shimin, Hu Yungong, and Zha Ruizhen, "Japanese Imperialism and the Massacre in Nanjing."

On atrocities with zhuizi needles, see an article written by a soldier (identity unknown) who escaped from Nanking, "Jingdi shouxing muji ji (Witnessing the Beastly Action of the Japanese in Nanking)," *Hankou Dagongbao*, February 7, 1938, reprinted in *Source Materials Relating to the Horrible Massacre*, p. 129.

87. *Death by fire:* Xu Zhigeng, *Nanjing datusha* (*The Rape of Nanking*) (Nanking: Jiangshu Wenyi Chubanshe [Jiangshu Literary Publisher], November 1994), p. 74; Gao Xingzu, Wu Shimin, Hu Yungong, and Zha Ruizhen, "Japanese Imperialism and the Massacre in Nanjing"; *Archival Documents Relating to the Horrible Massacre* (1987), pp. 68–77.

88. *Death by ice:* Gao Xingzu, Wu Shimin, Hu Yungong, and Zha Ruizhen, "Japanese Imperialism and the Massacre in Nanjing."

88. *Death by dogs: Archival Documents Relating to the Horrible Massacre* (1987), pp. 68–77.

88. *The Japanese saturated victims in acid:* Gao Xingzu, Wu Shimin, Hu Yungong, and Zha Ruizhen, "Japanese Imperialism and the Massacre in Nanjing."

88. *impaled babies:* Xu Zhigeng, *The Rape of Nanking*, p. 138.

88. *hung people by their tongues:* Chia Ting Chen, "Hell on Earth: The Japanese Army in Nanking During 1937–1938: A Barbaric Crime Against Humanity," *Chinese American Forum* 1, no. 1 (May 1984).

88. *One Japanese reporter who later investigated:* Wilson, *When Tigers Fight*, p. 82.

88. *Even genitals, apparently, were consumed:* "Witnessing the Beastly Action of the Japanese in Nanking," p. 128. (Stories of castration, along with pierced vaginas and anuses, are also mentioned on page 68 of *Draft Manuscript of the History Relating to the Horrible Massacre Committed by the Japanese Troops in Nanking in December 1937.*)

89. *Susan Brownmiller, author of the landmark book* Against Our Will: Susan Brownmiller, telephone interview with the author.

89. *Estimates range from as low as twenty thousand:* Rosair, "For One

Veteran, Emperor Visit Should Be Atonement"; Fitch, "Nanking Outrages," January 10, 1938, Fitch Collection; Li En-han, "Questions of How Many Chinese Were Killed by the Japanese Army in the Great Nanking Massacre," *Journal of Studies of Japanese Aggression Against China* (August 1990): 74.

89. *Many such children were secretly killed:* Oral history interview with Lewis Smythe by Cyrus Peake and Arthur Rosenbaum, Claremont Graduate School, December 11, 1970, February 26 and March 16, 1971, box 228, record group 8, Yale Divinity School Library.

90. *"uncounted":* "Deutsche Botschaft China," report no. 21, starting on page 114, in the German diplomatic reports, National History Archives, Republic of China, submitted by the farmers Wang Yao-shan, 75, Mei Yo-san, 70, Wang Yun-kui, 63, and Hsia Ming-feng, 54, "to the German and Danish gentlemen who were staying in the cement factory near Nanking on 26 January 1938."

90. *The Japanese raped Nanking women from all classes:* Hu Hua-ling, "Chinese Women Under the Rape of Nanking."

90. *Some actually conducted door-to-door searches:* Minnie Vautrin, diary 1937–40, March 8, 1938, p. 212.

90. *This posed a terrible dilemma:* Ibid., December 24, 1937, p. 127.

90. *For instance, the Japanese army fabricated stories:* Hsu Shuhsi, ed., *Documents of the Nanking Safety Zone,* no. 266 (Shanghai, Hong Kong, Singapore: Kelly & Walsh, 1939), p. 128.

90. *Some soldiers employed Chinese traitors:* Gao Xingzu, Wu Shimin, Hu Yungong, and Zha Ruizhen, "Japanese Imperialism and the Massacre in Nanjing."

90. *An estimated one-third of all rapes:* Fitch, "Nanking Outrages," January 10, 1938, Fitch Collection.

90. *Survivors even remember soldiers:* Hou Zhanqing (survivor), interview with the author, Nanking, July 29, 1995.

90. *No place was too sacred:* Fitch, "Nanking Outrages," January 10, 1938, Fitch Collection.

91. *"Every day, twenty-four hours a day":* Quote in *Dagong Daily* reprinted in Gao Xingzu, Wu Shimin, Hu Yungong, and Zha Ruizhen, "Japanese Imperialism and the Massacre in Nanjing."

91. *"clean the penis by her mouth":* Hsu Shuhsi, *Documents of the Nanking Safety Zone,* no. 436, p. 154.

91. *"rammed a stick up her instead":* Dick Wilson, p. 76; Hsu, p. 123.

91. *Many women in their eighties:* Hu Hua-ling, "Chinese Women Under the Rape of Nanking"; "All Military Aggression in China Including Atrocities Against Civilians and Others: Summary of Evidence and Note of Argument," submitted to IMTFE by David Nelson Sutton, November 4, 1946, p. 41, National Archives.

91. *Little girls were raped so brutally:* Shuhsi Hsu, *Documents of the Nanking Safety Zone,* no. 428, p. 152.

91. *Chinese witnesses saw Japanese rape girls under ten:* Hou Zhan-qing interview.

91. *In some cases, the Japanese sliced open:* "Deutsche Botschaft China," report no. 21, starting on page 114, in the German diplomatic reports, National History Archives, Republic of China. Another account reads: "Since the bodies of most of these young girls were not yet fully developed, they were insufficient to satisfy the animal desires of the Japanese. Still, however, they would go ahead, tear open the girls' genitals, and take turns raping them"; Du Chengxiang, *A Report on the Japanese Atrocities* (Shidai Publishing Co., 1939), p. 55, reprinted in Gao Xingzu, Wu Shimin, Hu Yungong, and Zha Ruizhen, "Japanese Imperialism and the Massacre in Nanjing."

91. *Even advanced stages of pregnancy:* Hu Hua-ling, "Chinese Women Under the Rape of Nanking"; Robert Wilson, letter to family, December 30, 1937, folder 3875, box 229, record group 11, Yale Divinity School Library.

91. *One victim who was nine months pregnant:* IMTFE judgment, p. 451, National Archives.

91. *At least one pregnant woman was kicked:* Chu Yong Ung and Chang Chi Hsiang, in "All Military Aggression in China Including Atrocities Against Civilians and Others," p. 37.

91. *After gang rape, Japanese soldiers:* "A Debt of Blood: An Eyewitness Account of the Barbarous Acts of the Japanese Invaders in Nanjing," *Dagong Daily* (Wuhan), February 7, 1938; *Xinhua Daily,* February 24, 1951; Hu Hua-ling, "Chinese Women Under the Rape of Nanking"; Tang Shunsan, interview with the author, Nanking, People's Republic of China, July 26, 1995; Gao Xingzu, Wu Shimin, Hu Yungong, and Zha Ruizhen, "Japanese Imperialism and the Massacre in Nanjing."

91. *One of the most notorious stories of such a slaughter:* The story of Hsia's family (now Xia under the pinyin system) is told in a

document describing the pictures taken at Nanking after December 13, 1937, Ernest and Clarissa Forster Collection, box 263, record group 8, Miscellaneous Personal Papers, Yale Divinity School Library.

92. *She was to endure brain damage:* Xia Shuqing (then the eight-year-old survivor), interview with the author, Nanking, July 27, 1995.

93. *"While I was there":* Hsu Chuang-ying (witness), testimony before the IMTFE, Records from the Allied Operational/Occupation Headquarters, entry 319, record group 331, p. 2572, National Archives.

93. *A similar story, no less grisly:* Document about John Magee film no. 7 describing the pictures taken at Nanking after December 13, 1937, Ernest and Clarissa Forster Collection.

93. *Many other girls, tied naked to chairs:* Bergamini, *Japan's Imperial Conspiracy,* p. 27. See the photograph of one such victim in the illustrations section of this book. It is unclear whether the girl in the photograph is unconscious or dead.

93. *"According to eyewitness reports":* Gao Xingzu, Wu Shimin, Hu Yungong, and Zha Ruizhen, "Japanese Imperialism and the Massacre in Nanjing."

94. *During the mass rape the Japanese destroyed children:* For an account of smothering of infants, see George Fitch diary, entry dated December 17, 1937, quoted in Commanding Officer C. F. Jeffs to the Commander in Chief, U.S. Asiatic Fleet (letterhead marked the U.S.S. *Oahu*), intelligence summary filed for the week ending February 13, 1938, folder A8–21/FS#3, box 195, entry 81, record group 38, National Archives; and James McCallum diary, January 7, 1938, Yale Divinity School Library. For an example of a child choking to death from clothes stuffed in her mouth while her mother was raped, see Chang Kia Sze, testimony of April 6, 1946, Records from the Allied Operational/Occupation Headquarters, IMTFE transcript, entry 319, record group 331, pp. 4506–7, National Archives.

94. *"415. February 3, about 5 P.M.":* Hsu Shuhsi, editor, *Documents of the Nanking Safety Zone.* Prepared under the Auspices of the Council of International Affairs, Chung King (Shanghai, Hong Kong, Singapore: Kelly & Walsh, Ltd., 1939), p. 159.

94. *"stuck a wire through his nose":* Wong Pan Sze (24 at the time of the tribunal, 15 at the time of the Rape of Nanking), testimony before the IMTFE, Records of the IMTFE, court exhibits,

1948, World War II War Crimes Records Collection, box 134, entry 14, record group 238, National Archives.

94. *Perhaps one of the most brutal forms of Japanese entertainment:* "Sometimes the soldiers would use bayonets to slice off the women's breasts, revealing the pale white ribs inside their chests. Sometimes they would pierce their bayonets into the women's genitals and leave them crying bitterly on the roadside. Sometimes the Japanese took up wooden bats, hard reed rods, and even turnips, forced the implements into the women's vaginae, and violently beat them to death. Other soldiers stood by applauding the scene and laughing heartily"; quote from Military Commission of the Kuomingtang, Political Department, "A True Record of the Atrocities Committed by the Invading Japanese Army," compiled July 1938, reprinted in Gao Xingzu, Wu Shimin, Hu Yungong, and Zha Ruizhen, "Japanese Imperialism and the Massacre in Nanjing"; Wong Pan Sze testimony before the IMTFE; Hu Hua-ling, "Chinese Women Under the Rape of Nanking."

94. *For instance, one Japanese soldier:* Forster to his wife, January 24, 1938, Ernest and Clarissa Forster Collection.

94–95. *And on December 22, in a neighborhood near the gate:* Zhu Chengshan, *The Testimony of the Survivors of the Nanjing Massacre,* p. 50.

95. *Chinese men were often sodomized:* see Shuhsi Hsu, *Documents of the Nanking Safety Zone,* no. 430, p. 153. Also Dick Wilson, p. 76.

95. *At least one Chinese man was murdered:* "Shisou houde nanjing (Nanking After the Fall into Japanese Hands)," *Mingzheng yugongyu* 20 (January 1938). This article is based on interviews with people who escaped from Nanking and arrived in Wuhan on January 18, 1938. It is reprinted in *Source Materials Relating to the Horrible Massacre* (1985), p. 150.

95. *A Chinese woman had tried to disguise herself:* Xu Zhigeng, *The Rape of Nanking,* p. 115; Sun Zhaiwei, *1937 Nanjing Beige,* p. 353.

95. *Guo Qi, a Chinese battalion commander:* Ko Chi (also known as Guo Qi), "Shendu xueluilu (Recording with Blood and Tears the Fallen Capital)," written in the first half of 1938, published in August 1938 by *Xijing Pingbao,* a Xian newspaper (Xijing is an older name for Xian), reprinted in *Source Materials Relating to the Horrible Massacre* (1985), p. 13.

95. *His report is substantiated:* "Deutsche Botschaft China," report no. 21, starting on page 114, in the German diplomatic reports, National History Archives, Republic of China.

95. *One such family was crossing the Yangtze River:* Hsu Chuang-ying (witness), testimony before the IMTFE, Records from the Allied Operational/Occupation Headquarters, entry 319, record group 331, p. 2573, National Archives. One survivor, Li Ke-he, witnessed four Japanese soldiers who, after raping a 40-year-old woman, forced her father-in-law and son to have sex with her; see Hu Hua-ling, "Chinese Women Under the Rape of Nanking," p. 68. The IMTFE records also mention a father being forced by the Japanese to rape his own daughters, a brother his sister, and an old man his son's wife. "Breasts were torn off, and women were stabbed in the bosoms. Chins were smashed and teeth knocked out. Such hideous scenes are unbearable to watch," the record added; court exhibits, 1948, box 134, entry 14, record group 238, p. 1706, World War II War Crimes Records Collection, National Archives.

96. *Many were able to hide from the Japanese for months:* Minnie Vautrin, diary 1937–40, January 23 and February 24, 1938, pp. 167, 201.

96. *In the countryside women hid in covered holes:* Ibid., February 23, 1938, p. 200.

96. *One Buddhist nun and a little girl:* John Magee to "Billy" (signed "John"), January 11, 1938, Ernest and Clarissa Forster Collection.

96. *Some used disguise—rubbing soot on their faces:* Bergamini, *Japan's Imperial Conspiracy,* p. 37; Minnie Vautrin, diary 1937–40, December 17, 1937, p. 115.

96. *One clever young woman disguised herself as an old woman:* Minnie Vautrin, diary 1937–40, January 23, 1938, p. 168.

96. *Others feigned sickness, such as the woman:* Hsu Shuhsi, *Documents of the Nanking Safety Zone,* no. 408, p. 158.

96. *Another woman took the advice:* Forster's undated letter to his wife, Ernest and Clarissa Forster Collection.

96. *One girl barely avoided assault:* John Magee, letter to his wife, January 1, 1938, archives of David Magee.

96. *Those who defied the Japanese:* Gao Xingzu, Wu Shimin, Hu Yungong, and Zha Ruizhen, "Japanese Imperialism and the Massacre in Nanjing."

96. *A schoolteacher gunned down five Japanese soldiers:* Hu Hua-ling,

"Chinese Women Under the Rape of Nanking," p. 68.

97. *In 1937, eighteen-year-old Li Xouying:* Li Xouying, interview with the author, Nanking, July 27, 1995.

100. *"The question is so big":* Miner Searle Bates testimony before the IMTFE, pp. 2629–30.

100. *The Chinese military specialist Liu Fang-chu:* Li En-han, "Questions of How Many Chinese Were Killed by the Japanese Army in the Great Nanking Massacre," *Journal of Studies of Japanese Aggression Against China* (August 1990).

100. *Officials at the Memorial Hall of the Victims of the Nanking Massacre by Japanese Invaders:* Author's interviews with museum officials. The number 300,000 is inscribed prominently on the museum's entrance. Honda Katsuichi, a Japanese writer, went back to Nanking a few decades later to check the stories for himself. He thinks that 200,000 Chinese were killed by the second day of the capture of the city and that by February the death toll had risen to 300,000. (Wilson, *When Tigers Fight,* pp. 81–82.) The Chinese historian Li En-han said that "the estimate of the total number of deaths . . . as 300,000 is absolutely reliable." (Hu Hua-ling, "Commemorating the 53rd Anniversary of the Great Nanking Massacre: Refuting Shintaro Ishihara's Absurdity and Lie," *Journal of Studies of Japanese Aggression Against China,* November 1990, p. 27.)

100. *The IMTFE judges concluded that more than 260,000 people:* "Table: Estimated Number of Victims of Japanese Massacre in Nanking," document no. 1702, box 134, IMTFE records, court exhibits, 1948, World War II War Crimes Records Collection, entry 14, record group 238, National Archives.

100. *Fujiwara Akira, a Japanese historian:* Hu Hua-ling, "Commemorating the 53rd Anniversary," p. 72.

100. *John Rabe, who never conducted a systematic count:* John Rabe, "Enemy Planes over Nanking," report to Adolf Hitler, in the Yale Divinity School Library. Rabe writes: "According to Chinese reports, a total of 100,000 Chinese civilians were murdered. But that seems to be an overassessment—we Europeans estimate the number to be somewhere between 50,000 and 60,000."

100. *The Japanese author Hata Ikuhiko claims:* Cook and Cook, *Japan at War,* p. 39.

100. *Still others in Japan:* Ibid.

100. *In 1994 archival evidence emerged:* United Press International, May 10, 1994.

100. *Perhaps no one has made a more thorough study:* Sun Zhaiwei, "The Nanking Massacre and the Nanking Population," pp. 75–80; "Guanyu nanjing datusa siti chunide yenjou (On the Subject of Body Disposal During the Nanking Massacre)," *Nanjing Shehui Kexue* 44, no. 4 (1991): 72–78.

100. *Nanjing zizhi weiyuanhui:* The setting up of such a puppet government was a longstanding custom of the Japanese in areas of China they occupied and it enabled the Japanese to preserve local structures of power and make some local elites beholden to them.

101. *However, this statistic balloons still larger: Archival Documents Relating to the Horrible Massacre* (1987), pp. 101–3; "150,000 Bodies Dumped in River in Nanking Massacre Affidavit," Reuters, December 14, 1990.

102. *For instance, in his paper:* Wu Tien-wei, "Let the Whole World Know the Nanking Massacre: A Review of Three Recent Pictorial Books on the Massacre and Its Studies," report distributed in 1997 by the Society for Studies of Japanese Aggression Against China.

103. *The authors James Yin and Shi Young:* Shi Young, telephone interview with the author.

103. *They dismiss arguments from other experts:* It is difficult to say how many bodies washed up along the river were eventually buried along the banks. On April 11, 1938, Minnie Vautrin wrote in her diary that a man mentioned to her that "there are reported still many dead bodies on both sides of the Yangtze and many bloated ones floating down the river—soldiers and civilians. I asked him if he meant tens or hundreds and he said it seemed to him to be thousands and thousands"; diary 1937–40, p. 247.

104. *"Since return (to) Shanghai a few days ago":* "Red Machine" Japanese diplomatic messages, no. 1263, translated February 1, 1938, record group 457, National Archives. *Manchester Guardian* correspondent H. J. Timperley originally wrote this report, which was stopped by Japanese censors in Shanghai. (See "Red Machine" Japanese diplomatic messages, no. 1257.) His estimate of 300,000 deaths was later included in the message sent by Japanese Foreign Minister Hirota Koki to Washington, DC. The significance of this message is that the Japanese government not only knew about the 300,000 figure given by Timperley but tried to suppress the information at the time.

CHAPTER 5: THE NANKING SAFETY ZONE

106. *In November 1937, Father Jacquinot de Bessage:* Tien-wei Wu, "Let the Whole World Know the Nanking Massacre," p. 16.

106. *When the Presbyterian missionary W. Plumer Mills:* Angie Mills to the author, February 16, 1997. In her family archives, Mills found a copy of a speech given by John Rabe on February 28, 1938, at the Foreign YMCA in Shanghai to a group of Westerners. In it he said, "I must tell you Mr. Mills is the man who originally had the idea of creating the Safety Zone. I can say that the brains of our organization were to be found in the Ping Tsang Hsiang No. 3 [the address, according to Angie Mills, of Lossing Buck's house, where nine or ten of the Americans were living during this period, near Nanking University]. Thanks to the cleverness of my American friends: Mr. Mills, Mr. Bates, Dr. Smythe, Mr. Fitch, Mr. Sone, Mr. Magee, Mr. Forster and Mr. Riggs, the Committee was put on its feet and thanks to their hard work it ran as smoothly as could be expected under the dreadful circumstances we lived in."

107. *Interestingly enough, the* Panay *would later be bombed:* "Sinking of the U.S.S. *Panay,*" ch. 11 of *Some Phases of the Sino-Japanese Conflict* (July–December 1937), compiled from the records of the Commander in Chief, Asiatic Fleet, by Captain W. A. Angwin (MC), USN, December 1938, Shanghai, Office of the Chief of Naval Operations, Division of Naval Intelligence, general correspondence, 1929–42, folder P9-2/EF16#23, box 284, entry 81, record group 38, National Archives; "The *Panay* Incident," Records of the Office of the Chief of Naval Operations, Records of the Deputy Chief of Naval Operations, 1882–1954, Intelligence Division—Naval Attaché Reports, 1886–1939, box 438, entry 98, record group 38, National Archives; "The Bombing of the U.S.S. *Panay,*" drawn by Mr. E. Larsen after consultation with Mr. Norman Alley, December 31, 1937, box 438, entry 98, record group 38, National Archives; Weldon James, "Terror Hours on *Panay* Told by Passenger," *Chicago Daily News,* December 13, 1937; A. T. Steele, "Chinese War Horror Pictured by Reporter: *Panay* Victims Under Japanese Fire for Full Half Hour; Butchery and Looting Reign in Nanking," *Chicago Daily News,* December 17, 1937; Bergamini, pp. 24–28.

108. *"We were not rich":* Marjorie Wilson, telephone interview with the author.

108. *"Would they kill us?":* Alice Tisdale Hobart, *Within the Walls of Nanking* (New York: Macmillan, 1928), pp. 207–8.

108. *"We were more prepared for excesses from the fleeing Chinese":* "Deutsche Botschaft China," German diplomatic reports, document dated January 15, 1938, starting on page 214, National History Archives, Republic of China.

109. *The son of a sea captain:* Details of John Rabe's early life come from correspondence between the author and Rabe's granddaughter, Ursula Reinhardt, and from the archives of the Siemens Company, Berlin Germany.

109. *"I believe not only in the correctness of our political system":* Rabe's account of the Rape of Nanking can be found in his report to Adolf Hitler, entitled "Enemy Planes over Nanking," copies of which are now at Yale Divinity School Library, the Memorial Hall of the Victims of the Nanking Massacre by Japanese Invaders, and the Budesarchiv of the Federal Republic of Germany. Information and quotes in this section not otherwise attributed come from this report.

112. *"the mayor of Nanking."* Letter from John Rabe of the International Committee for Nanking Safety Zone to the Imperial Japanese Embassy, December 27, 1937, enclosure to report entitled "Conditions in Nanking," January 25, 1938, Intelligence Division, Naval Attaché Reports, 1886–1939, Records of the Office of the Deputy Chief of Naval Operations, 1882–1954, Office of Naval Intelligence, box 996, entry 98, record group 38, National Archives.

113. *lost an eye:* Fitch, *My Eighty Years in China*, p. 101.

113. *only a fraction of the total food:* Hsu, p. 56.

116. *Han Chung Road:* Hsu, p. 2.

116. *mingled with civilians:* Letter from John Rabe to Fukuda Tokuyasa, December 15, 1937, box 996, entry 98, record group 38, National Archives.

116. *"We knew that there were a number of ex-soldiers":* George Fitch, diary entry for December 14, 1937, reprinted in *My Eighty Years in China*, p. 106. One of the original copies can be found in Commanding Officer C. F. Jeffs to the Commander in Chief, U.S. Asiatic Fleet (letterhead marked the U.S.S. *Oahu*), February 14, 1938, intelligence summary filed for the week ending February 13, 1938, Office of the Chief of Naval Operations, Division of Naval Intelligence, general correspondence, 1929–42, p. 5, folder A8–21/FS#3, box 195, entry 81, record group 38, National Archives. In the diary, Fitch wrote:

"Not a whimper came from the entire throng. Our own hearts were lead. . . . How foolish I had been to tell them the Japanese would spare their lives!"

118. *"All 27 Westerners in the city"*: Letter from John Rabe to the Imperial Japanese Embassy, December 17, 1937, enclosure no. 8 to report entitled "Conditions in Nanking," January 25, 1938, box 996, entry 98, record group 38, National Archives. This letter can also be found in Hsu Shuhsi, ed., *Documents of the Nanking Safety Zone: Prepared under the Auspices of the Council of International Affairs, Chungking* (Shanghai, Hong Kong, Singapore: Kelly & Walsh, 1939).

118. *"We did not find a single Japanese patrol"*: Rabe to Imperial Japanese Embassy, December 17, 1937; Hsu Shuhsi, *Documents of the Nanking Safety Zone*, p. 12.

118. *"Yesterday, in broad daylight"*: Rabe to Imperial Japanese Embassy, December 17, 1937; Hsu Shuhsi, *Documents of the Nanking Safety Zone*, p. 20.

118. *"If this process of terrorism continues"*: Rabe to Imperial Japanese Embassy, December 17, 1937; Shuhsi Hsu, *Documents of the Nanking Safety Zone*, p. 17.

118. *During the great Rape some Japanese embassy officials*: IMTFE judgment, National Archives. See "Verdict of the International/Military Tribunal for the Far East on the Rape of Nanking," *Journal of Studies of Japanese Agression Against China*, November 1990, p. 75.

118. *"if you tell the newspaper reporters anything bad"*: Fu Kuishan's warning to Rabe, recorded in John Rabe diary, February 10, 1938, p. 723.

119. *Once there, he would chase Japanese soldiers away*: Robert Wilson, letter to family, January 31, 1938, p. 61.

120. *failed to take the matter seriously*: Even the Japanese embassy staff seemed secretly gleeful of the excesses of the Japanese army. When Hsu Chuang-ying caught a Japanese soldier raping a woman in a bath house and informed Fukuda, vice-consul of the Japanese embassy, of the situation, he saw that Fukuda had "a little smile on his face." Transcript of the International Military Tribunal of the Far East. Testimony of Hsu Chuang-ying, witness. RG 311, Entry 319, page 2570-2571. Records from the Allied Operational/Occupation Headquarters, National Archives, Washington, D.C.

120. *"when any of them objects [Rabe] thrusts his Nazi armband"*: Copy of George Fitch diary, enclosed in file from Assistant

Naval Attaché E. G. Hagen to Chief of Naval Operations (Director of Naval Intelligence), Navy Department, Washington, D.C., March 7, 1938, Office of the Chief of Naval Operations, Division of Naval Intelligence, general correspondence, 1929–42, folder P9–2/EF16#8, box 277, entry 81, record group 38; also reprinted in Fitch, *My Eighty Years in China*, p. 114.

121. *Once, when four Japanese soldiers in the midst of raping and looting:* "Cases of Disorder by Japanese Soldiers in the Safety Zone," filed January 4, 1938, in Hsu Shuhsi, *Documents of the Nanking Safety Zone*, p. 65.

121. *"bad business to shoot a German subject":* "Cases of Disorder by Japanese Soldiers in the Safety Zone," subenclosure to enclosure no. 1–c, Intelligence Division, Naval Attaché Reports, 1886–1939, Records of the Office of the Deputy Chief of Naval Operations, 1882–1954, Office of Naval Intelligence, folder H–8–B Register#1727A, box 996, entry 98, record group 38, National Archives.

121. *During one of his visits to the zone:* Minnie Vautrin, diary 1937–40, February 17, 1938, p. 198.

121. *"almost wear a Nazi badge":* Fitch, "Nanking Outrages," January 10, 1938, Fitch Collection.

121. *"He is well up in Nazi circles":* Robert Wilson, letter to family, Christmas Eve 1937, p. 6.

122. *Born in 1904:* Early biographical information on Robert Wilson comes from Marjorie Wilson (his widow), telephone interviews with the author.

122. *The first two years for the Wilsons:* Ibid.

122. *After the Marco Polo Bridge incident in July:* Robert Wilson, letter to family, August 18, 1937.

123. *"He saw this as his duty":* Marjorie Wilson, telephone interview.

123. *No doubt to dispel loneliness:* Robert Wilson, letter to family, October 12, 1937, p. 15.

123. *Most contained gruesome descriptions:* Ibid., August 20, 1937, p. 9.

123. *"a respectable museum":* Ibid., December 9, 1937, p. 35.

123. *On September 25, in one of the worst air raids:* Ibid., September 25 and 27, 1937; Minnie Vautrin, diary 1937–40, September 26, 1937, p. 33.

124. *Heavy black curtains were drawn:* Robert Wilson, letter to family, August 23, 1937.

124. *There were approximately one hundred thousand wounded Chinese veterans:* Commander Yangtze Patrol E. J. Marquart to Commander in Chief, U.S. Asiatic Fleet (letterhead marked

"Yangtze Patrol, U.S.S. *Luzon* [Flagship])," intelligence summary for week ending October 24, 1937, October 25, 1937, Office of the Chief of Naval Operations, Division of Naval Intelligence, general correspondence, 1929–42, folder A8-2/FS, box 194, entry 81, record group 38, National Archives; Minnie Vautrin, diary 1937–40, October 26 and November 8, 1937, pp. 55, 64 (she writes that some 100,000 soldiers have been injured or killed in the Shanghai area).

124. *Soldiers who healed were returned:* Ibid.

124. *Chinese doctors and nurses:* Minnie Vautrin, diary 1937–40, December 5, 1937, p. 96; Ernest and Clarissa Forster, letter to parents, December 7, 1937, Ernest and Clarissa Forster Collection.

124. *Ultimately, however, he was unable to convince them:* Robert O. Wilson (witness), testimony, Records of the Allied Operational/Occupation Headquarters, IMTFE transcript, entry 319, record group 331, pp. 2531–32, National Archives.

124. *By the end of the first week of December:* Mrs. E. H. Forster report, December 12, 1937, from newsletter in Ernest and Clarissa Forster Collection.

124. *When Richard Brady:* Robert Wilson, letter to family, December 2, 1937; A. T. Steele, "Tells Heroism of Yankees in Nanking," *Chicago Daily News,* December 18, 1937.

125. *"It is quite a sensation":* Robert Wilson, letter to family, December 7, 1937.

125. *"naturally pretty shaky":* Ibid., December 14, 1937.

125. *Wilson saw Japanese flags fluttering:* Ibid.

125. *They broke into the main hospital:* Durdin, "Japanese Atrocities Marked Fall of Nanking"; Rabe, "Enemy Planes over Nanking"; an excerpt from a verbal presentation by Mr. Smith of Reuters about the events of Nanking on December 9–15, 1937, document no. 178, Hankow, January 1, 1938, in "Deutsche Botschaft China," German diplomatic reports, National History Archives, Republic of China.

125. *"swift kick":* Robert Wilson, letter to family, December 18, 1937.

125. *He also watched soldiers burn a heap of musical instruments:* Ibid., December 28, 1937.

126. *"The crowning insult":* Ibid., December 19, 1937.

126. *"December 15: The slaughter of civilians is appalling":* Ibid., December 15, 1937.

126. *"December 18: Today marks the 6th day":* Ibid., December 18, 1937.

126. *"December 19: All the food is being stolen"*: Ibid., December 19, 1937.

126. *"Christmas Eve: Now they tell us"*: Ibid., December 24, 1937.

126. *"The only consolation"*: Ibid., December 30, 1937.

127. *Frequently Wilson and the others saw the Japanese:* Durdin, "Japanese Atrocities Marked Fall of Nanking."

127. *After the fall of Nanking, the big trenches:* Robert Wilson, letter to family, December 24, 1937.

127. *The Japanese soldiers he confronted:* Robert Wilson, letter to family, December 21, 1937, p. 6; Marjorie Wilson, telephone interview with the author; John Magee to "Billy" (signed "John"), January 11, 1938, Ernest and Clarissa Forster Collection.

127. *One of the worst scenes:* Marjorie Wilson, telephone interview with the author.

127. *He told his wife that he would never forget the woman:* Ibid.

127. *"This morning came another woman in a sad plight"*: J. H. McCallum, diary entry for January 3, 1937, reprinted in *American Missionary Eyewitnesses to the Nanking Massacre, 1937–1938*, ed. Martha Lund Smalley (New Haven, Conn.: Yale Divinity School Library, 1997), p. 39.

128. *Incredible account of survival:* Robert Wilson, letter to family, January 1, 1938, p. 11.

128. *Struggled with a fever of 102 degrees:* Ibid., December 26, 1937, p. 7.

129. *Survivors of the massacre remember:* James Yin (coauthor of *The Rape of Nanking*), telephone interview with the author. The information about McCallum comes from his research in China.

129. *When the massacre and rapes gradually subsided:* Margorie Wilson, telephone interview with the author.

130. *Vautrin, the daughter of a blacksmith:* Early biographical details about Vautrin come from Emma Lyon (Vautrin's niece), telephone interview with the author, October 28, 1996.

130. *In her diary, she never ceased to marvel:* Most of the information for this section comes directly from Vautrin's diary, 1937–40, Yale Divinity School Library. Although she used her own page-numbering system (on the top of the middle of each page), I have used the Yale Divinity School page numbers, which were stamped on the top right-hand corner of each diary page.

130. *In the summer of 1937, while vacationing:* Minnie Vautrin, diary 1937–40, July 2–18, 1937, p. 2.

130. *Still, Vautrin refused to join the other Americans:* Ibid., September 20, 1937, p. 27.

131. *The embassy staff also gave her:* Ibid., December 1 and 8, 1937, pp. 91, 100; Commanding Officer C. F. Jeffs to the Commander in Chief, U.S. Asiatic Fleet (letterhead marked the U.S.S. *Oahu*), intelligence summary for the week ending February 13, 1938, February 14, 1938 (includes excerpt of missionary letter, which was not given to the press for fear of reprisals from the Japanese); George Fitch diary (name not given in report), Office of the Chief of Naval Operations, Division of Naval Intelligence, general correspondence, 1929–42, folder A8–21/FS#3, box 195, entry 81, record group 38, National Archives.

131. *She labored to prepare the campus for female refugees:* Minnie Vautrin, diary 1937–40, December 3, 6, and 7, 1937, pp. 94, 97, 98.

131. *Vautrin also commissioned the sewing:* Ibid., October 6, 1937, p. 41.

131. *By the second week of December:* Minnie Vautrin, "Sharing 'the Abundant Life' in a Refugee Camp," April 28, 1938, box 103, record group 8, Jarvis Collection, Yale Divinity School Library.

131. *Refugees were passing through the city:* Letter to parents, probably from Forster, October 4, 1937, from Hsiakwan, Ernest and Clarissa Forster Collection.

131. *Many of them, exhausted, bewildered, and hungry:* 793.94/12060, report no. 9114, December 11, 1937, restricted report, General Records of the Department of State, National Archives.

131. *"From 8:30 this morning":* Minnie Vautrin, diary 1937–40, December 15, 1937, p. 111.

131. *Vautrin allowed the women and children:* Ibid.

132. *Vautrin's heart sank:* Ibid., December 16, 1937, pp. 112–13.

132. *They certainly would have been killed:* Ibid., December 16, 1937, p. 113.

132. *A truck went by with eight to ten girls:* Ibid., December 16, 1937, p. 114. In her diary, Vautrin records that the women screamed "Gin Ming," but a more accurate translation of the Chinese expression for help is "Jiu Ming."

132. *"What a heartbreaking sight!":* Ibid., December 17, 1937, pp. 115–16.

133. *"Never shall I forget that scene":* Ibid., pp. 117–18.

134. *On at least one occasion Japanese soldiers:* Ibid., December 27, 1937, p. 130.

134. *"the lottery":* Source Materials Relating to the Horrible Nanking Massacre (1985), pp. 9–10.

134. *On New Year's Day 1938, Vautrin rescued:* Minnie Vautrin, diary 1937–40, January 1, 1938, p. 137.

134. *"fierce and unreasonable":* Ibid., December 18, 1937, pp. 119–20.

134. *"The request was that they be allowed":* Ibid., December 24, 1937, p. 127.

135. *"Group after group of girls":* Ibid.

135. *A week after the city fell:* Enclosure to report, "Conditions in Nanking," January 25, 1938, Intelligence Division, Naval Attaché Reports, 1886–1939, Records of the Office of the Deputy Chief of Naval Operations, 1882–1954, Office of Naval Intelligence, box 996, entry 98, record group 38, National Archives; Hu Hua-ling, "Chinese Women Under the Rape of Nanking," p. 69.

135. *Vautrin noticed that the men who arrived:* Minnie Vautrin, diary 1937–40, December 28, 1937, p. 131.

135. *In a few cases the zone leaders were successful:* Fitch, *My Eighty Years in China*, p. 117.

135. *"This proved to be a bluff":* John Magee, letter to his wife, December 30, 1937, archives of David Magee.

136. *The Draconian threats of the Japanese:* Hsu Shuhsi, *Documents of the Nanking Safety Zone*, p. 84.

136. *"You must follow the old customs of marriage":* Minnie Vautrin, diary 1937–40, December 31, 1937, p. 135.

136. *Vautrin observed that the Japanese soldiers:* Ibid., January 4, 1938, p. 141.

136. *The soldiers also forced the women:* Ibid., January 6, 1938, p. 144.

136. *"because a mother or some other person could vouch for them":* Ibid., December 31, 1937, p. 135.

136. *After registration, the Japanese tried to eliminate the zone itself:* Ernest Forster, letter of January 21, 1938, Ernest and Clarissa Forster Collection.

136. *February 4 was given as the deadline:* (Authorship unknown, but probably Lewis Smythe), letter of February 1, 1938, box 228, record group 8, Yale Divinity School Library.

137. *Vautrin was wary of these promises:* Minnie Vautrin, diary 1937–40, February 4, 1938, p. 183.

137. *crammed themselves into verandas:* Minnie Vautrin, diary 1937–40, December 18, 1937.

137. *"slept shoulder to shoulder":* (unidentified author at 145 Hankow Road), letter of February 12, 1939, Ernest and Clarissa Forster Collection.

137. *"Oh, God, control the cruel beastliness"*: Minnie Vautrin, diary 1937–40, December 16, 1937, p. 114.

137. *"Don't you people worry"*: Hsu Chi-ken, *The Great Nanking Massacre: Testimonies of the Eyewitnesses* (Taipei, 1993), pp. 56–57.

137. *"You do not need to wear this rising sun emblem"*: Ibid., p. 60.

138. *"China has not perished"*: Hua-ling W. Hu, "Miss Minnie Vautrin: The Living Goddess for the Suffering Chinese People During the Nanking Massacre," *Chinese American Forum* 11, no. 1 (July 1995): 20; from Ko Chi, "Recording with Blood and Tears the Fallen Capital," in *Source Materials Relating to the Horrible Nanking Massacre* (1985).

138. *"She didn't sleep from morning till night"*: Huang Shu, interview with filmmaker Jim Culp; transcript from the personal archives of Jim Culp, San Francisco.

138. *"It was said that once she was slapped"*: Ko Chi, "Blood and Tears," p. 16; Hua-ling W. Hu, "Miss Minnie Vautrin," p. 18.

138. *Christian Kröger, a Nazi member*: Christian Kröger, "Days of Fate in Nanking," unpublished report, January 13, 1938, archives of Peter Kröger.

138. *Looting and arson made food so scarce*: Minnie Vautrin, diary 1937–40, March 4, 1938, p. 208; on mushrooms, see Liu Fonghua, interview with the author, Nanking, People's Republic of China, July 29, 1995.

138. *They not only provided free rice*: Lewis S. C. Smythe to Tokuyasu Fukuda, Attaché to the Japanese Embassy, enclosure no. 1 to report entitled "Conditions in Nanking," January 25, 1938, Intelligence Division, Naval Attaché Reports, 1886–1939, Records of the Office of the Deputy Chief of Naval Operations, 1882–1954, Office of Naval Intelligence, box 996, entry 98, record group 38, National Archives.

138. *Yet they acted as bodyguards*: James McCallum, diary, December 30, 1937, Yale Divinity School Library.

139. *"threatened Riggs with his sword"*: Hsu Shuhsi, *Documents of the Nanking Safety Zone*, p. 24.

139. *A Japanese soldier also threatened professor Miner Searle Bates*: "Cases of Disorder by Japanese Soldiers in Safety Zone," subenclosure to enclosure no. 1-c, Intelligence Division, Naval Attaché Reports, 1886–1939, Records of the Office of the Deputy Chief of Naval Operations, 1882–1954, Office of Naval Intelligence, folder H–8-B Register#1727A, box 996, entry 98, record group 38, National Archives.

139. *Another soldier pulled a gun on Robert Wilson:* Diary of John Magee in long letter to his wife, entry for December 19, 1937, archives of David Magee.

139. *Still another soldier fired a rifle at James McCallum:* "Cases of Disorder by Japanese Soldiers in Safety Zone," subenclosure to enclosure no. 1-c, Intelligence Division, Naval Attaché Reports, 1886–1939, Records of the Office of the Deputy Chief of Naval Operations, 1882–1954, Office of Naval Intelligence, folder H–8–B Register#1727A, box 996, entry 98, record group 38, National Archives.

139. *When Miner Searle Bates visited the headquarters:* John Magee to "Billy" (signed "John"), January 11, 1938, Ernest and Clarissa Forster Collection.

139. *Hatz defended himself with a chair:* John Rabe diary, December 22, 1937, entry, pp. 341–42.

139. *The zone eventually accommodated:* In "Days of Fate in Nanking," Christian Kröger states his belief that 200,000–250,000 refugees fled into the zone on December 12; Miner Searle Bates ("Preliminary Report on Christian Work in Nanking," archives of Shao Tzuping) echoes the figure of 250,000; the estimate of 300,000 refugees in the zone comes from the IMTFE testimony of Hsu Chuang-ying, who was in charge of housing for the zone; see IMTFE transcript, entry 319, record group 331, p. 2561, National Archives.

Chapter 6: What the World Knew

144. *Special meals of Nanking noodles:* Morris-Suzuki, *Showa*, p. 34.

144. *Durdin, a twenty-nine-year-old reporter from Houston:* Frank Tillman Durdin, telephone interview with the author, January 1996.

144. *Steele was an older correspondent:* A. T. Steele Collection, Arizona State University Library.

144. *McDaniel was perhaps the most daring:* C. Yates McDaniel, "Nanking Horror Described in Diary of War Reporter," *Chicago Tribune*, December 18, 1937.

144. *Not only did they write riveting stories:* The first American reporter to break the full story of the massacre was Archibald Steele. When the correspondents boarded the *Oahu*, the twenty-nine-year-old Durdin was unable to send any dispatches out by radio because the operator said it was against regulations. But somehow Steele got his stories out. "I think

he slipped him a $50 bill or something!" Durdin exclaimed decades later in "Mr. Tillman Durdin's Statement on the News Conference—Refuting the Distortions of His Reports on the Great Nanking Massacre by the Japanese Media" (*Journal of Studies of Japanese Aggression Against China*, August 1992, p. 66). "I was new and young, Steele was an old hand. So he scooped me on the story."

145. *During the massacre most were so frightened:* C. Yates McDaniel, "Nanking Horror Described in Diary of War Reporter," *Chicago Tribune,* December 18, 1937.

146. *"I didn't know where to take him or what to do":* "Mr. Tillman Durdin's Statement on the News Conference—Refuting the Distortions of His Reports on the Great Nanking Massacre by the Japanese Media," *Journal of Studies of Japanese Aggression Against China,* August 1992, p. 66.

146. *"I could do nothing":* McDaniel, "Nanking Horror Described in Diary of War Reporter."

146. Details of Durdin's and Steele's last day in Nanking can be found in their news reports, Fitch's diary, and in "Mr. Tillman Durdin's Statement on the News Conference."

146. *There were also two American newsreel men:* For information on Norman Alley and Eric Mayell filming the attack, see "Camera Men Took Many *Panay* Pictures," *New York Times,* December 19, 1937.

146. *Though they survived the attack unscathed:* Steele, "Chinese War Horror Pictured by Reporter."

146. *While hiding with the surviving* Panay *passengers:* Hamilton Darby Perry, *The* Panay *Incident: Prelude to Pearl Harbor* (Toronto: Macmillan, 1969), p. 226.

146. *On December 13, President Franklin D. Roosevelt:* United Press story printed in *Chicago Daily News,* December 13, 1937.

146. *Filthy, cold, and wearing only blankets:* "Sinking of the U.S.S. Panay," ch. 11 of *Some Phases of the Sino-Japanese Conflict* (July–December 1937), compiled from the records of the Commander in Chief, Asiatic Fleet, by Capt. W. A. Angwin (MC), USN, December 1938, Shanghai, Office of the Chief of Naval Operations, Division of Naval Intelligence, general correspondence, 1929–42, folder P9-2/EF16#23, box 284, entry 81, record group 38, National Archives.

147. *When Alley's and Mayell's footage hit the theaters:* United Press story printed in *Chicago Daily News,* December 29, 1937;

793.94/12177, General Records of the Department of State, record group 59, National Archives.

147. *"The embassy cuts no ice"*: Copy of George Fitch diary, enclosed in file from Assistant Naval Attaché E. G. Hagen to Chief of Naval Operations, March 7, 1938, National Archives.

147. *In February they allowed a few American naval officers:* Commanding Officer to the Commander in Chief, U.S. Asiatic Fleet (letterhead marked the U.S.S. *Oahu*), intelligence summary for the week ending February 20, 1938, February 21, 1938, Office of the Chief of Naval Operations, Division of Naval Intelligence, general correspondence, 1929–42, folder A8–21/FS#3, box 195, entry 81, record group 38, National Archives.

147. *As late as April:* "Red Machine" Japanese diplomatic messages, no. 1794, translated May 4, 1938, boxes 1–4, record group 457, National Archives.

147. *"The assumption I made"*: "Deutsche Botschaft China,"document no. 214, German diplomatic reports, National History Archives, Republic of China. According to this report, the German diplomats returned to the city on January 9, 1938.

148. *A machine cipher had protected:* For information on the American Red Machine, see David Kahn, "Roosevelt, Magic and Ultra," in *Historians and Archivists,* ed. George O. Kent (Fairfax, Va.: George Mason University Press, 1991).

148. *"If they do return"*: "Red Machine" Japanese diplomatic messages, no. 1171, record group 457, National Archives.

148. *For example, Norman Alley:* Perry, *The Panay Incident,* p. 232.

149. *"utmost secrecy"*: "Red Machine" Japanese diplomatic messages, box 2, record group 457, National Archives.

149. *"If that is all the news coming out of Nanking"*: Robert Wilson, letter to family, December 20, 1937.

149– *"Carefully they were herded"*: George Fitch diary, reprinted in
150. *Reader's Digest* (July 1938).

150. *"tremendously pleased"*: George Fitch, *My Eighty Years in China,* p. 115.

150. *"spontaneous" celebrations: Reader's Digest* (July 1938).

150. *"these acts were not repeated"*: The Smythes, letter of March 8, 1938, box 228, record group 8, Yale Divinity School Library.

150. *"the Imperial Army entered the city"*: Archives of David Magee. A copy of the article can also be found in George Fitch diary, enclosed in file from Assistant Naval Attaché E. G. Hagen to Chief of Naval Operations, March 7, 1938, National Archives.

151. *"Now the Japanese are trying to discredit"*: James McCallum, diary entry for January 9, 1938 (copy), box 119, record group 119, Yale Divinity School Library, reprinted in Smalley, *American Missionary Eyewitnesses to the Nanking Massacre*, p. 43.

151. *"We have seen a couple of issues"*: copy of George Fitch diary, entry for January 11, 1938, enclosed in file from Assistant Naval Attaché E. G. Hagen to Chief of Naval Operations, March 7, 1938, National Archives.

151. *"In March, a government radio station in Tokyo"*: Reader's Digest (July 1938).

151. *"Now the latest is from the Japanese paper"*: Lewis and Margaret Smythe, letter to "Friends in God's Country," March 8, 1938, box 228, record group 8, Yale Divinity School Library.

152. *"All good Chinese who return"*: Reader's Digest (July 1938).

152. *"a charming, lovable soldier"*: "Deutsche Botschaft China," document starting on page 107, March 4, 1938, National History Archives, Republic of China.

152. *In early February a Japanese general:* Ernest Forster, letter of February 10, 1938, Ernest and Clarissa Forster Collection.

153. *"a mother of an 11-year-old girl"*: "Deutsche Botschaft China," document starting on page 134, February 14, 1938, National History Archives, Republic of China.

153. *The Japanese government barred other reporters:* "Red Machine" Japanese diplomatic messages, D(7–1269) #1129–A, boxes 1–4, record group 457, National Archives.

153. *Superior training in the verbal arts:* John Gillespie Magee, Sr., was the father of John Gillespie Magee, Jr., who served in the Royal Canadian Air Force and wrote the famous World War II poem, "High Flight." ("Oh! I have slipped the surly bonds of earth/And danced the skies on laughter-silvered wings . . .").

154. *"Complete anarchy has reigned"*: copy of George Fitch diary, diary entry for December 24, 1937, enclosed in file from Assistant Naval Attaché E. G. Hagen to Chief of Naval Operations, March 7, 1938, National Archives, reprinted in Fitch, *My Eighty Years in China*, p. 98.

154. *"It is a horrible story to try to relate"*: James McCallum, diary entry for December 19, 1937 (copy), box 119, record group 8, Yale Divinity School Library, reprinted in Smalley, *American Missionary Eyewitnesses to the Nanking Massacre*, p. 21.

155. *"I think I have said enough"*: John Magee, letter to his wife, December 31, 1937, archives of David Magee.

155. *"Please be very careful of this letter"*: John Magee, letter to "Billy" (signed "John"), January 11, 1938, Ernest and Clarissa Forster Collection.

155. *"sensation"*: Fitch, *My Eighty Years in China*, p. 92.

155. *"What I am about to relate"*: copy of George Fitch diary, diary entry for December 24, 1937, enclosed in file from Assistant Naval Attaché E. G. Hagen to Chief of Naval Operations, March 7, 1938, National Archives, reprinted in Fitch, *My Eighty Years in China*, pp. 97–98.

156. *"It is unbelievable that credence could be given"*: Reader's Digest (October 1938).

156. It is believed that John Gillespie Magee was the only Westerner who possessed a motion picture camera during the massacre, and that George Fitch may have borrowed this camera to capture the images of Chinese prisoners taken away by the Japanese. David Magee, son of John Magee, still owns the 16-mm-film motion picture camera used by his father to film scenes in the University of Nanking Hospital. Copies of the films are located in the family archives of Tanya Condon, granddaughter of George Fitch; David Magee, son of John Magee; and Margorie Wilson, widow of Robert Wilson. An English-language summary of the contents of the films can be found in "Deutsche Botschaft China," document starting on page 141, German diplomatic reports, National History Archives, Republic of China.

156. *"as unsavory a crowd"*: Fitch, *My Eighty Years in China*, p. 121.

156. *There was no doubt in his mind:* Tanya Condon, telephone interview with the author, March 27, 1997.

157. *At least one, George Fitch, suspected:* Ibid.

157. *"The Japanese military hate us"*: John Magee, letter to family, January 28, 1938, archives of David Magee.

CHAPTER 7: THE OCCUPATION OF NANKING

159. *"You cannot imagine the disorganization"*: John Magee, undated letter (probably February 1938), archives of David Magee.

159. *"several feet of corpses"*: Durdin, *New York Times*, December 18, 1937.

160. *Observers estimated that Japanese damage:* For estimates of the

damage, see Lewis Smythe, "War Damage in the Nanking Area" (June 1938), cited in Yin and Young, *The Rape of Nanking*, p. 232.

160. *In a sixty-page report released in June 1938:* Lewis Smythe to Willard Shelton (editor of the *Christian Evangelist*, St. Louis), April 29, 1938, box 103, record group 8, Jarvis Collection, Yale Divinity School Library.

160. *Fires in Nanking began:* Testimony of Miner Searle Bates (witness), Records from the Allied Operational/Occupation Headquarters, IMTFE transcript, pp. 2636–37, entry 319, record group 331; see also verdict in Tani Hisao's trial in Nanking, reprinted in *Journal of Studies of Japanese Aggression Against China* (February 1991): 68.

160. *Soldiers torched buildings:* Harries and Harries, *Soldiers of the Sun*, p. 223.

160. *The zone leaders could not put out these fires:* Hsu Shuhsi, *Documents of the Nanking Safety Zone*, p. 51.

160. *By the end of the first few weeks:* IMTFE judgment; "German Archival Materials Reveal 'The Great Nanking Massacre,'" *Journal of Studies of Japanese Aggression Against China* (May 1991); Lewis and Margaret Smythe, letter to friends, March 8, 1938, Jarvis Collection.

160. *They burned down the Russian legation embassy:* Hsu Chuang-ying (witness), testimony before the IMTFE, p. 2577; A. T. Steele, "Japanese Troops Kill Thousands: 'Four Days of Hell' in Captured City Told by Eyewitness; Bodies Piled Five Feet High in Streets," *Chicago Daily News*, December 15, 1937; James McCallum, diary entry for December 29, 1937, Yale Divinity School Library.

160. *The Japanese reserved American property for special insult:* *Reader's Digest* (July 1938).

160. *"remarkable":* "Deutsche Botschaft China," document starting on page 214, German diplomatic reports, National History Archives, Republic of China; Kröger, "Days of Fate in Nanking."

161. *Japanese soldiers devastated the countryside:* "Deutsche Botschaft China," report no. 21, document starting on page 114, submitted by Chinese farmers on January 26, 1938, German diplomatic reports, National History Archives, Republic of China.

161. *The Japanese also used acetylene torches:* Bates, testimony before the IMTFE, pp. 2635–36; Kröger, "Days of Fate in Nanking."

161. *Soldiers were permitted to mail back:* IMTFE judgment; Bergamini, *Japan's Imperial Conspiracy*, p. 37.

161. *More than two hundred pianos:* Bates, testimony before the IMTFE, p. 2636.

161. *In late December the Japanese:* History Committee for the Nationalist Party, Revolutionary Documents, 1987, vol. 109, p. 311, Taipei, Republic of China.

161. *They coveted foreign cars:* Lewis and Margaret Smythe, letter to friends, March 8, 1938, Jarvis Collection.

161. *(Trucks used to cart corpses:* Hsu Shuhsi, *Documents of the Nanking Safety Zone,* p. 14 (John Rabe to Japanese embassy, December 17, 1937, document no. 9).

161. *But the Japanese also invaded Nanking University Hospital:* Robert Wilson, letter to family, December 14, 1937; Bates, testimony before the IMTFE, pp. 2365–36.

161. *A German report noted that on December 15:* An excerpt of a verbal presentation by Mr. Smith of Reuters about the events in Nanking on December 9–15, 1937, in "Deutsche Botschaft China," document starting on page 178, written in Hankow on January 1, 1938, German diplomatic reports, National History Archives, Republic of China.

161. *"Even handfuls of dirty rice":* "The Sack of Nanking: An Eyewitness Account of the Saturnalia of Butchery When the Japanese Took China's Capital, as Told to John Maloney by an American, with 20 Years' Service in China, Who Remained in Nanking After Its Fall," *Ken* (Chicago), June 2, 1938, reprinted in *Reader's Digest* (July 1938). George Fitch was the source behind this article.

161. *In January 1938, not one shop:* Fitch, "Nanking Outrages," January 10, 1938, Fitch Collection.

162. *The harbor was practically empty of ships:* Commanding Officer to the Commander in Chief, U.S. Asiatic Fleet (letterhead marked the U.S.S. *Oahu*), intelligence summary for the week ending February 20, 1938, February 21, 1938, Office of the Chief of Naval Operations, Division of Naval Intelligence, general correspondence, 1929–42, folder A8–21/FS#3, box 195, entry 81, record group 38, National Archives.

162. *Most of the city lacked electricity:* Hsu Shuhsi, *Documents of the Nanking Safety Zone,* p. 99. By late January electricity was available in certain selected buildings in Nanking and water sometimes ran from lower hydrants; Minnie Vautrin, diary 1937–40, December 29, 1937; "Work of the Nanking International Relief Committee, March 5, 1938," Miner Searle Bates Papers, Yale Divinity School Library, p. 1; Xingzhengyuan

xuanchuanju xinwen xunliansuo (News Office of the Executive Yuan Publicity Bureau), *Nanjing zhinan* (*Nanking Guidebook*) (Nanking: Nanjing xinbaoshe, 1938), p. 49. (Information here comes from Mark Eykholt's unpublished dissertation at the University of California at San Diego.) For more information on the Japanese massacre of power plant employees, see Minnie Vautrin, diary 1937–40, December 22, 1937, p. 125; and George Fitch diary, copy enclosed in file from Assistant Naval Attaché E. G. Hagen to Chief of Naval Operations, National Archives. Fitch reported that the employees "who had so heroically kept the plant going" had been taken out and shot on the grounds that the power company was a government agency (it was not). "Japanese officials have been at my office daily trying to get hold of these very men so they could start the turbines and have electricity. It was small comfort to be able to tell them that their own military had murdered most of them."

162. (*Many women chose not to bathe:* Mark Eykholt (author of unpublished dissertation on life in Nanking after the massacre, University of California, San Diego), telephone interview with the author.

162. *People could be seen ransacking houses:* Minnie Vautrin, diary 1937–40, February 10, 1938, p. 189.

162. *On Shanghai Road in the Safety Zone:* Ibid., January 9, 1938, p. 149; January 12, 1938, p. 153; January 27, 1938, p. 172.

162. *This activity jump-started the local economy:* Ibid., January 20, 1938, p. 163.

162. *On January 1, 1938, the Japanese inaugurated:* "A Short Overview Describing the Self-Management Committee in Nanking, 7 March 1938," in "Deutsche Botschaft China," German diplomatic reports, document starting on page 103, National History Archives, Republic of China; Minnie Vautrin diary 1937–40, December 30, 1937, and January 1, 1938; IMTFE Records, court exhibits, 1948, World War II War Crimes Records Collection, box 134, entry 14, record group 238, p. 1906, National Archives; Commanding Officer C. F. Jeffs to the Commander in Chief, U.S. Asiatic Fleet (letterhead marked the U.S.S. *Oahu*), intelligence summary for the week ending April 10, 1938, April 11, 1938, Office of the Chief of Naval Operations, Division of Naval Intelligence, general correspondence, 1929–42, folder A8–21/FS#3, box 195, entry 81, record group 38, National Archives.

162. *Running water, electric lighting:* Commanding Officer C. F. Jeffs to the Commander in Chief, U.S. Asiatic Fleet (letterhead marked the U.S.S. *Oahu*), intelligence summary for the week ending April 10, 1938, April 11, 1938, Office of the Chief of Naval Operations, Division of Naval Intelligence, general correspondence, 1929–42, folder A8–21/FS#3, box 195, entry 81, record group 38, National Archives.

162. *Chinese merchants endured:* Ibid.; "Deutsche Botschaft China," document dated March 4, 1938, starting on page 107, German diplomatic reports, National History Archives, Republic of China; "A Short Overview Describing the Self-Management Committee in Nanking, 7 March 1938," in "Deutsche Botschaft China," document no. 103.

162. *The Japanese also opened up military shops:* "Deutsche Botschaft China," document dated May 5, 1938, starting on page 100, German diplomatic reports, National History Archives, Republic of China.

162. *The Chinese puppet government compounded the poverty:* "A short Overview Describing the Self-Management Committee in Nanking, 7 March 1938," in ibid., document starting on page 103.

163. *"We are now doing an authorized plundering":* Ibid.

163. *Far more alarming than the exploitation of the populace:* For information on the drug trade, see Bates, testimony before the IMTFE, pp. 2649–54, 2658.

163. *Some even tried to use opium to commit suicide:* Elizabeth Curtis Wright, *My Memoirs* (Bridgeport, Conn.: Winthrop Corp., 1973), box 222, Yale Divinity School Library.

163. *Others turned to crime:* "Deutsche Botschaft China," document dated March 4, 1938, starting on page 107, German diplomatic reports, National History Archives, Republic of China.

163. *Japanese employers treated many of the local Chinese laborers:* Tang Shunsan, interview with the author, Nanking, People's Republic of China, July 26, 1995.

164. *The Japanese even inflicted medical experiments:* Sheldon Harris, *Factories of Death: Japanese Biological Warfare, 1932–1945, and the American Cover-up* (London: Routledge, 1994), pp. 102–12.

165. *The Japanese authorities devised a method of mass control:* "From California to Szechuan, 1938," Albert Steward diary, entry for December 20, 1939, private collection of Leland R. Steward.

165. *The dreaded famine never struck:* Lewis Smythe, "War Damage

in the Nanking Area," pp. 20–24; Minnie Vautrin, diary 1937–40, May 5, 1938.

166. *The gardens and farms inside the city walls:* Minnie Vautrin, diary 1937–40, May 21, 1938; "Notes on the Present Situation, March 21, 1938," p. 1, Fitch Collection, Yale Divinity School Library.

166. *But there is no evidence to suggest:* Mark Eykholt, telephone interview with the author.

166. *They also began an aggressive inoculation program:* Ibid. While the Japanese used deadly biological warfare against other cities, it is clear that they took precautions to protect Japanese-occupied territories like Nanking from epidemics, probably because of the presence of Japanese nationals in those areas.

166. *Children of Western missionaries also remember:* Angie Mills, telephone interview with the author.

166. *sprayed with Lysol:* letter dated February 12, 1939, by unidentified author, Forster Collection, RG 8, Box 263, Yale Divinity School Library.

166. *In the spring of 1938, men started to venture back to the city:* Eykholt interview.

167. *Occasionally there was underground resistance:* Ibid.

167. *The Japanese remained in the former capital:* Author's interviews with survivors.

CHAPTER 8: JUDGMENT DAY

169. *In March 1944, the United Nations:* "Judgment of the Chinese War Crimes Military Tribunal on Hisao Tani, March 10, 1947," *Journal of Studies of Japanese Aggression Against China* (February 1991): 68.

170. *During the trials:* Xu Zhigeng, *The Rape of Nanking,* pp. 219, 223, 226, 228.

170. *One of the most famous exhibits:* Television documentary on Wu Xuan and Luo Jing, aired July 25, 1995, Jiangsu television station channel 1.

171. *A Japan Advertiser article:* Xu Zhigeng, *The Rape of Nanking,* pp. 215–16.

171. *The focal point of the Nanking war crimes trials:* Ibid., pp. 218–30.

172. *The scope of the trial was staggering:* For statistics on the IMTFE,

see Arnold Brackman, *The Other Nuremberg: The Untold Story of the Tokyo War Crimes Trials* (New York: Morrow, 1987), pp. 9, 18, 22; *World War II* magazine, January 1996, p. 6.

173. *"At the IMTFE, a thousand My Lais emerged"*: Ibid., p. 9.

173. *The prosecution learned:* IMTFE transcript.

173. *Only one in twenty-five American POWs died:* Ken Ringle, "Still Waiting for an Apology: Historian Gavan Daws Calling Japan on War Crimes," *Washington Post*, March 16, 1995; author's telephone interview and electronic mail communication with Gavan Daws. According to Daws, the death-rate figure for all Allied POWs for the Japanese was 27 percent: 34 percent for Americans, 33 percent for Australians, 32 percent for the British, and under 20 percent for the Dutch. In contrast, the death rate for all Western Front Allied military POWs of the Germans (excluding Russians) was 4 percent. For more information, see Gavan Daws, *Prisoners of the Japanese: POWs of World War II in the Pacific* (New York: Morrow, 1994), pp. 360–61, 437.

173. *"The Rape of Nanking was not the kind of isolated incident"*: Brackman, *The Other Nuremberg*, p. 182.

174. *"let loose like a barbarian horde"*: IMTFE judgment.

174. *"chastise the Nanking government"*: IMTFE judgment.

174. *To atone for the sins of Nanking:* Bergamini, *Japan's Imperial Conspiracy*, pp. 3–4.

175. *"I am happy to end this way"*: Ibid., p. 47.

175. *"either secretly ordered or willfully committed"*: IMTFE judgment, p. 1001.

175. *Unfortunately, many of the chief culprits:* Buruma, *The Wages of Guilt*, p. 175; Bergamini, *Japan's Imperial Conspiracy*, pp. 45–48.

175. The information about Nakajima Kesago comes from Kimura Kuninori, *Koseiha shogun Nakajima Kesago* [*Nakajima Kesago, General of the Individualist Faction*]. Tokyo: Kôjinsha, 1987.

176. The information about Yanagawa Heisuke comes from Sugawara Yutaka, *Yamatogokoro: Fukumen shogun Yanagawa Heisuke Seidan* [*Spirit of Japan: Elevated Conversation from the Masked Shogun Yanagawa Heisuke*]. Tokyo: Keizai Oraisha, 1971, p. 166. (Mention of his death by heart attack on January 22, 1945, is on p. 234.)

176. *"Many would find it difficult"*: Herbert Bix, "The Showa Emperor's 'Monologue' and the Problem of War Responsibility." *The Journal of Japanese Studies*, summer 1992, vol. 18, no. 2, p. 330.

177. *"a priceless historical treasure"*: author interview with John Young of the China Institute. In 1957, Young was a professor at Georgetown University and part of a group of scholars who had secured permission to microfilm some of the Japanese Army and Navy Ministries archives seized by American occupation forces in 1945. The following year came the abrupt decision of the United States government to return the documents to Japan—a tremendous blow to Young and the others. ("I was beyond shock, I tell you," Young recalled. "I was flabbergasted!") As a result of this decision, only a small portion of the Japanese military archives were microfilmed before they were boxed up and returned to Japan in February 1958. The greatest regret of his life, Young said, was his failure to foresee this decision, which would have given him and the other scholars the time to microfilm the most important papers in the collection.

The circumstances behind the return were mysterious, and continue to baffle to this day the historians involved in the microfilm project. "This was something I could never understand," Edwin Beal, formerly of the Library of Congress, said during a telephone interview in April 1997. "We were told that returning these documents was a matter of high policy and should not be questioned."

Years later, John Young heard rumors that the returned documents were used by the Japanese government to purge those from their ranks who had not been sufficiently loyal to the wartime regime.

177. *seriously criticized:* In all fairness, it must be pointed out that many of the facts in Bergamini's book are accurate and that he did discover, in the course of his research, many important new Japanese-language documents for World War II historians. Therefore, scholars have often found *Japan's Imperial Conspiracy* to be a valuable—even if flawed and confusing—resource.

178. *"In order to conquer the world"*: W. Morton, *Tanaka Giichi and Japan's China Policy* (Folkestone, Kent, Eng.: Dawson, 1980), p. 205; Harries and Harries, pp. 162–63.

178. *Currently no reputable historian*: Letter from Rana Mitter to author, July 17, 1997.

178. *"inconceivable"*: Information about Herbert Bix's opinion comes from author's telephone interview with Bix.

179. *Back in 1943, Prince Mikasa Takahito*: "A Royal Denunciation of Horrors: Hirohito's Brother—an Eyewitness—Assails Japan's

Wartime Brutality," *Los Angeles Times*, July 9, 1994; Merrill Goozner, "New Hirohito Revelations Startle Japan: Emperor's Brother Says He Reported WWII China Atrocities to Him in 1944; National Doubts Them Now," *Chicago Tribune*, July 7, 1994; *Daily Yomiuri*, July 6, 1994, p. 7.

179. *"It helps them acquire guts"*: *Daily Yomiuri*, July 6, 1994, p. 7.

179. *"bits and pieces"*: Goozner, "New Hirohito Revelations Startle Japan," *Chicago Tribune*, July 7, 1994.

179. *"extreme satisfaction"*: *Asahi*, Tokyo edition, December 15, 1937.

179. Prince Kanin's telegram: Ibid.

179. *silver vases*: *Asahi*, Tokyo edition, February 27, 1938.

180. *Prince Asaka, for one, retired:* Bergamini, *Japan's Imperial Conspiracy*, p. 46. Information about Asaka's golf course development comes from *Daijinmei Jiten* [*The Expanded Biographical Encyclopedia*] (Tokyo: Heibonsha, 1955), vol. 9, p. 16.

CHAPTER 9: THE FATE OF THE SURVIVORS

183. *According to Karen Parker:* Karen Parker, telephone interview with the author. For Parker's legal analyses on *jus cogens* and Japan's debt to its World War II victims, see Karen Parker and Lyn Beth Neylon, "*Jus Cogens:* Compelling the Law of Human Rights," *Hastings International and Comparative Law Review* 12, no. 2 (Winter 1989): 411–63; Karen Parker and Jennifer F. Chew, "Compensation for Japan's World War II War-Rape Victims," *Hastings International and Comparative Law Review* 17, no. 3 (Spring 1994): 497–549.

At a seminar for the 58th anniversary of the Japanese invasion of China, scholars urged Chinese victims to demand reparations from Japan. Tang Te-kang, a professor at Columbia University, said that the victims have a precedent in pressing Japan for compensation—set by Japan itself when it demanded and received reparations from China after it and seven other countries invaded China during the Qing dynasty. According to the historian Wu Tien-wei, Chinese victims are entitled to these reparations according to international law; Lillian Wu, "Demand Reparations from Japan, War Victims Told," Central News Agency, July 7, 1994.

184. *One man who was nearly roasted alive:* Author's interview with a survivor (name withheld on request).

184. *Another woman whose father was executed:* Liu Fonghua, interview with the author, Nanking, July 29, 1995.

185. *In the local newspaper, Lewis Smythe saw articles:* Oral history interview with Lewis Smythe by Cyrus Peake and Arthur Rosenbaum, Claremont Graduate School, December 11, 1970, February 26, and March 16, 1971, box 228, record group 8, Yale Divinity School Library.

185. *"not only responded well to the imperialist policies":* "Zhuiyi Rikou zai Nanjing da tusha (Remember the Great Massacre at Nanking)," reprinted in *Xinhua Yuebao* 3, pp. 988–91.

185. *"Dr. Smythe, there are 100,000 people in this city":* Peake and Rosenbaum oral history interview with Smythe.

186. *In 1951 he left his position:* "Biographic Sketch and Summary of Contents," in Peake and Rosenbaum oral history interview with Smythe.

186. *Bates also left Nanking:* Morton G. Bates, letter to the author, October 7, 1996.

186. *David Magee, son of the Reverend John Magee, is certain:* David Magee, telephone interview with the author.

186. *For example, Edith Fitch Swapp:* Edith Fitch Swapp, telephone interview with the author; Fitch, *My Eighty Years in China*, p. 125. In his book, Fitch describes his problems with memory loss and his visit to a neurologist. "To my considerable relief the doctor reported there was nothing wrong with my brain; I was just suffering from nerve fag. I had been leading a pretty strenuous life, of course, and possibly the terrible memories of those Nanking days had something to do with it too" (p. 125).

186. *Robert Wilson, the University of Nanking Hospital surgeon:* Marjorie Wilson, telephone interview with the author.

187. *"I'm about at the end of my energy":* Minnie Vautrin, diary 1937–40, April 14, 1940, p. 526.

187. *"In May 1940 Miss Vautrin's heath broke":* Minnie Vautrin, diary 1937–40, handwritten note on the bottom of the last page.

187. *Her niece recalls that Vautrin's colleagues:* Description of Vautrin's journey back to the United States, her electroshock treatment, her last communication with her family, and her suicide comes from Emma Lyon, telephone interview with the author.

187. *Before he was summoned back to Germany:* For Rabe's last days in Nanking, see Minnie Vautrin, diary 1938–40, February 21, 1928, entry, p. 199; George Rosen report "Deutsche Botschaft China," document no. 122, National History Archives, Republic of China.

188. *Also, an oral history interview with one of his friends:* Peake and Rosenbaum oral history interview with Smythe.

189. *"I am happy I could help you":* Martha Begemann, letter to the author, April 26, 1996.

189. *Rabe kept his promise to the Chinese:* Description of Rabe's efforts to publicize the Nanking atrocities and his downfall in Germany comes from Ursula Reinhardt, letters to the author, 1996–97.

190. *"My grandfather looked embarrassed":* Ursula Reinhardt, letter to author, April 27, 1996, p. 2.

191. *"There is no job for me at Siemens":* John Rabe diary, entry for the years 1945 and 1946, translated September 12, 1996, by Ursula Reinhardt in letter to the author, September 18, 1996.

191. *"Last Sunday I was with Mommy":* Ibid.

191. *"Now Mommy weighs only 44 kg":* Ibid.

191. *"We suffer hunger and hunger again":* Ibid., April 18, 1946.

191. *"Yesterday my petition to get de-nazified":* Ibid., April 18, 1946.

192. *"If I had heard of any atrocities":* Ibid., April 18, 1946.

192. *"On June the 3rd finally I was de-nazified":* Ibid., June 7, 1946.

193. *"Today Mommy is out":* Ibid., June 7, 1946.

193. *Within a matter of days:* Renmin Zibao (People's Daily), December 25, 1996, p. 6.

193. According to Reinhardt, the family of W. Plumer Mills also sent packages of food (CARE packages) to Rabe, which helped cure him of the skin disease that was caused by malnutrition.

193. *The Kuomingtang government even offered Rabe free housing:* Ibid.; see also Ursula Reinhardt, letter to the author, April 27, 1996; and *Renmin Zibao,* December 27, 1996.

193. *In June 1948 the city of Nanking learned:* Renmin Zibao, December 25, 1996.

194. *Rabe died from an artery stroke:* Ursula Reinhardt, letter to the author, April 27, 1996.

194. *Reinhardt was pregnant and immersed in school examinations:* Renming Zibao, December 27, 1996.

194. *Rabe's previous status as a Nazi:* Ursula Reinhardt, telephone interview with the author.

195. *Shortly after the discovery of the Rabe papers:* Peter Kröger, letter to the author, October 23, 1996.

195. *"Contrary to the current opinions of the Hitler government":* Kröger, "Days of Fate in Nanking."

195. *The contents were violent beyond her wildest expectations:* Renming Zibao, December 27, 1996.

195. *She saw the diaries as political dynamite:* Ursula Reinhardt, presentation, December 12, 1996, New York City; Reinhardt, telephone interview with the author.

195. *She spent fifteen hours:* Ursula Reinhardt, letter to the author, December 3, 1996.

195. *Shao, who was fearful that right-wing Japanese:* Shao Tzuping, telephone interview with the author.

196. *"It's an incredibly gripping and depressing narrative":*   David Chen, "At the Rape of Nanking: A Nazi Who Saved Lives," *New York Times*, December 12, 1996, p. A3.

196. *"What makes this report significant":* Asahi Shimbun, December 8, 1996.

197. *"The meaning of this report":* Ibid.

CHAPTER 10: THE FORGOTTEN HOLOCAUST:
A SECOND RAPE

201. *"People say that the Japanese made a holocaust":* "Playboy interview: Shintaro Ishihara—candid conversation," David Sheff, interviewer, *Playboy*, October 1990, vol. 37, no. 10, p. 63.

201. *"Japan's denial of the rape of Nanjing":* Yoshi Tsurumi, "Japan Makes Efforts to Be Less Insular," *New York Times*, December 25, 1990.

201. *In his rebuttals:* Reprinted in *Journal of Studies of Japanese Agression Against China* (February 1991): 71.

202. *"The raping of the women":* John Magee, letter to "Billy" (signed "John"), January 11, 1938, Ernest and Clarissa Forster Collection.

202. *"dead bodies in every street alley":* Ibid.

203. *"I think the Nanking Massacre and the rest was a fabrication":* Sebastian Moffet, "Japan Justice Minister Denies Nanking Massacre," Reuters, May 4, 1994.

203. *The violent reaction to his statements:* Accounts of Nagano being burned in effigy and eggs being thrown at Japanese embassies can be found in Reuters, May 6, 1994. For information regarding his resignation, see Miho Yoshikawa, "Japan Justice Minister Quits over WWII Gaffe," Reuters, May 7, 1994.

203. *"just a part of war":* Karl Schoenberger, "Japan Aide Quits over Remark on WWII," *Los Angeles Times,* May 14, 1988.

203. *That month Japanese Prime Minister Yasuhiro Nakasone dismissed him:* Ibid.

203. *"There was no intention of aggression":* Ibid.

203. *"I didn't say Japan wasn't an aggressor":* Ibid.

203. *By May, Okuno had been forced to resign:* Ibid.

204. *In August 1994, Sakurai Shin:* Mainichi Daily News, August 17, 1994.

204. *"the Chinese government regrets that":* Kyoto News Service, August 13, 1994.

204. *"inappropriate":* Ibid.

204. *While Japan was aggressive toward China:* Robert Orr, "Hashimoto's War Remarks Reflect the Views of Many of His Peers," *Tokyo Keizai,* December 13, 1994.

204. *"went for the money":* "Japanese Official Apologizes," Associated Press, January 28, 1997.

204. *"caused some unpleasantness":* Ibid.

205. *In 1990 he was forced to resign from his position:* Ibid.

205. *The entire Japanese education system:* Hugh Gurdon, "Japanese War Record Goes into History," *Daily Telegraph,* April 20, 1994.

205. *The first thing they wanted to know was who won:* New York Times, November 3, 1991. Psychology professor Hiroko Yamaji told me that even Japanese college students have asked him the same question: Which country won World War II, the United States or Japan? (Interview with Yamaji, March 30, 1997, during a workshop in San Francisco.)

206. *For example, in 1977 the Ministry of Education:* Brackman, *The Other Nuremberg,* p. 27.

206. *"Immediately after the occupation of Nanking":* The passages in Ienaga's textbooks and the censors' comments come from "Truth in Textbooks, Freedom in Education and Peace for Children: The Struggle Against the Censorship of School Textbooks in Japan" (booklet) (Tokyo: National League for Support of the School Textbook Screening Suit, 2nd. ed., June 1995).

207. *In 1970, when he actually won his case:* Buruma, *The Wages of Guilt,* p. 196.

207. *"politically tone deaf":* David Sanger, "A Stickler for History, Even If It's Not Very Pretty," *New York Times,* May 27, 1993.

208. *"It was not fair to describe the Nanking atrocity":* Shukan Asahi, August 13, 1982, p. 20.

208. *Before Fujio's dismissal:* Information on the treatment of the Nanking massacre in textbooks before and after Fujio's dismissal comes from Ronald E. Yates, " 'Emperor' Film Keeps Atrocity Scenes in Japan," *Chicago Tribune,* January 23, 1988.

209. *"The Sasaki unit":* Mainichi Daily News, May 30, 1994.

On August 29, 1997, Ienaga won a partial victory in the last of his three lawsuits against the Education Ministry. The Supreme Court ordered the central government to pay Ienaga 400,000 yen in damages and concluded that the ministry had abused its discretionary power when it forced him to delete from his textbook a reference on live human experiments conducted by the Imperial army's Unit 731 during World War II. However, the Supreme Court continued to uphold the textbook-screening system itself, ruling that the process did not violate freedom of expression, academic freedom, or the right to education, which are guaranteed under the Japanese constitution. (*Japan Times,* August 29, 1997)

209. *"How long must we apologize":* The military historian Noboru Kojima, quoted in *New York Times,* November 3, 1991.

209. *"hitting the lottery":* Quoted in Sonni Efron, "Defender of Japan's War Past," *Los Angeles Times,* May 9, 1997.

209. *Ono Kenji, a factory worker:* Charles Smith, "One Man's Crusade: Kenji Ono Lifts the Veil on the Nanking Massacre," *Far Eastern Economic Review,* August 25, 1994.

210. *In 1996, he coedited:* Ono Kenji, Fujiwara Akira, and Honda Katsuichi, ed., *Nankin Daigyakusatsu o kirokushita Kogun heishi-tachi: daijusan Shidan Yamda Shitai heishi no jinchu nikki. [Soldiers of the Imperial Army Who Recorded the Nanking Massacre: Battlefield Journals of Soldiers from the 13th Division Yamada Detachment]* (Tokyo: Otsuki Shoten, 1996).

210. *"Not only did the Japanese distributor":* Yates, " 'Emperor' Film Keeps Atrocity Scenes in Japan."

210. *"confusion and misunderstanding":* Ibid.

211. *Suzuki charged that some of Honda's and Hora's stories:* Most of the information on the debate between the illusion and

massacre factions, the *Kaikosha* survey, and the tampering with Matsui's diary comes from Yang Daqing, "A Sino-Japanese Controversy: The Nanjing Atrocity as History," *Sino-Japanese Studies* 3, no. 1 (November 1990).

212. *"enemy propaganda"*: Quoted in Buruma, *The Wages of Guilt*, p. 119.

212. *"not only on the Japanese officers"*: Ibid., pp. 121–22.

213. *"no less than tens of thousands"*: Yang Daqing, "A Sino-Japanese Controversy: The Nanjing Atrocity as History," *Sino-Japanese Studies* vol. 3, no. 1 (November 1990): 23.

213. *"there was no excuse"*: Ibid.

213. *What happened to Azuma Shiro*: Catherine Rosair, "For One Veteran, Emperor Visit Should Be Atonement," Reuters, October 15, 1992.

213. *The troubles for Motoshima Hitoshi*: Buruma, *The Wages of Guilt*, pp. 249–50.

EPILOGUE

215. *"Loot all, kill all, burn all"*: Rummel, *China's Bloody Century*, p. 139.

215. *"I have received orders"*: Quoted in Wilson, *When Tigers Fight*, p. 61.

216. *At least one author on China*: Jules Archer, *Mao Tse-tung* (New York: Hawthorne, 1972), p. 95.

216. *R. J. Rummel, author of* China's Bloody Century, *points out*: Rummel, *China's Bloody Century*, p. 139.

216. *In areas that may have served as landing zones*: Ibid., p. 138.

216. *We now know that Japanese aviators sprayed fleas*: Ibid., pp. 140–41.

216. *The final death count was almost incredible*: Ibid., pp. 149, 150, 164.

217. *"the transfer of oppression"*: George Hicks, *The Comfort Women* (New York: Norton, 1994), p. 43.

217. *Japanese soldiers were forced to wash the underwear of officers*: Nicholas Kristof, "A Japanese Generation Haunted by Its Past," *New York Times*, January 22, 1997.

217. *"act of love"*: Tanaka Yuki, *Hidden Horrors*, p. 203.

218. *"To be frank, your view of Chinese"*: Xiaowu Xingnan, *Invasion—Testimony from a Japanese Reporter*, p. 59.

218. *A Japanese officer in Nanking who bound Chinese captives:* Xu Zhigeng, *The Rape of Nanking,* p. 74.

218. *"a pig is more valuable now":* Azuma Shiro diary, March 24, 1938.

218. *"Every single bullet":* General Araki speech, quoted in Maruyama Masao, "Differences Between Nazi and Japanese Leaders," in *Japan 1931–1945: Militarism, Facism, Japanism?,* ed. Ivan Morris (Boston: D. C. Heath, 1963), p. 44.

219. *"Who is greater, God or the emperor":* Joanna Pitman, "Repentance," *New Republic,* February 10, 1992.

219. *"I am going to the front":* Bergamini, *Japan's Imperial Conspiracy,* p. 10.

219. *"The struggle between Japan and China":* Toshio Iritani, *Group Psychology of the Japanese in Wartime* (London and New York: Kegan Paul International, 1991), p. 290.

221. *The less restraint on power within a government:* R. J. Rummel, *Death by Government* (New Brunswick, N.J.: Transaction Publishers, 1995), pp. 1–2.

222. *The German government has paid:* Information on German postwar restitution comes from the German Information Center, New York City.

223. *"Those who ignore history":* "Japan Military Buildup a Mistake, Romulo Says," UPI, December 30, 1982.

224. *In April 1997, former U.S. Ambassador Walter Mondale:* Barry Schweid, AP, April 9, 1997.

224. *The Rape of Nanking even made its way:* William Lipinski (D-IL) drafted the resolution, copies of which can be obtained directly from his office or from the world wide web site of www.sjwar.org.

224. *"In the past war":* Chinese American Forum 12, no. 3 (Winter 1997): 17.

INDEX

ABC-TV, 196
Academic community, 209–10
Acton, Lord, 220
Addresses to Young Men (Hashimoto), 26
Afghanistan, 190
Africa, 3, 109
African Americans, 205
Against Our Will: Men, Women, and Rape (Brownmiller), 89
Agriculture, 25–26, 165–66
Ai-no-muchi ("whip of love"), 217
Air raids, 5–6, 64–66, 70–71; and biological warfare, 216; by Britain, 6; kamikaze suicide missions, 20; and the Safety Zone, 107, 111, 112, 113–15, 123–24; on the U.S.S. *Panay*, 107, 144, 146–49
Akutagawa Ryunosuke, 14

Aizu Wakamatsu Battalion, 209
Alley, Norman, 146–49
Alliance in the Memory of Victims of the Nanking Massacre, 8, 195
Allied Powers, 20, 169
American Heritage Picture History of World War II, The, 7
Anhwei (Anhui) Province, 76, 130
Araki Sadao, 26–27
Archer, Jules, 216
Arson, 138, 153, 160, 170
Asahi Shimbun, 44–45, 196, 211, 212
Asaka Yasuhiko, Prince, 38–42, 51–52, 174–76, 179–80
Associated Press, 144–46
Atami, 175
Atomic bombs, 6, 15, 167, 199, 202

Auden, W. H., xi

Auschwitz concentration camp, 105, 199

Australia, 26

Austria, 105

Authority, pressure to conform to, 31–32

Azuma Shiro, 42–44, 49–50, 58, 213, 218

Baguazhou, 45

Bataan Death March, 173

Bates, Miner Searle, 99–100, 139, 163, 170, 185–86

Bavaria, 189

Begemann, Martha, 189

Belgium, 5

Benedict, Ruth, 54

Bengali women, 89

Bentatsu ("act of love"), 217

Bergamini, David, 37, 39, 177

Berlin, 189–91

Bertolucci, Bernardo, 210

Bessage, Jacquinot de, 106

Biological warfare, 216

Bix, Herbert, 176

Blood on the Sun (film), 178

Body disposal, 45–46, 127, 143, 159–60, 164. See also Burial

Bosnia, 89, 221

Boxer Indemnity Scholarships, 30

Boycotts, of Japanese goods, 25, 29

Brackman, Arnold, 173

Brady, Richard, 123, 124

Britain, 5–6, 191, 204; air raids by, 6; capital ship limitation treaty with, 27; correspondents from, 38; Japanese trade with, 21; military academies in, 32

Brownmiller, Susan, 89

Buck, J. Lossing, 123

Buck, Pearl, 122, 123

Buddha, statue of, 170

Buddhism, 37, 61, 109, 175. See also Religion

Buddhist monks, 95

Buddhist nuns, 90, 96

Bungei Shunju, 203, 211

Burdick, Charles, 189

Burial: grounds, excavation of, 171; mass, 46, 85, 127, 171; records, 101–2; services, 51. See also Body disposal

Bushido (Way of the Warrior), 20

Cagney, James, 178

Calligraphy, 61

Canada, 9, 26, 223

Cannibalism, 88, 173

Cantonese language, 71

Capra, Frank, 157, 193

Carlowitz & Company, 114

Carthage, 5

Cease-fire, three-day, 113

Censorship: and history textbooks, 6–7, 205–9; self-imposed, 210–11

Central China Expeditionary Force, 174

Central Hospital, 123

Chahar, 4

Chang Siao-sung, 64–65

Chang Su Hsiang, 94

Chang Tien-Chun, 65–66

Chang Tsolin (Zhang Zuolin), 29

Changsha, 69

Changteh, 216

Chiang Kai-shek, 33, 103, 113, 151–52, 182; battle with the warlords under, 28; and the fall of Shanghai, 67; flight of, from Nanking, 70; retreat ordered by, 74, 75; and Tang Sheng-chih, 67–70, 73–75

Chicago Daily News, 144–45

Chicago Tribune, 153

Chichibu, 39

China's Bloody Century (Rummel), 216

China Weekly Review, 38

Chinese Expeditionary Force High Command, 164

Chinese language, 61

Cholera, 166

Choy, Christine, 8

Christ, 62

Christianity, 5, 54–55, 62, 153. *See also* Religion

Chrysanthemum and the Sword, The (Benedict), 54

Chunghua Gate, vii, 171

Chungking (Chongqing), 69, 71

Chungshan Gate, 47

Chungshan (Zhongshan) Road, 46, 77, 78, 114, 115

Chuo University, 52

Churchill, Winston, 7

CNN (Cable News Network), 196, 221

Cold War, 182, 223

Colonialism, 25, 27

Comfort women, 52–53, 209, 223

Communism, 11, 181–82, 187, 213, 223

Communist Party, 213

Confucianism, 53

Cook, Haruko Taya, 54

Cook, Theodore, 54

Coppening, Max, 153

Council of Princes of the Blood, 180

Coup d'états, 28, 37

Crusades, 5, 218

Currency, 162–63

Dagong Daily, 91

Death: and desensitization exercises, 56–58; by dogs, 6, 88–89, 164; by fire, 87–88; by ice, 88; meaning of, to the samurai warrior class, 20; and military training, 10, 56–59; statistics, 4–6, 8, 20, 99–104, 139, 212, 216–217; and torture, 87–89. *See also* Suicide

Delhi, 5

Delivered from Evil: The Saga of World War II (Leckie), 7

Democide, 220

Department of Justice, 224

Depression, 25–26

Desensitization exercises, 56–58

Diseases, sexually transmitted, 53

Documentaries, 8–9; *In the Name of the Emperor*, 8, 13, 49, 157; *Testament*, 157; *Why We Fight: Battle of China*, 157

Documents of the Nanking Safety Zone (Hsu), 155

Dogs, death by, 6, 88–89, 164

Domei news agency, 149

Dresden, 6

Drug addiction, 163

Drum Tower, 62

Durdin, Frank Tillman, 144–45, 153, 201–2

Earthquakes, 25, 48

Eastern Europe, 181–82

Economic crises, 24–26

Education, 12–13, 15, 29–33, 200–201, 218, 223–24; and military training, 10, 32–33, 56–59; and textbook content, 6–7, 205–9

Ethics, 20, 23. *See also* Morality

Ethiopia, 3

Executions: and killing contests, 56, 83–87, 143; and Matsui, 51–52, 53; near Mufu Mountain, 44–46; ordered by Asaka, 40–48; squads, motives behind, 54–59; and torture, 87–89

Expansionism, 21, 25, 27–28

Experiments, medical, 164–65, 216, 223

Fabrication of the "Nanking Massacre," The (Tanaka), 212

Families, slaughter of entire, 91–92

Far Eastern magazine, 155

Far Eastern Conference of 1927, 178

Farming, 25–26, 165–66

Ferguson, John, 122

Feudal lords, 19–20

Fillmore, Millard, 21

Films, 9, 11; *Blood on the Sun*, 178; *It's a Wonderful Life*, 193; *Last Emperor, The*, 210; *Rashomon*, 14; *Schindler's List*, 185. *See also* Documentaries

Fitch, George, 116–17, 133, 147, 150–57, 161, 186; film smuggled out of China by, 156–57; on Japanese propaganda, 151; reports/diaries of, 116–17, 120, 121, 154, 155–56

Foreign intelligence, 37, 147–49

Fox Movietone, 146

France, 5, 24; capital ship limitations treaty with, 27; Japanese army intelligence in, 37; Japanese trade with, 21, 27; priests from, 106

Frank, Anne, 105, 129, 199

Fujio Masayuki, 203, 208

Fujiwara Akira, 100

Fukuda Tokuyasu, 118

Fuxuan war criminal camp, 101

Gambling, 24
Gas, poison, 123, 124, 164
Genocide, 200–21
Germany, 3–4, 148; and
    Christianity, 55; former
    colonies of, 25; and Israel,
    11; militarism of, 23;
    property of, damage of,
    160–61; Rabe's return to,
    188–90; and the Shantung
    Peninsula, 25; war
    reparations payments by, 12,
    222. *See also* Holocaust;
    Nazis
Gestapo, 190, 194
Giep, Mies, 105
Ginling Women's Arts and
    Science College, 64, 93, 96,
    106, 129–33, 135–38
Global Alliance for Preserving
    the History of World War II,
    9
Göring, Hermann, 187
God, 27, 54, 219
Great Britain. *See* Britain
Great Depression, 25–26
Guo Qi (Ko Chi), 95
Gu Zhutong, General, 73–74

Hague Convention, 172
Hamburg, 188, 189
Hanchung Gate, vii
Han Chung Road, 116
Hangchow (Hangzhou), 5, 36
Hankow (Hankou), 69
Hara-kiri, ritual of, 20
Harvard Medical School, 122

Harvard University, 7, 122,
    196
Hashimoto Kingoro, 26
Hashimoto Ryutaro, 204
Hashimoto Tokio, 30
Hata Ikuhiko, 100, 196–197
Hatz, 139
*Hidden Horrors: Japanese War
    Crimes in World War II*
    (Yuki), 217
Hirohito, Emperor, 12, 37–39,
    205; death of, 213–14; and
    the IMTFE, 176–80
Hiroshima, 6, 11, 57, 199–202,
    206
Hirota Koki, 103, 148, 175
History curricula, 12–13, 15,
    200–201, 223–24; in
    military academies, 32–33;
    and textbook content, 6–7,
    205–9
Hitler, Adolf, xi, 147–48, 111,
    187; death of Jews under, 5;
    and foreign intelligence,
    147; Luftwaffe and Panzer
    divisions of, 3; pictures of,
    160; and Rabe, 119, 121,
    187–88, 190, 195–97; as a
    war criminal, 12
Hofei (Hefei), 130
Holocaust, the, 11–13, 15–16,
    188, 201, 221; and
    Auschwitz concentration
    camp, 105, 199; memory of,
    13, 16; number of Jews
    killed during, 5. *See also*
    Jews
Honda Katsuichi, 211–12

Hong Kong, 68
Hong Xiuquan
    (Hung Hsiu-ch'üan), 62
Hopeh (Hebei), 4
Horace, 20
Hora Tomio, 211–12
House of Representatives, 224
Hsia (Xia), Mr. and Mrs., 92
Hsiakwan (Xiaguan), vii, 48,
    70, 75, 77, 87, 101, 124,
    147
Hsing Lu Kao (Xinglukou), 92
Hsu Shuhsi, 155

Ice, death by, 88
Ichang (Yichiang or Water
    Gate), 77
Identity, Japanese, 19–20
Ienaga Saburo, 206–7
"Illusion of the Nanjing
    Massacre, The" (Suzuki), 211
Imai Masatake, 47–48
Imperial Rescript on
    Education, 31
IMTFE (International Military
    Tribunal of the Far East), 4,
    99–102, 172–81, 201, 203
In the Name of the Emperor
    (documentary), 8, 13, 49,
    157
Incest, 95
Individualism, 32
Industrial Revolution, 21
Infanticide, 90
Inflation, 25
Inoculation programs, 166
Instinct, 55, 220

International Committee for
    the Nanking Safety Zone,
    72, 75, 90, 92–97, 105–39,
    145, 153–57, 160–62, 174,
    182, 184–85, 192, 194–95
International Red Cross, 67,
    100, 115, 125, 137, 189
Interventionism, 28
Intimidation, 213–14
Inukai Tsuyoshi, 28
Iritani Toshio, 32
Iron Production, 24
Ishihara Shintaro, 201,202
Ishiwara Kanji, 30
Israel, 11
It's a Wonderful Life (film), 193
Italy, 27, 71
Iwo Jima, 20

Japan Advertiser, 56, 171
Japan at War: An Oral History
    (Cook), 54
Japanese Fellowship of
    Reconciliation, 224
Japanese Terror in China
    (Timperley), 155
Japan's Imperial Conspiracy
    (Bergamini), 177
Japan That Can Say No, The
    (Ishihara), 201
Jennings, Peter, 196
Jews, 5, 13, 105, 109, 185. See
    also Holocaust, the
Jiang Jieshi. See Chiang Kai-
    shek
Jiangsu Academy of Social
    Sciences, 100
Jim Crowism, 13

Journalists, 143–57; American, 144–46, 196; and debates on the Nanking Massacre, 211–13; and the defense of Nanking, 70; and the fifty-ninth anniversary of the fall of Nanking, 196; Japanese, 47–48; and Japanese damage control, 147; and Matsui, 50–51; and the motives behind Nanking, 55, 56; newsreels from, 146–47, 148–49; and recent mass killings, 221; and the stories of survivors, 83; and textbook censorship, 207–8. See also Documentaries; Films; specific publications
Judeo-Christian tradition, 54–55. See also Christianity
Jus cogens, principle of, 184
Justice Department, 224

Kaikosha, 212–13
Kajiyama Seiroku, 204–5
Kamikaze suicide missions, 20
Kanin, Prince, 179
Kasahara Tokushi, 196
Kawano Hiroki, 48
Kidnapping: of men for military service, 71; of women, for military prostitution, 52–53, 93
Killing contests, 56, 83–87, 143
Kimura Kuninori, 37, 176
Kim Young-sam, 204
Kirby, William, 196

Korea, 23, 52–53, 203–5, 206; and the Korean War, 182, 185; and the 1885 treaty, 23
Kriebel, Mr., 111
Kröger, Christian, 114, 138, 139, 195
Kröger, Peter, 195
Kuang To (Official Earth), 163
Kubotani Motoyuki, 210
Kuling, 123
Kurihara Riichi, 45
Kuomintang (Guomingdang) government, 193
Kutwo (ship), 111
Kwantung army, 178
Kyoto, 14, 213

Labor strikes, 25
Last Emperor, The (film), 210
Latin America, 188
Leaflets, dropped by airplanes, 72, 149, 152
League of Nations, 29
Leckie, Robert, 7
"Let the Whole World Know the Nanking Massacre" (Wu Tienwei), 102
Lethal gases, 123, 124, 164
Lexington Theological Seminary, 186
Liaodong Peninsula (Manchuria), 23–24
Liaoning Province, 101
Liberal Democratic Party, 201, 204, 214
Life (magazine), 157
Liu Fang-chu, 100
Li Xouying, 96–99

Lootings, 138, 160–61, 170, 215, 216
Luftwaffe division, 3

MacArthur, Douglas, 177, 223
McCallum, James, 123, 129, 139, 151, 154
McDaniel, C. Yates, 144–46, 153
Magee, David, 186, 202
Magee, John Gillspie, 8, 155–57, 186, 188, 190, 201–2
Magee's Testament (videotape), 8
Mainichi Shimbun, 202–3
Manchester Guardian, 115
Manchukuo, 29. *See also* Manchuria
Manchuria, 3–4, 28–30, 62, 100, 152; Kwantung army in, 178; seizure of, in 1931, 29; and Tang, 68
Mandarin language, 71
Mao Tse-tung (Mao Zedong), 182
Marco Polo, 62
Marco Polo Bridge, 33, 122–33
Martial law, 28
Master-race mentalities, 3–4
Matsui Iwane, General, 7, 37, 38–39, 50–52, 72, 75, 174–75, 179, 212, 219
Matsumoto, 51
Mausoleum Park, 70
Mayell, Eric, 146, 147
Media, 143–57; American, 144–46, 196; and debates

on the Nanking Massacre, 211–13; and the defense of Nanking, 70; and the fifty-ninth anniversary of the fall of Nanking, 196; and Japanese damage control, 147; and Matsui, 50–51; and the motives behind Nanking, 55, 56; newsreels, 146–47, 148–49; and recent mass killings, 221; and the stories of survivors, 83; and textbook censorship, 207–8. *See also* Documentaries; Films, Photographs; *specific publications*
Medical experiments, 164–65, 216, 223
Meiji, Emperor, 22, 178
Meiji Restoration, 23, 26, 31
Memoirs of the Second World War (Churchill), 7
Memorial Hall of the Victims of the Nanking Massacre, 100
Methodists. *See also* Christianity
Michel, Henri, 7
Middle class, 24
Mikasa Takahito, Prince, 179
Militarism, 23, 29–33, 223
Military Academy at Ichigaya, 32
Military: prostitution, 52–53, 209, 223; training, 32–33, 55–59
Mills, W. Plumer, 106, 133
Ming dynasty, 62, 63, 130

Ministry of Education, 203, 205–9
Ministry of Foreign Affairs, 125
Ministry of Health, 123
Mitter, Rana, 30
Mondale, Walter, 224
Mongolia, 28, 178
Morality, 15, 39. *See also* Ethics
Morison, Samuel Eliot, 21
Motoshima Hitoshi, 12, 213–14
Mountain Gate, 73
Movies. *See* Films
Müller, Rastor, 189
Mufu Mountain, 44–46
Mukai Toshiaki, 56, 171
Munitions factories, 25
Mussolini, Benito, 3
My Lai massacre, 173

Nagako, Empress, 33
Nagasaki, 6, 15, 167, 199, 201–2, 213–14
Nagatomi Hakudo, 59, 218–19
Nakajima Kesago, 35, 37, 39–40, 46, 175–76
Nanking Self-Government Committee (*Nanjing Zizhi Eiyuanhui* or *Nanking Tze Chih Wei Yuan Hwei*), 162
Nanking-Shanghai railway, 35, 64
Nanking (Nanjing) Wall, 183
Nanking War Crimes Trial, 170–72
Narcotics, 163
National Archives, 188

National Conference for the Defense of Japan, 208
Nationalist Party, 63, 66–68, 108, 166
Nazis, 12, 105, 182, 196, 200; and American POWs, 173, and Christianity, 55; and the IMTFE, 177; in Nanking, 6, 109–10, 114, 117, 120–21, 138–39, 157, 160, 177, 194–95. *See also* Germany; Holocaust, the
Netherlands, 5
New Year's Day, 128, 134
New Year's Eve, 150
New York Times, 9, 51, 144–45, 196, 201–2, 221
Newsreels, 146–47, 148–49
Nichi Mainichi Shimbun, 47
Ningpo (Ningbo), 216
Nobukatsu, Fujioka, 209
Noda Takeshi, 56, 171
North Korea, 182. *See also* Korea
Nuclear weapons, 6, 15, 167, 199, 202. *See also* Atomic bombs

Obedience, 31–32
Ohta Hisao, 101
Oka, Major, 110
Okamura, Mr., 147
Okuno Seisuki, 203–4
Ono Kenji, 209–10
Opium, 163
Opium Wars, 61
Orwell, George, 217

Other Nuremberg: The Untold Story of the Tokyo War Crimes Trials, The (Brackman), 173

Paimou Inlet, 35, 36
Pakistan, 89
Palace Museum, 70
Panay gunboat, 36, 73, 106–7, 131, 144, 146–49
Panay Incident, The (Perry), 149
Panzer division, 3
Parker, Karen, 183–84
Passivity, of Chinese soldiers, 42–44
Pearl Harbor, 3, 200, 213
Peking (Bejing), 4, 62, 130, 178
Peking Palace, 113
Perry, Hamilton Darby, 149
Perry, Matthew, 21, 23
Pescadores, 23
Philippines, 52, 223
Photographs, 7, 9–11, 13, 143, 146; and Japanese propaganda, 150; and war crimes trials, 170
Pine River, 36, 38. *See also* Sungchiang
Plague, 216
Playboy (magazine), 201, 202
Poison gas, 123, 124, 164
Poland, 3, 181
Porcelain Pagoda, 62
Poverty, 162–63, 191
POWs (prisoners of war), 42–46, 82, 173
Pregnancy, 85–86, 91, 92

Presbyterians, 106, 133. *See also* Christianity
Princeton University, 122
Pro-democracy, movements, 9
Propaganda, 145–57, 212, 218
Property, lost, 160, 222
Prostitution, 25, 203–4; and the comfort women, 52–53, 209, 223; and the registration of Chinese women, 136; and the Safety Zone, 133, 135
Psychological programming, 29–33
Pu Yi (P'u-i), 29, 210
Pukow (Pukou), 74
Purple Mountain, 62, 113

Qing (Ch'ing) dynasty, 23, 28, 62–63
Quakers, 105

Rabe, Dora, 121, 191
Rabe, John, x, 100, 109–21, 134, 139, 157, 187–97; death of, 194; and Hitler, 119, 121, 187–88, 190, 195–97; during the postwar period, 188–96; return of, to Germany, 188–90
Rabe, Margarethe, 189
Rabe, Otto, 189, 194
Railways, 29, 35, 64, 66
Rain Flower Terrace, vii, 172. *See* Yuhuatai
Rape, 6, 89–96, 153, 170; in the film *Rashomon*, 14; in the former Yugoslavia, 89;

and Matsui, 51–52, 53; Magee on, 202; Rabe's efforts to stop, 118–21; and the registration of Chinese women, 136; and the Safety Zone, 118–21, 126–28, 133–34, 136; "second," the forgotten Holocaust as, xi, 199–214, 221–22

Rashomon (film), 14

Reader's Digest, 151, 155, 156

Reagan, Ronald, 223

Red Cross, 67, 100, 115, 125, 137, 189

Red Swastika Society, 117

Refugees, 65, 66, 81, 106–39

"Regarding the Recruitment of Women for Military Brothels" (Japanese Defense Agency), 53

Registration procedures, 135–36, 165

Reinhardt, Ursula, 109, 189, 190–96

Rekishi to jinbutsu, 213

Religion, 54–55, 218–19. *See also* Buddhism; Christianity

Remorse, lack of, 59

Renming Ribao (People's Daily), 195, 196

Reparations payments, 11–12, 181, 183–84, 222

Revolution: in China (1911), 30; in Japan (1868), 22–23

Rice Imports, 26

Riggs, Charles, 139

Romans, 5

Romulo, Carlos, 223

Roosevelt, Franklin D., 146, 149

Rummel, R. J., 216, 220–21

Russia, 5, 21, 24, 152, 178, 191. *See also* Soviet Union

Russo-Japanese War of 1905, 24, 152

Rwanda, 221

Saipan, 20

Saito Hirosi, 148

Saito Mitsuhiro, 211

Sakhalin Islands, 24

Sakurai Shin, 204

Samurai warrior class, 14, 20

San Francisco Bay Area, 9, 223

San Francisco Peace Treaty, 222

Santayana, George, 16

Sarajevo, 130

Sasaki Motomasa, 48

Schindler, Oskar, 105, 109, 185, 20

Schindler's List (film), 185

Second World War (Michel), 7

Seiron, 212

Shao Tzuping, 8, 195–96

Shanghai, 29, 37; fall of, 4, 33–34, 67, 70–71; Fitch's escape to, 156–57; and Japanese propaganda, 150–51; Nanking railway, 35, 64; outbreak of fighting in, 64; ratio of Chinese to Japanese forces in, 33

Shansi Road Circle, 115

Shantung Peninsula, 25

Shinto, sun cult of, 22

Shintoism, 54

Shochiku Fuji Distribution Company, 210–11

Shogun, 20, 22

Shokun!, 212

Showa era, 214

Shukan Kinyobi (magazine), 210

Siam-Burma Death Railway, 173

Siemen, Carl Friedrich von, 190

Siemens China Company, 109–10, 120, 190–92

Signal Intelligence Service (U.S. Army), 148

Silence, 11, 14, 50–51, 53, 218

Sin Shun Pao (newspaper), 150

Slavery, 13, 38, 163

Smythe, Lewis, 133, 150–52, 160, 170, 185–86

Socialism, 110. See also Communism

South Gate, 70, 93

South Korea, 204–5. See also Korea

Soviet Union, 181. See also Russia

Spanish Inquisition, 5, 218

Sperling, Eduard, 75, 121

Stalin, Joseph, 5

Starvation, 26, 138, 166, 173, 216

Steel production, 24

Steele, Archibald, 144–45, 153

Steward, Albert, 165

Stock market crash (1929), 25

Suchow (Suzhou), 36, 37

Sugawara Yutaka, 37, 176

Sugimoto Ryokichi, 207

Suicide, 31–32, 121, 163, 176; and comfort women, 53; missions, 20; among Nanking survivors, 185, 187; and rape, 90; and torture, 88

Sungchiang (Songjiang or Pine River), 36, 38

Sun Goddess, 20

Sun Yat-sen, 30, 61, 64, 66

Sun Yat-sen Memorial Park, 130

Sun Zhaiwei, 100–101

Suzuki Akira, 211, 212

Swapp, Edith Fitch, 186

Sweden, 105

Switzerland, 193, 222

Syria, 5

Ta Chung Chiao (Da Zhang Chao, literally "Big Middle Bridge"), 94

Tai Hu Lake, 37, 38, 66

Taiping, 62

Taiping Road, 87–88

Taisa Isamo, 40n

Taiwan, 7, 23, 52

Tajima, Private, 56–57

Takehiko, Nakane, 211

Takokoro, Kozo, 49

Tanaka Gi-ichi, 177-78

Tanaka Masaaki, 213, 213

Tanaka Ryukichi, 40n

Tanaka Yuki, 217

Tanaka Memorial, 178

Tang Sheng-chih, General, 67–68, 71–79, 111, 184n

Tang Shunsan, 83–87

Tani Hisao, 50, 171–72

Tariffs, 26

Taxes, 162, 163

Taylor, John, 188

Tekken seisai ("the iron fist"), 217

Terrorism, 28, 216

Testament (documentary), 157

Textbooks, 6–7, 205–9

Textile exports, 26

Thomas, Jeremy, 210

"Three-all" policy, 215–16

Tiananmen Square massacre, 9

Tientsin (Tianjin), 4, 33

Tientsin-Peking region, 33

Time (magazine), 155

Timperley, Harold John, 155

Timur Lenk, 5

Tokugawa family, 21–22

Tokyo, 6, 27–28, 40, 169, 216

Tokyo Nichi Nichi (newspaper), 151

Tokyo Bay, 21

Tokyo War Crimes Trial. *See also* IMTFE (International Military Tribunal of the Far East)

Tokyo University, 105, 209

Tominaga Shozo, 57–58

Tong, Nancy, 8

Tongjimen, 95

Toronto, 9

Torture, 87–89, 173

Trade, 11, 21–25; boycotts of Japanese goods, 25, 29; during the Depression, 26; and Perry's visit to Japan, 21, 22; and tariffs, 26

Treaties, 23–24, 27, 61, 222

Trials. *See* IMTFE (International Military Tribunal of the Far East)

Tribalism, 22

Trimmer, C. S., 124, 128, 139

Tsingtao (Qingdao), 130

Tsushima, 24

Turkey, 190

Typhoid, 166, 216

Unit Ei 1644, 164–65

United Nations, 8, 169, 195

United Christian Missionary Association, 130

United Christian Missionary Society, 187

United Press, 173

Universal Studios, 146

University of Chiba, 197

University of Illinois, 8

University of Nanking, 99, 106, 122, 133, 139, 160, 163, 186

University of Nanking Hospital, 98, 122, 124–25, 129, 156, 161, 186

U.S. Army, 148

U.S.S. *Panay* gunboat, 73, 106–7, 131, 144, 146–49

Utsunomiya University, 196

Vancouver, 9
Vautrin, Wilhelmina
  ("Minnie"), 129–39,
  186–87
Versailles Treaty, 25

Wallenberg, Raoul, 105
Warlords, 28
Waseda University, 211
Watanabe Shoichi, 212
Water Gate, 145, 159–60. See
  also Ichang
"Water treatment," 173
Weapons: biological, 216;
  nuclear, 6, 15, 167, 199, 202;
  poison gases, 123, 124, 164
Weinberg, Gerhard, 7
Why We Fight: Battle of China
  (documentary), 157
Wiesel, Elie, 16
Wilson, Elizabeth, 123
Wilson, Marjorie, 123
Wilson, Robert, 121–29, 139,
  149, 186
Women: comfort women,
  52–53, 209, 223; and
  modernization, 24. See also
  Prostitution; Rape
World at Arms, A (Weinberg), 7
World War I, 24–25
Wuhu, 124
Wulong Mountain, 45
Wu Tienwei, 102

Xenophobia, 21
Xiaomenkou, 83
Xing, Frank, 65
Xinhua Yuebao (journal),
  185

Yalta Conference, 181
Yanagawa Heisuke, General,
  37, 39, 52, 176, 179
Yangtze (Yangzi) River, ix, 8,
  35, 36, 45–46, 62, 64–65,
  75–79, 101, 164–65, 175;
  and acts of suicide, 90,
  95–96; and agriculture,
  165–66; evacuation via,
  77–79, 83, 115
Yasuhimo, Nakasone, 203
Yasukuni Shrine, 203
Ying, James, 103
YMCA (Young Men's Christian
  Association), 117, 120, 133,
  186
Yokoto, 44–45
Yoshima Yoshiaki, 52, 53
Young, Shi, 103
Yuan Shikai, 30
Yugoslavia, 89, 130, 221
Yuhuatai, vii, 73. See also Rain
  Flower Terrace

Zaimoku, 164
Zhuizi, 87

IRIS CHANG graduated with a degree in journalism from the University of Illinois at Urbana-Champaign and worked briefly as a reporter in Chicago before winning a graduate fellowship to the writing seminar program at The Johns Hopkins University. Her first book, *Thread of the Silkworm*, told the story of Tsien Hsue-shen, father of the People's Republic of China's missile program. Her second, the international bestseller *The Rape of Nanking*, examined one of the most tragic episodes in World War II. Her third and last book was *The Chinese in America*, an epic history spanning 150 years. As one of America's leading young historians, Iris Chang received numerous honors, including the John T. and Catherine D. MacArthur Foundation's Program on Peace and International Cooperation Award, the Woman of the Year Award from the Organization of Chinese Americans, and honorary doctorates from the College of Wooster in Ohio and California State University at Hayward. In 1991, she married Brett Douglas and together they had a son. Her work appeared in many publications such as *Newsweek*, the *New York Times*, and the *Los Angeles Times*, and she was featured on numerous television and radio programs, and she lectured widely. She committed suicide in November 2004.